Beverley Steffert lectures in psychology for the extra-mural department of London University. She also runs relationship, business and education seminars on all aspects of psychological communication from enhancement of learning and work-place compatibility to emotional exchange between men and women. She lives near Cambridge and is often a guest on radio and television programmes.

The Rhythms of Love

Beverley Steffert

Thorsons

An Imprint of HarperCollins*Publishers*

Thorsons
An Imprint of HarperCollins*Publishers*
77–85 Fulham Palace Road,
Hammersmith, London W6 8JB

Published by Thorsons 1992
1 3 5 7 9 10 8 6 4 2

A catalogue record for this book
is available from the British Library

ISBN 0 7225 2473 0

Typeset by Harper Phototypesetters Limited,
Northampton, England
Printed in Great Britain by
Mackays of Chatham PLC, Chatham, Kent

Contents

Acknowledgements

To the classes of Chiswick, Chelmsford and the City Literary Society, Heston and Hounslow, Kensington and Camden, Marylebone and Mill Hill, London and Loughton, Wanstead and Westminster, all of whom taught me quite as much as I taught them.

And to all the couples who completed their questionnaires and talked in depth and sincerity about their relationships, from Scotland to the Shires.

For everything there is a season and a time to every purpose under heaven. A time to be born and a time to die, a time to plant and a time to pluck . . . and, Ecclesiastes might have continued, a time to reach out in intimacy and a time to withdraw in understanding.

Introduction

My dear old red setter used to sit at my feet when I was writing, alternating hazily between his world of doggie philosophy, and predicting my likely comings and goings and whether he would be included. Cushioned between me and the radiator, he would open his eyes every twenty minutes or so, give a lazy tail-wag which said 'Glad you're still here' and fall back into his musings until walk time.

It was summer-time that brought his worst dilemma — whether to sit within six inches of me by the now cold radiator under the dark table, or luxuriate on the soft sun-bathed settee, twelve feet away from me. He solved it by snoozing on the sunny patch for about one and half hours, during which he would pad sleepily across to me several times for a stroke of approval and a few words of love. Reassured that he was indeed the best dog in the whole world he would sink back, satisfied. At walk-time he would spring up and look expectantly through the glass door at the green fields beyond. Walk over, it was back to the settee, the sequence to be repeated several times throughout the day.

The sociability cycles of humans are much more complex than dogs, of course, but even in humans the physical is usually also a reflection of the psychological. Wherever you are standing – in a bookshop, on public transport, at work or anywhere – when you look at the people around you you can tell who is with whom, just on the basis of how closely they stand together, look at each other, talk and touch each other. Sometimes in a situation where physical distance is impossible (rush hour tubes or divorcing couples forced to share the same house), distancing mechanisms such as averted eyes, stiffened body and emotionless or cold expressions emphasize the message: this is not how close I feel.

The same mechanisms regulate the intimacy cycles of love. Every minute of every hour of every day, the shifts of closeness and withdrawal regulate an intimacy equilibrium which fits a couple's changing circumstances.

Having the capacity to judge ourselves against others gives us a particularly human predicament. Like all social animals, we need to be close enough to each other to have a sense of community and involvement, to feel at least one person on earth cares whether we live or die! To that end we emphasize similarity and conformity to human rules, but the more conformity the greater the feeling of being swamped; to be swept along with the trend willy nilly gives us no chance to do it 'my way'. Being unique, independent and autonomous has its own rewards. This predicament is emphasized in the way a couple communicates. They symbolize the balance of individuality and independence with the forces of involvement. It is the micro-cycles of speech-patterning, breathing, timing of pauses and responses, eye contact and facial muscles that carry the silent messages of indifference or involvement.

Relationship development is a complex process – like seeds or trees planted at the wrong seasonal cycle, relationships won't root and flourish, unless you match the rhythm of intimacy. The plants don't die but they stop growing – getting stuck in the wrong cycle – leafing away with no fruit, or growing tall without the petals unfolding, until the gardener comes along with some bottled or canned remedy.

Similarly with people, unless each psychological seed pushing out the emergent properties of trust, warmth and intimacy is allowed to develop in its own time, with its own rhythm, in the right sequence, the couple remain nearly as separate and unbonded as they were in their single days. The sequence of development isn't even. Like a flower it can remain the same for weeks and months, only to unfold literally overnight into a bright, vivid perfection – a relationship can go through days of doldrums to sudden exhilarating harmony and closeness.

Closeness has a rhythm. It is cyclical, it comes and goes naturally like appetite, thirst or any other physiological necessity. A good host is flattered when the guests reject the dessert with 'No, I'm just too full after that wonderful meal' but lovers frequently feel rejected when the love of their life says 'No, I'd like to be alone now/see a friend/get on with my work', or anything else that makes up the daily round. Intimacy-overload is not as acceptable as digestive-overload.

Love isn't some sort of magic radiation elicited from the other. It's as mundane and necessary as food and water. We search for it when we haven't enough and turn away from it when we've had too much. Happiness is when each matches the peaks and troughs of the other's intimacy cycle. For some, like my old dog, the cycles of closeness are long and interspersed only briefly with periods of withdrawal – his walks and meal times. For others it's an inevitable decline to the other way round.

This book is for the ordinary couples of basic goodwill who find to their puzzlement and distress that things aren't going as well as they could and, to their dismay, that boredom and bickering have eroded that initial love.

Matching the other person's micro-cycles of intimacy and withdrawal creates a synchrony that reflects the internal world of the relationship. This rhythm of relationship alters perception of similarity and difference, compatibility and incongruity. And mostly it is unaware. Keeping in synchrony with each other is only a matter of sensitive timing and catching the rhythm.

The three parts of this book parallel the three stages of closeness in relationships, closeness which is ever-opposed by cycles of distance and withdrawal: thesis – antithesis – synthesis.

Attraction, guided by similarity, promises the safety of familiarity and harks back to the security of the cradle. But we base our similarity rating on one fundamental difference, a difference that eventually brings frustration and sometimes separation, and certainly ushers in the least happy period of relationship.

From the day of birth men and women live in different worlds, with different conditioning histories. This conditioning gives men and women opposing views of love, expectations of relationships, defense mechanisms, ways of coping and processing information, perception of events, storage of memory, direction of attention and just about anything and everything that can affect a relationship, including emotional bonding and communication style. The very qualities that most attracted them become, eventually the things that irritate them the most.

Men and women tend to have two different styles of communication, she the language of involvement, and he the language of independence. This is expressed in non-verbal ways as well as in the minutiae of speech patterning, and the microrhythms of conversation which make up speech style. His style is divergence and hers convergence. This is why when a man and a woman fall in love and promise each other everything, they can find their relationship slowly fading into disillusion, bickering, confusion, despair, criticism and blame. The exhilaration of love, the close-ness of commitment, are now swamped by the dilemma of insurmountable difference. Moving together from strangeness or at least only prior friendship towards synchrony and becoming as close as two people can, physically and psychologically, they have formed an extremely close bond. As they each try to puzzle out the other's meanings and motivations, they each withdraw a little more, laying down the seeds of dissent for the next cycle of conflict in between the shortening periods of intimacy.

Each conflict produces stress – and promise. The euphoria of resolution moves a couple confidently into the next conflict resolution. If it is not resolved it may stay submerged, and the couple will be stuck at a lower level of intimacy than they could otherwise achieve.

These micro-cycles of intimacy and withdrawal are embedded in larger macro-cycles, which are periods of stability punctuated by periods of transition between qualitatively different relationship stages. They each have their inherent, predictable and – with knowledge – resolvable conflicts. If the conflicts are not resolved they are carried on to the next stage, germinating, congealing and spreading tendrils of dissatisfaction to choke the relationship, leaving the structure but suffocating the vitality and fertility of the first years.

Chapter 1 describes the timing between hope and uncertainty, matching every similarity to get to a total rapport and synchrony of mind and body. This is the stage of test and retest, which every lover does with as much determination as any scientist in a laboratory – but the phenomenon under scrutiny is love.

Chapter 2 is about commitment and how the rewards of close emotional involvement are balanced against the costs. Costs which are weighed differently by each individual according to their particular psychological makeup, family experience and cultural history. The rewards of involvement are less obvious to the 'freedom-seekers' than the 'team-builders', and it is this dilemma that shapes the different love-styles which are based on the three self-protective strategies of fight, flight or submit. Part 2 explains how attachment styles are the defences designed to preserve the individual's emotional safety. These love and attachment styles are communicated consciously and unconsciously to the partner, and those who are similar strike the best bargain they can. All relationships fall into the three major categories on this scale – traditional, separate or the interdependent therapeutics. Each type has its own characteristic preferences for closeness or distance, relationship ideology, means of communication, both verbal and body language, ways of controlling life and influencing each other.

If we all found our attachment style match and then slotted ourselves into the same position on the traditional to therapeutic relationship dimension, life would be harmonious, tranquil – and boring! We go through an unconscious and conscious search for similarity, familiarity and safety, but because we base it all on one fundamental difference, gender, it alters all the relationship style interactions. Whatever love-style a man is, he is similar to all men in ways peculiar to the male sex. And whatever love-style a woman is, she also shares more similarities with other women, no matter how different their love-style.

Romantic ideology is not consonant with the biological 'whispering within' which remain hidden, ready to spring up and take us unawares. Ideals and ideologies are poor matches for the powerful passions of jealousy, rejection, adoration, raw anger, physical ecstasy, revenge, blame and unbridled optimism that come unbidden with each relationship cycle. As we go through the stages of courtship, parenthood, middle age and beyond we feel different – sometimes in the grip of hormones, other times able to engineer our emotions to the vibrations of social forces. Evolution's blueprint for relationships fades as the children grow up, but unless we recognize that biology has laid down a model for relationships which can only be overridden with knowledge of the emotional input for the programme, we will be living at odds with the natural macro- and micro-cycles of intimacy and conflict, never being able to move naturally through the spiral to deepest intimacy and commitment. At 18 we want to be heroes and goddesses, but at 80 we want someone to cut our toenails!

Romantic love has existed since the first civilizations, although the concepts and names may have changed with varying cultural conditions, the emotions exchanged between men and women have remained the same, emotions that have evolved to guide us towards the benefits of social life and away from the dangers of isolation. Relationships are a developmental stage in the humanizing process, and underwrite the chemistry of health, happiness and optimum psychological functioning. We marry those we believe we have some influence over, we want to be able to predict and control events that affect our lives. But we also want a life of interest, challenge and creativity. In other words, an oscillation within certain limits, a tuning up or tuning down, according to what else is going on outside the relationship. An intimate relationship, with someone that we can feel an alliance with, talk to, touch, make plans with, is not only a joint hostage against life's fortune, it is an energy regulator.

In the majority of cases, this relationship will be between opposite sexes, but other varieties of pairs lead perfectly successful happy lives and the same forces of involvement and independence operate.

This book is about the social conditioning of boys and girls and how it gives them a biosocial personality that is biased. Men grow up emotionally inhibited, and women instrumentally inhibited. This makes love and intimacy the feminine province, something that men fear. If she does the emotional work to keep the relationship going, and manages his emotional life, he will feel controlled by her and withdraw. As she advances in intimacy he stonewalls. Her response then ranges from protecting him to despising him, and there is a measurable physiology behind these responses. Variations of this pursuer-withdrawal cycle are in some degree evident in every relationship, made worse by the differences in perception. Each thinks the other is being perverse when they can't agree that the milk was off, the sauce too salty, or the stereo too loud. Or that she changed her mind or he wasn't listening.

The tragedy of sex-differences in emotional communication is that it leads couples to conclude, usually inaccurately that 'we're just not compatible'. Thinking of intimate communication as a skill to be learned does not make us robots, in contrast to the criticisms the sceptical Anglo-Saxon culture makes of the 'human potential movements'. It is a very deep human desire to get closer to those we choose to share life with. Emotional competence is a prerequisite and not a neurotic or narcisstic self-absorption.

Biology is not destiny, but it can throw a spanner in the works of carefully laid social plans. Alone in the animal kingdom we can reflect upon our experience, our place in the world, our origins without and emotions within. Biology has provided us with mechanisms to assess each other, match our potentials, and either withdraw if the match is unsatisfactory, or dissolve our territorial boundaries into cooperativeness and form an attachment bond. A time sequence has evolved, a period of close cooperation and idealization, then a turning outwards, and later still a turning back – all promoted by a complex cascade of hormones and neuro-chemicals that alter our motivations, moods and emotional readiness to harmonize individual physiological cycles into the other's rhythms. Intimacy comes and goes in waves, each relationship stage presages the next conflict to be resolved. We alter this procession with damaging consequences to the psychological growth of relationship. Whirlwind marriages, shot gun weddings, cohabitation without commitment, can all be successful but they need a great deal of emotional understanding in matching each other's macro-cycle levels.

Maturity isn't a unitary concept, nor an ideal we all climb up to steadily, heaving ourselves with weary relief onto the plateau of safety from where we throw lifelines to all the other strugglers. It's more like air around us that we stop to breathe deeply when we can spare a moment out of the race. Maturity is situation-specific. When we understand ourselves in some area we can react to another stuck at that level empathetically, and with maturity. People change, emotional growth is uneven, even retrograde under bad circumstances and spurting under good. The trend toward therapeutic relationships, which are increasingly required to serve both partners' emotional development, calls up the capacity for closeness and intimacy. The development of the individual has emerged as an increasingly important objective, both of social policy and of the individuals concerned. The handling of technology, environmental problems and massive social change needs human adaptability, curiosity and creativity.

The history of human thought is characterized by a move from belief in inevitable fate to freewill and the individual's own ability to change and control their destiny. Ritual has become experimentation and manipulation, illness once believed to be of divine retribution we now stop with vaccines, but relationships are the last things to be released from the spell of mystery. The idea of marriage counselling has done something to dispel the notion of marriages made in heaven but even it still concentrates on patching up, a curative medicine rather than a preventive one. Researchers too, look for natural differences that occur between successful relationships and couples in counselling, as if the successful have some magic potion that can be isolated and given to the happy to 'immunize' them.

More output for less input is a business concept that can also revolutionize relationships. Instead of the disheartening injunction 'work at it', the answer is to *understand* the inherent conflicts that will inevitably come, and use that knowledge to gain a relaxed control of the dilemmas, approaching them with positive energy and avoiding unproductive, draining encounters.

Monitoring the non-verbal aspects of behaviour and speech helps good communication, which saves much misunderstanding and unnecessary input. Discussions of daily mood fluctuations and the insights gained, may be a better barometer than universal generalizations about love.

Thinking of a relationship as a product that needs updating, costing, comparison with similar other products, continual research and development, and quality control, will change both attitude and behaviour. Love may come naturally, but fades in intensity quickly. The idealization it brings is the product to be nurtured. Chapter 5 gives you a comparison guide of the relationship styles of others and their type of 'product'.

A quality relationship is life-enhancing, fully functioning and equal in give and take. The 'checklist' of relationships emphasizes commitment, change and implementation, and the 'charter' is set out in the appendix. A checklist for quality control of each specific conflict is itemized at the end of each chapter.

Even though the chemistry of pair bonding has been powerfully programmed by evolution we are not slaves of the genetically made molecules of desire. Our thoughts can control our emotions – if we're aware and seek to make different choices. And two people together with a common ideology can reinforce each other even more so. A partnership committed to exclusivity, intimacy, empathy and trust can rule over the *sotto voce* of biology, which can be urging infidelity, jealousy, selfishness or hostility as well as idealization. A prerequisite is understanding the evolutionary hangover and accepting the flickering, fleeting glimpses of negative emotions and replacing them with longer term, more satisfying, positive ones. Even the peacock's tail is of use to the peahen in judging compatibility!

Part I
Coming Closer: Searching for Similarity

Like is cured by like, not contrariwise.

Paracelsus (1493)

1

Attraction: hope v. uncertainty

The stooped old lady, who was gamely dragging a battered suitcase in one arm and a large handbag on the other, stopped to peer unsteadily at the street sign. With an anxious sigh she asked a pleasant-looking passerby directions to her friend's home. It turned out to be quite a complicated and lengthy route – and the old lady was near tears as she told the sympathetic woman how an impatient bus driver had put her off at the wrong stop half a mile back. She didn't have enough money for a taxi and was worried she wouldn't get to her friend's home before dark. Her confidante was sympathetic – her own mother had been attacked and robbed of a pathetic few pounds and her trust in humanity recently. From that day she had refused to leave her house alone and had become withdrawn and depressed.

The young woman admired this old lady's tenacity in a stressful situation. Her instinct was to take the case from her and walk her round to her friend's home but she herself was already late.

The rewards of involvement are always counterbalanced by the costs. Helping an old lady safely on her way calls out the boy scout in most of us. Vulnerability breeds altruism (at first! – longer-term vulnerability turns to dependency and later exploitation), and self-esteem is raised in proportion to the benefit to the other. But the costs are time, and unexpected, unwanted involvement. What if the old lady had the wrong address or collapsed on the way: all this agonizing for a five-minute interaction!

A committed relationship has endless possibilities for

involvement, closeness and the deepest levels of communication and rapport. But, unlike a friendship or work relationship, in which we can share feelings and then go away to other relationships and homes, a couple live in a close proximity which dictates the need for some emotional privacy.

Involvement and independence: the contradictory forces in every human relationship

Lovers, family, colleagues, friends and the person who asks you directions in the street all pose the same dilemma: how to move towards them and keep one's independence, and how to move away from them and keep an involvement – simultaneously and in harmony with their own needs for intimacy and withdrawal matched. All social species, from migrating wildebeest to cooperating ants and humans, have to cope with the problem of being close enough for comfort and far away enough to preserve autonomy and identity.

Human lovers require more than the social closeness animals seek; we look for a perfect, blissful union recapitulating the emotional closeness of babyhood, the days before the dreadful realization of difference and potential separation dawned.

Painful isolation or uncomfortable crowding

By the time we are adults we have established characteristic preferences in the way we relate to others between emotional closeness and emotional distance. The quills of the porcupine are a good metaphor for the psychological defences we establish to keep others from getting uncomfortably close. Porcupines, like humans, are a source of both comfort and pain to each other. The poor old porcupines can never solve their differences; they huddle together for warmth, but then their quills prick each other, so they move away a bit. Then they get cold, so they huddle together. Their dilemma is to freeze or get pricked, and ours is to be lonely or be swamped.

The body ballet of closeness

A couple signal to each other that they would like to get closer much like other species: a ritualized dance of show and countershow while they are each assessing the suitability and readiness of the other, before plunging into a major genetic investment – or, in the human case, an emotional commitment that has lifelong consequences. The sequence of synchronized ritual is orderly and regular, and observable to anyone who learns to become sensitive to non-verbal behaviour.

It's not so much the movements that are important in courtship and love, it's the degree to which they are reciprocated. Julie described how it seems to her:

> I saw this guy looking across at me several times, he looked quite nice but didn't come over or anything, I supposed he couldn't tell whether I was with anyone or not – we were all horsing around and joking. So when I got up to go to the ladies, I passed by his table and half-smiled at him. When I came back I could tell he was waiting for me so I slowed up a bit and he stood up and said a bit hesitantly, 'You seem to be having a good time over there, mind if I join you?' So I mumbled something about them being too noisy for me and perhaps I would join him! I wanted to add perhaps he would have just as good a time with me alone but I could see he felt that anyway, just from the way he was looking at me. I felt a bit daring, after all I didn't know him from Adam and yet within 5 minutes I felt as if I'd known him all my life. By the end of the evening I can honestly say I knew we were going to get married . . . and we did, 10 months later.

Sam had been bowled over by Julie's appearance, and had (uncharacteristically) made an approach, low-key enough for Julie to ignore should she wish, but she had not only matched his signals, she reciprocated and escalated his every move. In order to signal acceptance a definite and intentional response has to be made, although it can still be quite subtle – a move forwards, a light touch on the hand, a direct gaze and smile. To signal non-acceptance and shut down the unspoken enquiry, one simply keeps still, not looking or looking away, and stiffens the body. The feeling evoked by that is 'he/she doesn't like me'. Any non-matching response at any later point in the conversation will make the other feel things aren't going well, they're not on the same wavelength, whereas any matching response at the right time (about $\frac{1}{8}$ of a second, in our culture) keeps interest going, affects expectations of the encounter, and – with the right sequence – the outcome.

It is this subliminal chain of events, look-turn-touch-synchronization that culminates in intimacy and the magical state we call love: a smile, followed by a quick flash of the eyebrows, then a turning away, with the head cocked aside, eyes lowered and eyelids dropped. By the time Julie and Sam were fully synchronized they had communicated to each other by behaviour, look, touch, movements and talk that they could interact intimately. Their arousal levels and emotional readiness had created the preconditions for a sexual relationship. Hormones and neurochemicals that enhance the excited, trance-like state are released when full body synchrony is achieved. Good actors make conscious use of synchrony to suggest emotional involvement to the audience; research suggests that their hearts should have followed where the body went, but one scene is not enough (fortunately for the real husbands and wives of actors). Exchanged and reciprocated looks, touches, talk and synchronized movements will be repeated again and again before a sexual union is established.

The key is mutual, equal involvement – it hardly matters what is said at this stage, it is the behavioural synchronization that develops intimacy. Moving towards each other, turning towards each other, mutual gaze, all at the same beat as speech patterns and arm movements. Postural echo and body orientation are quite familiar to most people through popular body-language books, and there follows the harmonization of breathing rate, pause rate and speech patterns.

These matching rituals have been observed in other species, from rats to pygmy chimps, who gaze intently into each other's eyes during sex. Even monkey pairs have been observed to move to a common underlying rhythm. In humans, emotional and behavioural communication are also integrated. Animals react and respond to each other but don't need the symbolic aspect of communication like humans, who must synchronize their emotional feelings behaviourally and symbolically for the message to be understood as one of unspoken interest . . . I am like you and I like you. This appears to be communicated at 10 cycles per second, a close approximation to an alpha-rhythm, which is an indicator of feelings of relaxed interest.

Social cohesion is so important that we must have a non-verbal and private way of expressing 'not tonight, Josephine' before either party is really aware of the message being given and received. The human ability to create and then to integrate emotional symbols into behaviour elicits emotions in the other person as surely as pheromones once did. These courtship communicative 'feedback loops' alter the state of the receiver, then the original sender and so on. They are initially set low, 'just talking', then 'just checking', and as the regulator for intimacy is turned up higher, the signals become stronger, turning towards each other 'Yes, I'm interested too'. Each matching signal becomes more intense until there is a mutual accommodation at a point satisfactory to each.

Love chemistry

Sharing intense feelings is totally involving and changes our normal perception. The moment that two people (or sometimes more) are feeling the same emotion with the same intensity there is a resonance – call it a physical vibration – that harmonizes electrochemical events. For a few milliseconds the feeling appears to be outside the skin and the individuals are joined by that feeling. This psycho-physiological linkage is for many of us our first and only peak experience, which brings such powerful, unusual feelings there is no ready-made linguistic label for them. The closest attempts use synonyms of free-floating ecstasy – oceanic, all-embracing, ego-dissolving, cosmic, universal – all changes in perception due to being able to perceive oneself in a connected way. When the self is perceived as separate, with separate feelings and beliefs, without all the connections we have established with others over the years, we cut off many integrating perceptions. There are many invisible connections between us that we are unable to perceive with our normal senses. Some of these, at the edges of our sensory mechanism ranges, stretch under the influence of emotional intensity to take in new meanings. When love lends a colour, a texture and a hue to life, the daily irritants lose their grip. We look longer at the garden roses, with their scent, colour and sheer improbability, and pass over the flaking paintwork.

There is both a physical and psychological development in perception. Maturity is correlated with an increased understanding of diversity and other people's reality which is divergent to their own. The symbolic view of self changes from the centre of things with other people coming and going (this is called egocentric) to one of a more abstract knowledge of self and the role that self plays in the patterning of life, the influences to and from others, and the widening ripple of connections, coincidence, cause and effect. Maturity enlarges our frame of reference and the intensity of love can put us on the fast track to transformation of familiar thinking concepts. Relationship accentuates this development. Feelings that are not much promoted in the average family can be developed; positive love, forgiveness, faith and hope are perceptually enlarging emotions, and if not practised in childhood don't come easily. But romantic love gives us the ability to see the world through another's eyes – or more accurately, another's feelings. Everything else is relegated to the unimportant while those feelings last, even unattractive traits are turned into evidence of mere mortality in an otherwise god/goddess figure. Who hasn't had to sit indulgently humouring a friend giving an account of this wonderful new being on his horizon, and then meeting a perfectly ordinary person. There are times when sharing intense emotional feelings can be negative, lynch mobs for example, or crowds that get swept into actions that any individual would not perform alone. But the principle holds: sharing feeling changes normal perception.

When the love chemicals are aroused we overlook the warning signs, just as we overlook the flaking paintwork in order to admire the roses. The near-alcoholic becomes a roguish imp showing a too-staid society that life should be lived with panache. The anxious hypochondriac is transformed into a brave, suffering and fragile figure in the face of an uncaring world.

Those in love feel with absolute certainty that it will last forever, that there is no obstacle that can't be surmounted, and that nothing can disturb this love they are sure no one else has ever experienced before. Any overwhelming experience like this must have neurochemical as well as psychological components, and it has been discovered that people in love have a higher rate of production of a highly stimulating brain chemical called enkephalin. Through a series of chemical steps this increases their attention, alertness and initiative, and gives them a powerful feeling of being able to conquer anything. At very high levels it can even cause a trance-like state, with bouts of dizziness and sleeplessness. This release of the body's 'natural morphine' and associated chemicals originally developed out of the need to overcome physical and emotional pain, this gives us a clue to why we get 'hooked' on each other and suffer withdrawal symptoms when love is lost.

Our brains have vast neural networks which can perceive movements that are measured in milliseconds. Women more often have an inkling of what is going on, but mostly they are only aware of the feeling, not the signals making the feeling. There is much room for misunderstanding between the sexes already, and we're only at the first meeting stage!

The spellbinding quality of love

The vision of a world like that painted by Turner surrounds romantic love. Whenever I brought up the subject of falling in love, most couples fell into a mesmerized trance – as if I'd waved a magic wand. Smiles, shared glances, nostalgic sighs accompanied stories of how they suddenly found the buoyancy and energy to dance all night, renovate an entire flat within a week, or dismiss 'minor' obstacles like living continents apart. People in love took up aerobics, ancient Greek history, fell-walking, wrote poems and novels, went on diets, bought new clothes, collected for charities, organized office spring-cleaning parties, and a million more activities – not only in order to make themselves more attractive and interesting, but because they appeared to be generalizing their new-found joy to include the universe. The great thing about this aspect of love is that even after love is over the other changes can stay.

This impetus to empathy, creativity and altered perception can't be dismissed as a folly, as the modern-day 'rational' view would have it. These emotions have always been felt by lovers and our species would not have survived and proliferated without them. All mammalian species are capable of a rudimentary form of them. The only myth is the illusion of easy permanence – because it came so easily, we feel it must stay without any effort, or else it is not 'true love'. Seeing the world and the loved one through these rosy lenses gives us an artist's view, shifts the same old mundane things into a different perspective, adding colour, depth, and new meaning. Some lovers recounted instances of noticing flowers, birds, trees, butterflies in ways they hadn't before. Sometimes it did sound like an altered state of perception, like drug-induced euphoria.

How long the peak of intensity lasts depends on hope. Many did mention hope. Hope for a new beginning, a better self, a more satisfying life, an exciting future. These were more salient than sexual attraction – that was there of course, but everyone insisted love was much more than that.

But research suggests that once love is elicited its course depends on the balance between certainty and uncertainty of reciprocation. Uncertainty is the breeding-ground for emotional intensity, and this is influenced by self-esteem and inner confidence as much as what a lover says and does to reassure us. Certainty demarcates the pendulum swing of hope, on its way to boredom.

This is a most unflattering view of romantic passion, and not one all my respondents agree with. What about *The Tale of Two Cities*, they cried, where is altruism, the tragic passion of Romeo and Juliet, Tristan and Isolde? My answer was that in all cases the lovers that went to their deaths were at the unbearable peak of uncertainty and intensity, when reality would have been the most tenuous!

There is, however, sound evolutionary sense here. If the goal of the pair-bond is to create an emotional attachment fostering conception, then once that is cemented there is no point in leaving the pair like Shakespeare's lovers, totally besotted and not able to do anything productive or even bring up the baby for the intrusive obsessive thoughts and day-dreams.

The biological basis makes falling in love similar for all human beings, the relatively instantaneous feelings alighting far in advance of the rational. This is why love is sometimes compared to an addiction. Like addictions and obsessions it is irrational in the sense that very few know enough about a person to decide with such certainty that this person fulfils life's criteria. No one even knows that about themselves, or how they will change. But it is an irrationality that we long for. Most of us can recapture the thrill of our first love – and all the subsequent ones if we were so lucky. Lucky because although it can be misplaced and will eventually decline, it is nevertheless a transcendent emotion, giving us confidence to leave home and start a separate family and start the process of becoming a separate and unique individual.

Fool's paradise or not, it gives us hints of ourselves as we could be in a better world. Not only do people under the spell of the other's admiration manage to excel in many activities for the first time, they also just feel good, healthier, more active and alive.

One interviewee told me that she had been at daggers drawn with the man in the corner-shop from childhood. He had consistently short-changed her before she was able to cope with money properly, would never give change for the telephone or laundry, and regularly sold out-of-date food. After she fell in love she floated past the shop enveloped in her new cocoon of happiness and noticed how drab it was, how tired the proprietor inside looked, hung over his till haggling with down at heel customers over pennies, and realized that that man had worked 7 days a week for 12 hours a day for the last fifteen years that she knew of. On impulse, she went in, bought something small and commented on his long hours. He told her how he was paying for his children's private education so they didn't have to work like him. He told her how all the years of near-exhaustion had been made up for when his son topped the class in mathematics and won a sports prize in the same year. And later he told her how he didn't like what had happened to him over the years. Bad customers, he said, make bad shop-keepers. This was when she had become a regular – long after she'd fallen out of love.

Almost all of us fall in love at least once. There are a minority who either never do so or who are constantly doing so. Like all biological traits there will be some that don't feel much of it. There are people who feel puzzled by the agony and ecstasies they hear about going on around them. When, poor soul, someone else falls in love with them, these love-crippled individuals feel annoyed by the excessiveness, the claims for exclusive attention and pleas for demonstration of love. This is different from fear of intimacy – it is plain lack of the neurochemical functioning that helps to underwrite the romantic passion.

This is a hint that falling in love is a biologically determined state. All traits influenced by evolutionary pressures have such a normal distribution, and the love-blind are equalled in proportion to the love-crazy, those who are in a constant uproar over someone who is either transforming their life, *or*, if you meet them 3 weeks later, ruining it. The majority of us fortunately fall between these two extremes.

The instinct of love

The other telling clue that love is biologically based is that it is so universal. All historical epochs, and geographical areas, leave evidence of such idealizing passion. It wasn't always associated with marriage and was sometimes with the same sex: but love songs, poems and letters survive from ancient societies that today's lovers would recognize.

Falling in love is not something that has to be taught, unlike living together lovingly. It happens almost instantaneously, can't be thwarted, and is impossible to stop until it has run its course. These are all the criteria a biologist wants to see before they will recognize a behaviour as innate, and romantic love qualifies. It consumes all attention like other biologically motivated behaviours, and has been likened to an obsession, or religion, in which another person is believed in. It is also like an obsessive-compulsive disorder in that the evidence of the senses is not believed. No matter how many times you tell a compulsive doubter that you saw them turn off the gas, they worry. Maybe you were wrong, they 'know' they did, but better check – just in case. And then they must check again, perhaps their last check was inadequate and the gas suddenly turned on again, or something. Couples know they are loved but they constantly check the other's feelings – just in case.

The more towards the love-crazy end of the love spectrum one is, the more checking – which is counter-productive. To be constantly subjected to this barrage of 'do you *really* love me', 'prove it', and other 'tests' of love is pretty well bound to destroy it. In Chapters 3 and 4 there is an explanation of the neurochemical basis to the love-crazy state, and some antidotes!

Throughout the world the type of pair-bond formed is related to the species' optimal strategy for bringing up a family. In some species, particular kinds of birds for example, a lifelong bond develops and they can only be separated by force. They literally spend their whole life after meeting within a few inches of each other. When one dies the other will fly around agitatedly, calling, searching, watching every rustle of leaves that might mean its mate's return. Birds exist so marginally that both must cooperate for the young to survive, and their 'obsessive' love promotes this. So, attraction – the biological idealization of another – exists to ensure the survival of the species.

Although inspired by sexual attraction, most lovers vehemently deny this as a major motive – they feel it is something far more beautiful than the mere erotic. It is a whole constellation of feelings that makes them feel complete. Thus it is impossible to be in love with anyone else at the same time, not at this level of intensity, which seems to have an average duration of about six months.

The preoccupation index

Every whim and passing fancy of the lovers is monitored by each for evidence of similarity to themselves. Everything is geared to monitoring the lover's emotional state – do they feel the same way? – and most time-consuming of all is the sheer amount of time they spend thinking about each other. For some in the early stages there was hardly a minute of the day when fleeting images of the loved one didn't form a backdrop to their activities. A normally highly efficient secretary says:

> When I dialled a number for my boss I would inevitably think about David as I waited, then when the call connected I'd have forgotten who it was that I'd rung and either have to put the phone down or ask then who it was that I was ringing. Embarrassing. Even when I'd be

concentrating on a task I would have an image of David there –
just hovering disconnected in space. I'd find myself going over things
he'd said in my mind for months.

One researcher claims love can be measured solely in the
preoccupation of thoughts, of each about the other, from 100 per
cent of a day downwards. It is useful in the wild to know one's mate
intimately to avoid mistakes of recognition. This is what the modern
ethnological idea of imprinting is – a propensity of the offspring to
familiarize themselves with all aspects of their mother and keep
close to her. Later on, these features are stored in memory and will
be brought out, dusted off, and ready to act as a guide in aiding the
search for a mate. In the animal world this ensures that the same
species will be attracted to each other and it also acts as a warning
signal against inadvertent incest. The message is find someone
similar, not familiar. While couples tend to have a long list of
matching similarities, children who are not related but who grow
up together for at least the first 5 years, as on a Kibbutz, rarely
marry. Yet we manage to end up with people as similar to ourselves
as they could be without being related. The preoccupation of today's
lovers, the looking, touching and thinking of the other, is
reminiscent of the biological sexual imprinting stage.

Idealization and its uses

Once the label 'love' is attached, perception switches into 'eliminate
the negative, accentuate the positive' mode. It even denies reality
to the extent that a person in love will not see dangerous traits that
are perfectly obvious to everyone else.

Choice

We need the idealized stereotype we call love to justify the
monumental consequences of such a complex choice. Unlike our
ancestors' social set-up, where the balance of people of
marriageable age who could meet each other was small, we have
a highly mobile, technologically and communicatively sophisticated
society, and meet more new people in a day than some of our
grandparents met in a month or even a year. And proposals then
were limited to marriage. Other types of arrangements are
acceptable these days, including the choice of not marrying at all.
Joining lives with a partner in whatever way is a reflection of our

judgment in an important life decision, so in order to trust in our own judgment it is necessary to think well of, idealize, the object of choice!

Idealizing projection and growth

But idealization is more than self-serving, it is truly life-enhancing. It is like an artist's creation. The artist abstracts the inner essence, selects out the mundane reality, shows us the unrealized connections. The idealizing lover does the same, ignores faults to highlight good points, and goes beyond the superficial, even beyond the person and into him or herself to bring out a relationship perspective that neither had alone. They see what each could become. If the image of the other that partners hold is better than the image they have of themselves, they help each other to psychological growth and maturity. In effect each is conveying to the other, 'I think you're better than I am, and I think you're better than you think you are.'

Idealizing projection and similarity to ideal self

Psychoanalysts would say that the feeling of completeness that love brings is because the idealized lover is a construction of all one's own desired features, projected onto this stranger. You need a mysterious stranger to be able to project, someone known quite well has already established their qualities. This is their back-up argument to the one of memories of the mother-child blissful union evoked in romantic love.

Projection is the process by which traits in ourselves that we don't like are imagined to be in someone else ('It's *her* that's aggressive, not me') or in the case of idealizing projection, traits we would *like* to have more of – intelligence, altruism, or outgoingness – are simply imagined in the lover, and then of course the feeling that they complete you comes easily. They are a sort of super-self.

Actually, in all friendships, even children's, we tend to like people who are more like our 'ideal' self than we are ourselves. The more similar the potential partner to one's ideal self, the more likely one is to fall in love. As Maureen, a 32-year-old assistant producer said of Stephen:

> He looked nice, nothing extraordinary, but then as we talked I found out how much he knew. He was so knowledgeable about his own field but also knew as much about drama as I did and much more about music

and history and sailing. He seemed a universal man, yet so unassuming and modest. I see so many types in television who make such a noise about the little expertise they have it seemed so refreshing. I couldn't ever imagine this kind, gentle guy ever being like that. He would have been a wonderful GP [just like her kind, gentle GP father, it later transpired]. I hope I can keep my feet on the ground and keep on mastering subjects like him.

What counts as love is the degree to which each fulfils the other's projected image. These idealized images are not what others around perceive, but as long as they are not impossible extractions to live up to (a prince charming who will transform your life without any effort on your part, except for slipping your foot into the glass slipper) then the exaggeration of desirable qualities and the downgrading of the undesirable is the best policy in relationships. To eliminate the negative and accentuate the positive has ever been a good recipe, as Dale Carnegie promised millions.

Passionate, idealistic love is not so blind as folklore has it, when it provides a positive goal for the other to aspire to. Geraldine, for example, wrote whimsical little poems about the children she taught. Rhymes of no consequence, she was fond of saying to Pat, her council officer husband. But Pat had come from a matter of fact practical background and thought they were charming, off-key observations and talked her into sending them to the PTA newsletter, from where they were taken up by the teacher's magazine. Now she contributes regularly to parent's magazines. 'Imagine getting paid for them,' she glows, 'they must be better than I thought.'

Idealization may be the major defence mechanism for long-term relationship happiness. The goal is to predict and shape the other's behaviour, moods and personality sufficiently well to permit a smooth fit in getting on with each other. Each helps the other towards more sociably desirable qualities by such idealistic 'shaping-up'. Accuracy, then, is not so much of an issue; happy couples are those who agree on an idealized version of personality that each is satisfied with. While Glenys saw her husband as assertive, he would demur – well, a bit on the aggressive side perhaps. And David called Glenys understanding and sympathetic; she called it over-emotional:

I cry over snippets of information in the paper, about neglected animals, cruelly treated children and starving refugees and I don't know any of them.

If each partner helps the other to an acceptable view of themselves this is creative idealization, and it is a mutually rewarding, growth-enhancing experience, not a distortion. It is accurate in that the salient points are abstracted (aggression and emotion were traits of concern to David and Glenys) and reworked by the creative artist's rose tints.

I asked my volunteer couples to fill in a personality questionnaire as if it was their partner completing it. In other words they had to predict what their partner's responses would be to this questionnaire. Meanwhile the partner completed the questionnaire for themself and then the results were compared. The happier couples thought their partner should be much higher on the desirable scales like sociable, fitting in with others, honourable, pleasant, and so on, while the less happy thought their partners should be higher on neurotic behaviour, tough-mindedness and hostility scales than they actually were. It would be interesting to redo this exercise in another ten years with the same people. Self-fulfilling prophecies say that if you expect a neurotic, obsessive reaction you will surely get it – just as expecting the best will help your chances of getting it.

In one study, unhappy husbands saw their wives as immature, egocentric, suggestible, demanding and naive, while wives retaliated with aggressive, hostile, impulsive, unemotional and insensitive – in other words the very antithesis of idealization. These are not traits that any partner would wish to 'live up to'. When each is communicating to the other greater expectations than they have of themselves, they hold a view of each other that can weather bad or ambiguous situations.

The lover's conflict: uncertainty, hope and fear

The fear of rejection prolongs love (as does outside opposition), and uncertainty enhances the intensity. The smallest crumb of hope sends the 'ecstasy meter' through the roof, and often there is an incomprehensibility about the lack of return of this love, so ardently offered. Because of the intensity it is almost impossible to believe that the other doesn't feel the same way.

As in the playing of fruit machines, the combination of doubt and hope produces irrational behaviour. This is where love is quite rightly referred to as an addiction. It comes involuntarily, interrupts ongoing plans, and intrudes into one's daily thoughts so that little else can be done. The lover's conflict is declaring themselves at the same point between uncertainty and hope that their partner has reached. The growth of love can be smothered by too much affectionate pressure or extinguished by too distinterested a response. But, like the obsessive, we test love again and again, often to the point of destroying it.

Some said they just knew – without words, and this is the advantage of having similar attitudes to love and sex, the pacing to the commitment point is the same.

Men and women deal with the uncertainty of reciprocation in quite different ways. We intensify sex-role characteristics when in love, even more so when trying to prove ourselves under the strain of uncertainty and stress of possible rejection.

The fade out

This is the first seed of conflict and withdrawal. Fading passion is accompanied by a physiological return to 'stable state'; the high of the euphoric state subsides to a pleasant contentment.

The people who have never fallen in love, with the physiological excitement that literally sweeps them off their feet, may have felt slightly cheated when everyone around them swoons, but now they have an advantage, as they are insured against the painful disillusion and recriminations of the fade-out stage. Media and society in general make sure we all know about the passionate state of love, but not much about the decline. Nature, after sucking us in with the wonderful 'high', then cruelly sprinkles damp-down dust around, to make sure the couple can get on with providing and protecting the family and participating equally in community life.

Instead of looking inside at this chemical fall-out, couples may feel they have fallen out of love, or have chosen the wrong person. This point seems to be the most critical in the whole relationship cycle, and the way it is resolved affects the rest of the relationship.

A couple may still go on with their plans for marriage or living together, believing the dip in passion is due to their fear of commitment. (And sometimes this is so.) When the expected exhilaration doesn't return, the commitment is never really cemented – and they may break up. This is the divorce peak; the actual time is 3 years from marriage to divorce, but the process of crumbling behind it started earlier. If they do keep living together it is often in a state of temporariness, which makes both reluctant to invest emotional energy or time in the relationship.

In addition, of course, one can suffer the fade out while the other is still enthralled. And because men are quicker off the mark than women in the first flush of passion, they are also more likely to fade out sooner.

Ardent men and waiting women

Premarital sex figures have remained roughly the same over the centuries, if you accept some complicated inferences from the statisticians who compile these things. Studies show that, in both the animal and human world, it is the female that does the choosing. Even in human dating it is claimed that 50 per cent of initial advances are made by women; but the rate at which synchronization proceeds to sexual intimacy is different. In contrast to women who love too much, the women who wait can find emerging out of the crowd after everyone else has long disappeared a previously overlooked man, sticking around, being patient, being helpful, being trustworthy – and being the one who wins. As the sociobiologists say, 'Men are a vast breeding experiment, run by women.'

The traits women choose in a man are the ones that will be passed on to the next generation if there is any physiological backing to them. Some men don't understand the waiting game. They misinterpret caution as teasing, and think of it as a hostile game, for which they hate women. Men who hate women are men who feel they have no control over them. Misogynist men are those for whom intimacy means anxiety, and its corrollary, boredom. Their concern vanishes as soon as romantic ardour is dampened by the certainty of her commitment. Worse, he will blame her for his post-romantic neurochemical dip, and criticize her for not being attractive enough to turn him on any more. His need for intimacy is mixed with fears of being hurt, deprived, abandoned or engulfed, which start to surface again once he becomes adapted to the love chemicals coursing through his brain. The cultural model of femininity takes the place of real knowledge, since a man frightened of women has taken care to avoid close contact with them, and has had therefore no opportunity to revise his stereotypes. When he sees women through the distorting cultural projections of the media – films, television, books and so on – he can't help but view them as weaker than himself, passive and emotional and needing men more than men need women. That being the case, he reasons, she should be paying attention to him, caring for and nurturing him. However, culture can't explain these attitudes totally, or else all men would be misogynists.

In Chapter 3, personality and differences in early intimate experiences throw some light onto the 'lone rangers' of the intimacy scene – the cool, independent, unemotional and in-control man; control of himself *and* of his woman. These sex-differences in emotional and sexual arousal do much to explain men's attitude to women, from over-the-top idealization to violence, rape, and men's conviction of women's incomprehensibility. The differences in emotional and sexual arousal have a biological history that has stood the evolutionary test of time, and the consequences for the new demands of intimacy (his responsiveness to her expressivity), structure the differences in emotional communication between the sexes in a way that biology could never have predicted (a fuller explanation in Chapter 6).

From babyhood, most men are taught to control and eschew emotions, and are therefore totally unprepared for the experience of love. The hormones that flood their system alter their perception and motivations. When he sees the object that first triggered his biochemical flow, his whole world is reorganized, centred on her, planned around her. The emotional loneliness of which he has been largely unaware for years (speaking now of the average single western man) is suddenly dissipated, and it feels heavenly. This is even the case for men who have had dozens of sexual encounters, and are proud of 'never being short of a woman', but who have never been really emotionally involved.

Take, for example, James, who, at 48, has fallen in love for the second time: 'It is even stronger than my feelings at 22', he confides excitedly. 'I couldn't think it could ever happen to me again.' I believed James, a tall, dark and very attractive antique dealer, when he told me he had had several dozen women 'half in love with him' and he had had four long-term live-in relationships (sequentially). Very nice, interesting women, he said, erudite companions and pleasant sex partners, but not one had engaged his whole attention since the love affair, 26 years ago, which went wrong because of his immaturity:

> Nevertheless, I don't seem to have learned much in the intervening quarter century, I can feel myself doing all the same things again. I've just got to know where she is all the time, and I want to see her more than she wants to see me. So I find myself excuses to walk past her

house, even shutting up my shop in prime business time to do it. In fact, my business is going downhill because I can't bring myself to go away to auctions to buy if it means staying overnight, and the rate at which the tourists are buying I'll have nothing left to sell. People stop coming in if they see a half empty, uninteresting shop. I think about Carmen practically non-stop. Even mother being seriously ill doesn't enter my thoughts much once Carmen is there. When we're together, the whole world changes – I notice how beautiful the sun is shining on the sea, lovely scenes on the coast that are now associated with her. I can't even look at them if I'm not with her.

Realizing how un-macho this must sound, this successful businessman in the depths of despair about what seemed even to himself irrational behaviour cast around for an explanation:

I feel so at home with her, I love the way she holds the teapot when she pours the tea, the way she talks through her recipes when she's cooking. She does everything in a careful methodical way – always the same predictable movements. [All the easier to synchronize with?] The teapot and teacups are always in exactly the same place, beautiful china cups and Georgian teapot. Her kitchen walls are hung with lovely Victorian oils. In fact, everything in the house spells taste, discrimination, just the same way I would have done it myself. She even has the same birthday as my mother, and chose the same restaurant to celebrate as my mother did on her fiftieth – of which the family made a big occasion.

Carmen has evidently provided to James similarities that are to him signs of inner compatibility, more so than all the other women he knew. But all is not going well; Carmen is clearly suspicious of this wild knight proclaiming love eternally. She has every reason to be the proverbial woman who waits and watches, since her husband left her and their two children without warning some years ago. Now, at 36, she and her teenage children are stable and content. Every time James gets close, there follows a freeze for several days – as if she is testing his endurance:

If only I knew that. I'd go through hell and high water to prove I was the man for her, I know she needs me and I will stay around for as long as it takes. I try to be calm and the strong man she wants me to be but when she does relax and we have a wonderful day or night together I start getting overconfident and messing things up, just showing off I suppose. I hate myself afterwards but at the time I can't stop myself. Like you forget the resolution to have only one glass after you've had one drink. I prance around telling her wildly improbable things about my exploits and deals – I just get so over-involved, she called it manic once. I insist on doing things, like the other night, when the boiler went out. She'd struggled with the damn thing for 10 years so of course she knew more about it than me. But no, I had to brag about my knowledge of antique machinery and pushed her aside. Of course I took about 2 hours and she was furious, kept saying she could have done it in 10 minutes without all the soot over the floor too.

So while James is driven demented with love, Carmen waits . . . and tests. The only question is, can James stand it? He feels he is ever on the brink of depression, and was near suicide after the boiler episode. But if this relationship runs the usual course, Carmen will be like the dozens of other nice women in James's life. The peak of his intensity will start to decline just as hers starts to climb, and the struggle between each about their feelings will be this lack of matching. In no relationship James has ever had have they both wanted commitment at the same time, and he remembers recriminations – 'You said you loved me, and I gave up something for you' – over and over again. In spite of James's feeling that this time is *the* one, his friends say they notice no difference to all the other friendships he had previously.

In male and female differences in emotional arousal, it seems often to be the women who are the most disappointed. Every woman I spoke to commented on the difference in her man before and after emotional commitment. Angela:

> He would do anything for me, nothing was too much trouble, he talked about anything and everything under the sun, and I thought how lucky I was to have such an empathetic man. So when he started coming home, reading the newspaper and watching the news on television – even while we were eating – I thought it was something I'd done that he was upset about. We would have arguments about there being nothing wrong! And I truly believe he doesn't remember all the things he said to me, he's surprised when I comment on things he's told me about his family for instance – and he says 'How did you know that?'

For people (and this is usually men) who have been used to ignoring their emotions, it is like unblocking a dam – it all rushes out until equilibrium is restored, and then in the calm they start building the wall again.

Why men change

The powerful emotions aroused in the first stage of love need great control and men usually only let them out on high days and holidays. All women remarked in some way on the change from initial loving articulation to virtual mono-syllabic, or at least reluctant, emotional discussion.

Many men are enthusiastic suitors until they get their goal. Once commitment of some sort is made, women go from being chased and catered to, to being the caterer. They do not like it: well, who would? But, worse, the equality they had felt, the weight and seriousness given to their opinions and feelings evaporates as he picks up the role of decision-maker, this time for them both. The women who recounted the extravagant behaviour above were also the women that now sighed over precisely the opposite, the lack of concern and expressions of love: 'I seem to have become invisible,' as one woman put it! Now they had passed the test, achieved the goal, it seemed the men felt they deserved to be able to put their feet up and enjoy the fruits of battle. Janice sums it up for many of the women:

> I made a bit of a joke about him never mentioning love any more, and how we must be an old married couple (she's 31, married 3 years). He didn't even answer. So in the end I made a bit of an issue about it. When I wanted to know what he did feel then, all I got was a low-grade mumble, and 'Can't we ever talk about anything else?'

In the remaining chapters, the lack of men's emotional responsiveness, and the fears of many of them about becoming emotionally dependent, are fully examined and discussed. It starts after erotic 'desensitization', lessens the reward of being in love, and then the cost of emotional expressiveness increases. It is not a deliberate plot by men to get the women, and they are usually surprised at charges of 'You've changed.' He has, and so has she, but at different rates.

When women reach the palpitation stage, later than men, they make up for it. The sheer generosity of the women in love I interviewed was a credit to womankind. They happily scrubbed, cooked and sewed, did his accounts, the ironing, took his dog on holiday, mixed concrete, lent money, redecorated his house, nursed sick men, did companion duty on jogging exercises, tended his greenhouse, filled in on his job, mowed his lawn – in fact I can't think of any worthwhile area of human endeavour that women hadn't helped their men with. At this stage, women's only reward was the assurance of being loved. As his ardour is coming off flashpoint hers is just simmering up to boil, and once there, it sets – her emotional, romantic and sexual feelings are now cast, pushing her to loyalty and lasting commitment. So this first struggle between hope, uncertainty and commitment can have an intensity that neither is prepared for – heightened feelings also mean heightened conflict intensity. Romantic love is probably the greatest spur to action we experience, alongside survival and perhaps pathological revenge. And yet so often we allow this tremendous powerhouse to degenerate into alienation, and not the idealization it can sustain. Tolerance for uncertainty allows a lover to idealize instead of criticize and make the commitment towards coupledom.

Because the situation is emotional, most women don't ask for continued demonstration of it in an emotionally calm tone, thus creating an unhelpfully demanding atmosphere, which feels to him like manipulation. The partners of women who felt let-down and unloved were usually not willing to talk about it to me, but other men, who had passed through this conflict, remembered it. Mostly they remembered their uneasiness and puzzlement, as their women turned from loving expressiveness to demanding and tearful pleas for reassurance. This seemed to be the first critical point at which emotional sympathy between the two was lost. It was not inevitable that women would respond to this perceived loss of love with an escalation of demand, sometimes they would just find someone else, or withdraw emotionally themselves, matching their partner's perceived level of involvement. Some older women remembered it, they had accepted it with humour and managed to keep up their level of emotional input without expecting it returned. This probably speaks of women's changing status and increasing power: younger women feel they have the right to demand equal involvement.

But the tragedy is that each related the downturn to themselves, taking it as an indication that something was wrong, rather than recognizing the psycho-physiological inevitability of the fade out.

Men who love too much

Men in love come alive as at no other time. It is this overwhelming euphoria which leads them into such rash promises. Promises which wise women take with a grain of salt. In love, a man's whole perception changes. He believes himself capable of heroic feats, his old life looks dull in comparison, nothing else interests him but the consummation of his love. Old friends and prior family fade into insignificance – it is as if they had never been. This is what hurts a previous girlfriend or wife so much. Under the influence of a passionate new love affair, he is stone-cold and bored with prior commitments. He is sure that this time it is far stronger and more real than he *ever* felt before. To the outsider though, it looks the same every time – the onset, the duration, the things he says – only the woman's name is different.

There is a second, minor, pattern. The older man, who has more to lose in terms of home, children, respect and sometimes career, won't allow his feelings to run away with him quite so much and attempts to keep his wife, while still pursuing his new desire. And even less frequent, the man who manages to keep two separate families secret all his life. If there are any women doing this then they can keep up the double life better than the men, for it is unheard of in marriage research. But more of affairs later.

The following interview was from a grandmother's viewpoint, and illustrates perfectly the lack of insight some men have when emotionally and sexually aroused. She told me she had watched her normally affectionate son turn into a cool stranger, not once, but every time he fell in love. She was now particularly upset because his last love-tumble meant she would lose her close relationship with her two grandchildren. Her own husband had recently died and she felt she was losing all hope in her life, 'just because of those wicked hormones', she said vehemently. She had been so glad he'd married at last, not least because she looked forward to a stable period of friendship with him, now that she was alone. Three years and two children later, however, she was just as shocked as Heather, her daughter-in-law, when he fell in love with a woman at work. Nothing could convince him that he hadn't made a mistake in marrying. This new woman was his 'real' destiny, he was sorry for his previous 'dalliances' (including his marriage), but must be 'true' to himself. His mother says:

If only I'd taped what Godfrey said about Heather when they first met. It's word for word what he's saying about Anthea now, but I think any opposition just increases his determination. Heather and I have talked about it, and she first thought she could convince him to stay for the children's sake. But the more he tries to deny what they once were to each other, the less she tries, poor girl, she is so hurt. I'm so angry with him. Much as I would love it if Heather did succeed, I know him better, he will blunder on until he cools off again and I don't want to make so much fuss now that he'll feel too proud to come back once this passion for Anthea has burnt out. I keep telling Heather not to burn bridges, but of course that's so hard for her. I don't think she'll ever get over him saying that he wasn't really in love with her and that though he meant

what he said at the time he hadn't known enough to judge it properly.
Now I can remember him telling me that about the girl he was engaged
to before Heather came along. And I'm afraid Godfrey is a chip off the
old block, my husband had two affairs during our marriage, although
he never left me.

When idealization turns to criticism

The fade out starts with criticism. The sudden realization of how
irritating that nervous cough is when it was once a charming
manifestation of reserve and politeness. For some it feels like
deliberate betrayal, although of course it is their own expectations
of a life transformed responsible for the disenchantment. These are
the blamers, asking their partners what they have or haven't done
to explain their own decrease in ardour.

When love is conceived of as something that happens *to* us, it
stops us actively creating a good relationship. To imagine this wasn't
the right person after all is easier than changing our attitude. We
ask ourselves how we could have fallen for that person, not how
can we move from intense stimulation and attraction to intimate
attachment.

Couples still together after many years also remember the
downturn, but accept it quite philosophically – 'it's natural' – and
were even relieved – 'I couldn't have kept that up all my life.' Perhaps
an important point here is that the memory of obsessive thoughts
in the first stage didn't appear to be as intense and frequent as
among the more extreme reactors. Disillusion obviously hits harder
the earlier it falls.

Also revealing are the reflections of those who did break up and
either divorced or went on to find someone else, including those
who had drifted into perfectly good, companionable and secure
relationships, but felt somewhat cheated because it hadn't started
with the excitement of romantic passion. The old attachment was
dismissed as never having been 'real' love, even though they may
have had several contented, productive years. The yearning for
passionate, involving love can destroy solid friendships, but it is not
another person that brings involvement, it is knowing how to catch
the intimacy-conflict cycle at the right time with the right response.
The sad couples are those where one partner, thinking they had
fallen out of love, initiated divorce – but then regretted it. The other's
trust had been damaged, or they had found someone else, and
reconciliation was impossible. A third of people who divorce say

they wished they'd stuck it out and tried harder.

One interviewee, Nadia, told me:

> No one prepared me for the way I would feel. I only know now because
> I've been through the whole thing again, *twice*. I fall madly in love, think
> he's wonderful, then after 6 months or so I start being critical. When I
> was married it was like I'd fallen into a black hole – I thought how could
> I have *not* noticed all his faults before, they're just screaming at me now.
> I thought I'd better get out before we had children – he was very cut-up.
> The next time the urge to criticize my boyfriend hit me, I didn't make
> the connection – just thought, I couldn't be bothered with relationships.
> I was still seeing my husband at work, and I felt terrible. Then I met my
> last boyfriend and I'll never forget going into the kitchen one evening,
> yelling at him for throwing tea leaves down the sink (which blocks) and
> I just froze – it clicked. I hadn't worried about it much before, why did
> it upset me so much now? I'd let other relationships deteriorate through
> my criticism, I thought I couldn't help it, but I talked to a psychologist
> friend who said maybe I was really disappointed with myself. And I
> suppose I was. No one has ever been as kind or as much fun as my
> husband, and I left him. Of course someone else recognized a good man
> when they saw one, and so he's married again, expecting a child. I'm
> 32 and it's taken me all this time to find all this out, and to be honest
> I don't really trust myself again.

The ideal situation was voiced by those who said they'd realized
soon after living together they weren't as similar as they'd thought,
but began now to appreciate the differences. One lady showed me
her first wedding anniversary card, which had a picture of
Tweedledum and Tweedledee sitting like identical twins (in
synchrony) and identically dressed, with identical glum expressions.
The caption said 'compatibility is boring!':

> Once I'd admitted I was bored with football on television and was going
> to read upstairs, he said, 'Good, that means I don't have to go to anymore
> of those uplifting, culturally excellent concerts with you!' It turned out
> he'd been bored stiff by symphonies, and we had a good laugh over all
> the things we'd dragged each other along to for the sake of being
> together: we both went upstairs then, not to read though! (Mind you,
> he put the football on the video.)

So here, as in all good partnerships, the differences which once
would have separated them now drew them together more closely.
As they each told each other their real view of sports and classical
music they realized that each had put the relationship before their

own interests, and even been prepared to put up with a couple of hours of boredom just to be with each other. This they appreciated, even if they never learned to appreciate the other's interests.

Studies on friendship show the same patterning. While similarity, particularly of attitude and feelings, is what draws people together, it is the differences that make for long-term interest. These have to be revealed at precisely the right time for them not to be threatening, and the similarities and differences alternately expressed in the relationship as other stresses come along.

Which similarities and which differences are of course critical – and in Chapter 3 you will see the important similarities are physiological arousal cycles, and in Chapter 5, attitudes towards relationships. Successful differences are the subject of Chapter 4; these are coping strategies in the face of stress. It's a matter of having enough similarities to relax, confident that one will be understood, and enough differences to provide help with the other deficiencies, not to mention a little exciting unpredictability, variety and interest. We all have different levels of tolerance to un-predictability, excitement and risk. This is what fuels love and idealization.

It's not only our physiology to blame for the anger, confusion, bitterness, disillusion and desperation that so often replace romantic love. Those first few months are lived in an unreal haze, each keeping up the front, fitting in, avoiding conflict, the newly exciting sexual passion, the attention withdrawn from other people, and activities to please and benefit each other – all these are quite sufficient to be felt as serious deprivation when they stop and life goes on normally. And stop they must. Once a couple becomes 'at home' together, they usually feel it is a refuge from the stressful world, where hair can be let down, all can be understood and Sunday behaviour exchanged for weekday.

Negotiating a smooth passage from romantic love and idealization to intimate love needs a clear understanding about what's worth preserving, enhancing, and idealizing, and what will turn into a liability. Admirable self-discipline could, when the stress level rises, turn to mule-like obstinacy, or his sweet shyness turn to indifference and inability to express emotions. By contrast, honesty, empathy, trustworthiness are less variable and more easily judged attributes.

How to interpret criticism

The ideal is to get to the stage where you both see criticism as a catalyst to productive change which helps the relationship become stronger. But ideals and reality commonly diverge, and criticism is more often experienced as a rejection. This is due to childhood conditioning, when it was frequently accompanied by raised voices and disapproving looks. Thinking of criticism not as fault-finding, but as valuable feedback and guide to the other's emotional state, alters the negative sensitivity with which it is usually received.

You tell them how wonderful they are and then they think they're too good for you!

What we want is unadulterated admiration, and that's what our partner would like to be able to give us. But the fate of everyone who enjoys such a diet of positive attention, like the sychophantic flattery the boss gets, is to *believe* it. Without self-correcting feedback even mature adults can end up like spoilt brats.

Timing and collusion in self-revelation

As the neurochemical fade out returns perception to normal, each partner is dismayed to notice imperfections that had been previously invisible – but perception can be trained. That's the basis of Freudian insight into repression. When positive emotions like love hold perception in thrall, idealization can be maintained. But only if the partner colludes in keeping up the positivity, and refrains from tipping the balance too quickly.

Interpreting criticism as the entrance to the next stage – attachment

Attachment heralds the upgrading of the likeable qualities, the enhancing of the ideal self, and recognizing the emerging qualities of trust, solidarity and empathy. Attraction was there to promote the longer-term qualities, which are eventually more satisfying and necessary to health and happiness than sexual excitement.

Critical guide to fade out

You could keep a notebook of the criticism each makes, agreeing beforehand that neither is to be castigated for their considered criticism. Then, at an appointed time each week (or less) sit down and criticize each other – one at a time. The other one is *not* allowed to speak except, to nod sympathetically and profer a minimum apology – 'I'm sorry you felt like that, I'm sorry you took it that way', etc., and then each is never to mention that complaint again outside 'criticism time'. The idea is that each will think about the other's criticism, and understand the biological basis of idealization and fade out. They will be able to identify the expectations the criticism was based on, and decide if it merely reflects the criticizer's unrealistic expectations. Later, they can agree to criticize in reward terms rather than punishment ones, i.e. 'I would appreci-ate it if you did/didn't do . . .' rather than 'If you don't stop doing . . .'.

If you don't think your partner is going to take this seriously, then you just have to read the criticism yourself, and concentrate on turning their dissatisfaction and your upset into an opportunity for growth and strengthening of the relationship.

ALWAYS:
- Acknowledge their criticism in some way, don't ignore it, dismiss it or sulk about it. You don't have to agree with it . . . yet. As a first comment use neutral responses:
    'Do you think so?'
    'I'm sorry you think that'
    'It sounds as if I've upset you'
- Evaluate it – is it true/valid; is this fade out blues; are they emphasizing differences rather than similarities?
- Enquire how you can help them maintain their idealization. Assume they are only telling you this to help the relationship.
    'Yes, we do have different tastes in x, but look how we both think/enjoy y'
    'What can I do to show you you're wrong?'
    'Yes, I may be x, but wait until you see my y'
- If you can't change whatever the criticism is, acknowledge it and direct their attention elsewhere:
    'Yes I do have a hooked nose, so until we can afford cosmetic surgery you'd better look at me only from full frontal angle'

Remember that criticism is the first line of defence against overwhelming closeness.

No one bothers to criticize someone they don't care about.

Identifying strongly with a partner means their inadequacies become our own to the outside world. The joy of closeness inevitably becomes a close-up of their weakness. The purpose of idealization is to collude in *not* criticizing.

2

Attachment: closeness v. autonomy

Limpets have some similar problems to humans. They have to go out into the deep blue sea to maintain life, and then rush back home to cling tightly to a rock to prevent being eaten themselves. It helps to have a known safe spot to return to quickly, and limpet's safe spots are so worn that the resident limpet fits snugly into it, its curves fitting the rocks bumps like a lock and key.

On commitment to each other, humans create a spot like the limpet, a psychological 'safe house' that we return to after jaunts into the unknown. Finding a mutually comfortable balance between clinging together in this safe spot, creating a joint identity and being apart while maintaining one's unique self, is a life-long relationship problem. Like the tides that the limpet has to calculate, couples have to match external sources of satisfaction and danger which can interfere with their homing instinct.

The biology of distance

The forces of attraction are counterbalanced; even when the world was underpopulated there was this counteracting mechanism. When two people are attracted they stick to each other as exclusively as they can, thereby reducing other possibilities of attraction. The couple just don't 'see' anyone else – just as well, because most of these other possibilities have attachments of their own which mean they only have eyes for their own partner. All these separate, exclusive couple attachments mean that any social group, human or animal, spreads out and maintains intimate distances between those called friends, acquaintances, colleagues and so on. The change from traditional, close, mutually involved marriages to the loosely interdependent 'therapeutic' marriage parallels the changes in population density and dispersion.

The creation and balancing of a joint identity

It is not just a matter of two single people now becoming a couple which is the sum of the two parts. They must negotiate an interdependence which often precipitates a desperate struggle, usually for 6 months to a year, sometimes for a lifetime. For some couples this crusade starts immediately after the honeymoon, for others on setting up home together.

Many couples remember this period as being the worst of their relationship. Frustrations built up silently, resentments about being taken for granted, assumptions of easy harmony shattered, establishing domestic ground-rules, all often symbolically transferred to a single, stupid issue, like who leaves the top off the toothpaste. The sheer difficulty of adjusting to the closest relationship most of us have had since early childhood is never referred to on the wedding congratulation cards, and most couples are horrified and miserable at this unexpected disaster. The consequences range from being revolted by a touch that would once have been thrilling, to a frenzy of separate activities that necessitate days or evenings away from each other.

It is early childhood that is the model for much of what goes on now. The pivot is dependency versus autonomy. These issues were always there of course, in moving towards commitment, but they intensify once a high proportion of the couple's time is now spent together and they have a shared understanding of their emotional commitment towards each other. The confidence and trust brought to commitment is shaped by personality, early experience and the love attitude of the partner.

Attachment and growth

John Bowlby, the author of many books on attachment, loss and separation in early childhood and their consequences for adult intimate relationships, defines attachment as interdependence that creates a happiness and harmony for both. He coined the word 'attachment' to describe the emotions binding the mobile young of various species to their mother, and the later pair-bonding to their opposite sex partner. Much has been written by Bowlby and others about how the baby's first experiences with its mother, being held, stroked, looked at, gurgled over and so on, create a prolonged stimulation of the nervous system which strengthens neural pathways that have a lifelong responsiveness to tenderness and closeness, touching, gazing and sweet-talking.

The more a mother rat licks and touches her babies, the more they grow. If for some reason she doesn't (if the babies are hidden, for example), their growth stops; not from malnutrition, but from the alteration of brain chemicals that would normally be stimulated by the mother's touch. Within minutes of licking, body-building cycles are triggered, and are shut down within half an hour of separation. To start growing again, a baby rat had to be given back to its mother or the researchers had to spend their days stroking them with wet paint brushes! And it's the same with human babies – touched and massaged premature babies increase their weight by 50 per cent compared to those left alone; and their brain chemicals increase.

An excellent book *The Joy of Touch* describes how that neglected sense, touch, alters biological arousal, and is a necessary lifelong health-promoting motivation. But because it has become linked with sex, touch is taboo – to the detriment of western society, particularly men.

The heart-rending accounts of the utter despair of children and babies separated from their mothers, and observation of later adult separation panic and anxiety, left no one in any doubt that the deprivation of loving physical contact is stressful and harmful to the mind and the body. The repeated breaking of attachment bonds in childhood is believed by many psychoanalysts to lead to the formation of abnormal and sociopathic personalities, and to set the scene for individual differences in ability to form close relationships. The dependent clingers, who haven't formed a neurochemical system in childhood that easily produces their natural morphine, need an attachment to keep their neural reservoirs of opiates high enough to prevent panic attacks.

Even securely attached adults who lose a close relationship are more likely to suffer cancer, heart disease, ulcers and arthritis, or become depressed, involved in accidents or alcohol abuse. Figures from medical records tell the same story – securely attached couples have much better physical and psychological health than single, divorced, separated and unhappily married couples. The death of one half of a couple can even precipitate death in the healthy survivor.

In an amazing set of figures analysing over a million people in the United Kingdom between 15 and 64 years old, who had between them 200 different occupations, it was found that whatever the occupation of the husband when he died, the wife tended to die in the same 'mortality risk' band. So, if he was a coalminer she died, like him, shortly after retirement. If she was a cabinet minister's wife, she lived, like him, much longer. It seems likely that the attachment synchrony communicated the occupational health risk – with negative effects on the wives' well-being. They had established a neurophysiological synchrony, just like the early mother-baby attachment.

Attachment is the opium of the couple

The tie that binds is responsible for the resonating connections in the rhythms established between those that live together – and it can even be between human and animal. Not only could the majority of spouses tell when one of them was receiving bad treatment in the room next door, (as measured by a machine that picks up electrical changes on the skin) but so also did dogs get aroused at the precise moment an experimenter was putting ice cubes down the dog's master's neck, out of sight and hearing.

Blood sugar levels, hormone production, brain networks – all harmonize and synchronize with each other. They become 'attached' at this physiological level, as well as the emotional level. They become attuned to each other, and the daily experience of one has an influence on the other's arousal level. The relationship facilitates an optimal emotional growth stage that is attenuated by conflict or separation. When happy, they can keep the other's system humming away. Attention is directed outward, life's opportunities are maximized and each serves as a secure base for the other to return to for recharging.

The basic disposition of human nature is, like other social species, to feel secure with the familiar and be wary of the strange. These have been good past evolutionary guides, minimizing danger. Given a familiar other, the strange is not so alarming and silent communication between the physiological states is a reassuring 'I'm here, don't worry, relax.' Any change disrupts this synchronous attunement to each other, and the medical figures quoted previously attest to the suffering – the sleeping difficulties, a compulsion to pace up and down (as if searching for the disappeared person), depression, frequent crying, overworking of the fight/flight mechanism, which results in the increased heart and respiration rate, body temperature elevation, and a decrease in the immunological response. Sufficient change can bring clingingly anxious or aggressive behaviour.

Reunion after a separation restores the cheerful mood, the fight/flight system throttles back to lower surveillance, sleep and immune rhythms are restored. Even without separation, emotional distance and upset can disturb an attached couple. They are then 'not in tune' with one another. They will use metaphors to describe brain-wave incompatibility – like 'not being on the same wavelength'. This often happens to newly divorcing couples. They disagree, glare at each other across the solicitor's office – but they are still attached to each other at some level and often feel better in each other's presence even if throwing verbal insults. Detachment can take months, or even years, and until that happens some sensitive divorcees have trouble in accepting, or even remembering, other events of emotional significance. Life cannot be lived spontaneously without a certain level of opiate production which a secure attachment orchestrates. In many sad cases couples are surprised at their intense loneliness and preoccupation with thoughts of each other after the divorce or separation. They feel 'stuck' at a certain emotional level and unable to start over again with someone else.

There is, clearly, good reason to see attachment as the second stage of relationship growth. The chemical highs of falling in love with a new exciting person are now replaced by familiarity of the loved one, and the next cycle of feeling is mediated by the opiates. It is too stressful to the body not to pass from romantic love to attachment, or realistic, conjugal love as it is sometimes called. New levels of physical and psychological growth can only happen when one cycle is finished. Each cycle has it's own function and place in the hierarchy of relationship.

Sex differences in surrender

Conformity is the opposite of creativity. To hand over important life decisions to another, no matter how much they have our best interests at heart, is de-motivating. In marriage it means conforming to marital roles and accepting the standards of living together handed down over the generations when women were powerless – as well as doing most of the housework.

Therapeutic change in identity

Our partners become 'listening posts' in the process of self-clarification, to whom the account of change through experience is addressed. A major psychologist in this field believes people stop growing towards their natural maturity when they repress certain aspects of themselves, and maladjustment happens when they can't talk to anyone about their emotions. Then we succumb to the strait-jacket of social roles, and become less able to recognize our own motivations, feelings and wishes. This is the road to boredom, conformity and lack of confidence. We can only achieve lasting emotional security in our relationships if we have a clear idea of the other person as well as ourselves. People, says Sidney Jourard, become patients when they have not disclosed themselves fully to the significant people in their lives. There is no more rewarding experience than revealing to another one's thoughts, feelings, beliefs, wants, hopes, ambitions, fears – things another person cannot know unless told. The reward is assessing the other's probable reactions and then having those assumptions confirmed. If someone important agrees with our values, empathizes with our worries and exchanges their own, a new emotional perspective is created, a feeling bond that can endure much physical and material deprivation. By choosing as intimate partners those who share and support one's identity, it can be retained and developed.

However, choosing another on the basis of attractiveness, status, intelligence, availability, similarity or pheromones does not guarantee that a partner shares one's view of oneself – or even of one's idealized self. Two people can idealize each other for totally non-existent qualities that they perceive in each other, but the litmus test of durability is the degree to which they do share and support each other's actual identity. Idealization must be based on some reality. A mediocre piano player who dreams of being a national concert pianist is happy when their partner also shares that hope; but to imagine this player is going to be a new Chopin or Liszt is unrealistic and may prevent even the mediocre piano-playing.

Bad men and good women

It is still the norm that freedom to live life as one pleases, to define oneself without the veto of family, is considered by many men to be their prerogative. Throughout the world it is men who have more control over their lives than women. This is a psychological wealth and the lack of it is probably responsible for the higher rate of depression in married women.

While all of us seek some degree of freedom, novelty and individuality, letting go of familiarity and security is harder for some than others. The traditionalists will be those who place joint identity above uniqueness. Psychologists who study child development have noticed rules and rituals that illustrate their ideas of what should be. Even infants know what type of clothing is masculine and feminine, what toys, games, words and behaviours are or are not suitable for each sex. Toddlers less than two years old could say 60 per cent of the time whether a photo was of a man or a woman, so it is obvious that we learn these sex-appropriate distinctions early.

However, boys exaggerate things masculine and spend more time with each other, whereas girls don't use the gender rules so much. Perhaps this shows that boys perceive very early that boys' lives are freer – they get more toys, use more space, and get more play time than girls.

We all associate freedom with assertiveness, independence, boldness, courage and spirit. Most men believe that the last six traits are masculine, and little boys are approved of when they show any of them, much more so than girls. Boys are allowed more freedom to travel further from the house than their sisters, stay away longer and come back later. The model for sons is father's absence from the house – men on average spend much less time at home than even full-time working women. Home is associated with security and therefore boredom, and by definition away from home must be exciting and free from feminine rules.

It's not surprising that men tend to be the ones that hang onto their idea of traditional freedom. Women, on the other hand, have been taught as girls that independence can be dangerous, staying home and keeping the status quo is the way to win the approval of adults, but as girls they watched the more exciting life of their brothers enviously, laying down the idea that life with a man is better.

The whole social and economic system ensures that men can go further physically, geographically and materially. But men don't want their women cluttering up the playing field and boardroom. A boy's view of his contemporary opposite sex is that girls have to be looked after, protected from rough and tumble and bad language. Girls are a pain in the neck, said 99 per cent of 9-year-olds at one British school; furthermore, they added, girls were unfairly protected and cosseted.

Boys do carry many of their views about girls with them to adulthood. The powerful passions of sexual maturity leave a man resentful of the fact that the gender he has learnt to denigrate, to see as potential trouble now becomes the object of overwhelming desire. A mixture of fear and resentment threatens a man's control of his feelings. This is not a good recipe for equality because when anyone, man or woman, can't control their feelings, they are left with the option of controlling the stimulus. When you can't control your own feelings you try to control the actions and behaviour of the other, so they won't give you any nasty surprises. All in all, it's not that surprising that some men see alliances with women as a trap while a woman has buried memories of excitement and mystery attached to boys.

Fear, resentment and need to control all inhibit trust, the basic feeling which has to be present for the relationship even to survive, let alone be happy. Trust is a generalized expectancy that people can be relied on to keep their word, to mean what they say, to have a basic good will to others, and, in relationships, to keep loving. Biology lends a fraction of this trust equation (see Chapter 6) and adds to the differences between men and women in trust; men do not trust women as much as women trust men.

One reason is thought to be that it is women that give birth . . . to both boys and girls. A universal, unchangeable event, meaning that it is a woman who is the first attachment figure for both sexes. Growing girls can identify with mother and learn from her the behaviour appropriate to her sex – a girl experiences a continuity of experience so her sense of self develops within the maintenance of close relationships. Boys, by contrast, fear closeness, because at an early age they had to separate from mother, repress their dependence on her in order to learn male appropriate behaviour. By the age of 2, most little boys are already being told 'big boys don't cry or want to sit on mummy's knee', while their sisters can still do so. Feelings of dependence become associated with femininity and are threatening to masculinity. When men are forced into independence they will harbour a need for close relationships and a mistrust of any symbolic representation of the agent of his denial – the mother who pushed him away and the women who later remind him of that first close attachment.

When masculinity is tied to the denial of dependence in these circumstances it also goes with the devaluation of women.

Solving the I/we conflict the traditional way

Once a man decides that his particular love is unique and decides to chance the trap, he makes the commitment; but when idealization falters, all the years of childhood conditioning now creep back to taint his wife with echoes of 'girls are trouble, keep away from them'. He is now more likely to guard his independence.

A woman is inspired by her upbringing to think of herself in the centre of her family and group of friends. They come to her for support and advice, rather than to her husband. She tends to know much about their social and emotional lives and these intimate networks are important to her. She may be a career woman, play the harp or be a sports champion but usually a great measure of her self-esteem depends on this close interaction rather than on the other activities in her life.

Men are more likely to evaluate themselves in relation to their job and achievements. If you ask people to draw their lives in this symbolic way, women will people their artistic creations while the male universe will generally include cars and some representation of their occupation. Intimacy is less evident in a man's self-concept. Even men who have made a confident commitment can seek other freedoms to replace the loss they feel they have suffered, which damages their intimacy. A man may endorse the double standard (keep up his old, or new girlfriends) or request an extra room in the house, for a study, workroom, or whatever.

Intimacy makes demands, and counter-substitutions are tossed around like hot plates. When the I/we conflict is not understood, joint solutions are not attempted. As a response some women blame themselves. These are the women who have fallen in love with men who believe that 'we' means mostly him. To keep believing in their idealized expectation of married life, women who may have lead independent, capable lives before marriage become fearful of making decisions or taking responsibility, clinging to their husbands for reassurance, sometimes to the point of developing disabling phobias; a metamorphosis of competence and strength to married passivity and helplessness. Talents and abilities are gradually eroded, friends forsaken – in general a suppression of self and compression of a previous life. When it happens gradually, sophisticated tycoons or clever office workers succumb to the stereotype of femininity; helpless, ineffectual, dependent, and desperate for intimacy. In effect, they are saying to their men, 'I'm not so masculine and bossy as I appear and I'm proving it by becoming so feminine. I will give up "me" in the service of "us"'. Whether a direct response from their man or an imagined one, the unspoken message is: 'See, I'm not competing with you.' This is an injunction learnt early in childhood by most women, and ignored at their peril in areas considered a masculine preserve such as sports, senior management, executive boards, or the rarefied reaches of science and technology.

Successful sexual relations are one of the first casualties in the I/we conflict. Men can feel that their masculinity is threatened by a woman they perceive as superior in performance to themselves. But the answer is surely not for the woman to become as inadequate as the man!

The conformers and the freedom fighters

Traditional women easily toss the self aside for a couple identity, and accept the ideology of helpmates in life, even though the help will be sex-stereotyped. The freedom-seekers cling to self and resist, as they would resist anything that smacks of conformity and loss of self. Hence the refusal of the freedom-seekers to be really emotionally involved in relationships. Married or not, there will always be large psychological and physical areas that are sacrosanct, and not to be shared with the otherwise intimate partner.

Who are the conformers and the freedom-fighters? Each of us is both – according to the situation. We all hang on to the old norms when change threatens us. And we get bored when the situation is predictably familiar, safe and conforming. Temperament and personality have much to do with our eventual location on the 'togetherness to freedom' scale and it influences the intensity of the search for variety and novelty and what we perceive as a restriction to our freedom.

The extroverted sensation-seekers have different kinds of relationships to the anxious and emotional. There are many freedom-seeking women, those whose personality veers to extroversion, and adventurousness, but they are not frightened of initial commitment. It is a new experience that suits their need for variety and novelty. But it *is* those women who are more likely to divorce, and if they haven't done so by 16 years of marriage, when children have left the nest, they and their husbands tend to be unhappy with the relationship.

A particularly sinister influence on men, affecting their commitment, comes from magazines like *Playboy*, which promote the policy of not marrying, and forgetting about 'foolish notions about togetherness, home and family and all that jazz'.

Playboy portrayed women as gold-diggers looking for lifetime meal tickets, and made it clear it was a man's magazine, anti-wives, anti-alimony and pro parades of nude breasts, long legs and blonde hair. The damage was that it was more than a publishing phenomenon: it became the focus of male rebellion for men who decided they wanted to be 'free'. Free of the female domination media told them they were cowed down by. Free of the routine and boring jobs which they were chained to in support of the family, a togetherness which *Playboy* called conformity, anonymity and slow death.

Women's magazines played into the hands of the playboys, the beatnicks and the bohemians exemplified by characters like Mickey Spillane, John Wayne, James Dean and so on. They blamed women for driving men on to work harder to meet the escalating standards of family consumption. The grey flannelled rebellion of the 1960s brought articles in the American press about the cushy lives of housewives, inviting their husbands daily into their early graves. The *Playboy*-inspired vision of the ideal male life, (single, rich, surrounded by hi-fis, cadillacs, drinks cabinets and interchangeable bimbos – the quicker the turnaround the better) spread to Hollywood, and then pervaded western culture. Housework was dismissed as easy, whizzed off in between coffee and lunch parties. The contemporary feminist movement of the time agreed that sex roles were enslaving, and their promise to men was relief from the financial burden in return for the recognition for the equal routine of housework and childcare. Husbands would no longer be pressured to provide the status a woman could not win for herself, or to meet her exaggerated romantic expectations. A little economic advance for women has made the 1990s men less suspicious of a shared life, but the old stereotypes are available in abundance for men who want to rationalize and use them, even though research shows relationships to be more to their advantage than to a woman's. Furthermore, a new American influence is spreading to Europe. This is the 'Wildmen organization', and nearly every large city in America boasts one. They are designed to put men back in touch with the competitive, aggressive urges they are claimed to have lost. The four essential masculine energies distorted by modern family living (logic, language, creativity and power) are symbolized by this 'masculinity' movement, drawing on a picture of semi-mythological feral-man, living in balance with nature and lead by wise elders. The most enthusiastic recruits appear to be middle-class, middle-aged men. The similarity between the 1960s playboys and the 1990 wildmen is the struggle for perceived loss of male power.

How things got this way

The history of marriage, as opposed to the history of feeling between couples, reveals the way that the church and the state laid down rules and provided a legal and binding framework for the relationship of a couple, which has slowly evolved from concepts of duty, obligation and procreation to what historians call the 'companionate' marriage. Individuals began to have more freedom to choose a partner they could get along with, and more attention was paid to individual personality, philosophy and physical charms. This was the church and state catching up with the reality of love based on the feelings couples had towards each other. Generations ago the idea of falling in love and marrying because of it was unknown officially. Couples were expected to choose suitably according to family and property exchange, and *then* fall in love. At least this was the case in the propertied classes. But, rich and landed or poor and disenfranchised, many couples paid more attention to their subjective feelings about each other, as surviving fragments of love poems, letters and songs from antiquity onwards attest to. As now, there would have been those who paid more attention to what other people thought than to their own feelings, those who looked outward and used society's definition of relationship to label their feelings, rather than looking inward and taking a subjective stance. But society's objective view of the proper relationship between men and women caught up with the subjective in the last century, even if the division of labour on gender lines still holds today. They could help each other in their specialism, but never be truly equal in exchange, in that the woman wouldn't be happy to be the breadwinner forever, or the man the domestic. Even today, dual career couples have more problems than most couples. Husbands do not dash away with smoothing irons as happily as wives paste up a roll of wallpaper.

Even though sex roles still rule

All of us are born with a drive to become competent and control our environment. No one who has seen a baby's repeated attempts to balance blocks on top of one another, or fit the correct shapes into the corresponding holes, can doubt this. We take notice of our immediate surroundings and the people there in order to predict what is going to happen next and how it is going to affect us. As we grow, this desire for mastery takes different forms in boys and girls. Boys are encouraged to compete with other boys and expand the domain of their influence in the outside world by hard work, that bit of extra effort, ignoring discomfort and grimly maintaining self-control. Girls learn that competitiveness is not nice, and the best form of competence is directed towards improving self and the inside world – social skills, empathy and beautification. Artistic and academic accomplishments are very nice too – so long as she cheers up those she beat to attain the achievements!

Herb Goldberg, in his book on pursuing the mythical new man, makes the point that men are more motivated to competitive success by fear of failure, and the opposite for women is an internal competition – one where the prize is more to do with psychological growth. The essence of power is the ability to make the social world conform to how we think it should be, and much social strategy goes into achieving this. Persuading others to give up their resources, pay attention, join one in the same enterprise, needs more than coercion, threat or control of the rules. You have to make them believe they want to do it for you. Successful dominance starts in kindergarten, where the children who get their way are popular *and* persuasive. They wait for the first possible opportunity to ask actively for a go on the red fire-engine, instead of just pushing off the present rider as the unpopular dominant children do.

What constitutes success is different in the adult world, and also between cultures. For some it's money, for others political or academic eminence, still others favour athletic or media popularity. And in the sub-culture of morality, even crime can be considered a success, as well as its opposite, principle, as in spiritual leaders. But what is similar is the *feeling* that success brings. The sense of status elevates the hormones of victory – and as Kissinger is once reported to have remarked, 'Success is the ultimate aphrodisiac.' Men are pressured into power and success by the expectations of their family and friends. Many women are attracted by the sense of confidence that a successful man exudes through his hormonal arousal. And that maintains his virility. When men have difficulty in fulfilling their expectations of success, the sense of failure can lead to various psychological disorders, impotence being one. This is one of the reasons that less successful men, although initially attracted to successful women, feel compelled to denigrate and erode their success.

Women notice this bedtime correlation, consciously or unconsciously, and sometimes swap a successful career for a successful sex-life. Equality between men and women then may have a hidden cost for them both – until boys are brought up differently. A fair proportion of today's men can't perform successfully with a woman to whom they feel subordinate. But equality is necessary, both for intimacy, and for the new form of therapeutic relationship, with its possibilities for psychological change and growth to emotional maturity.

Training a boy for competitive endeavour, to be challenged when another's achievement exceeds his own, means that later his wife can become a threat. Taking care of women is so ingrained in male training they begin to see their wives' success as a threat to their own ability to protect them from the world's vicissitudes – a *sine qua non* of successful manhood.

At this stage, the man becomes the archetypal misogynist – believing that if he can make this woman weak and dependent on him, then he won't feel so much like a loser, and furthermore she won't be able to leave him. So, although power is a turn-on, men high on power motivation do have much less successful long-term relationships.

And it's not OK

It is the competent men that women stay with, those who earn higher wages than average but who are content with that. Power, status and competitiveness are inimical to intimacy in any relationship. In a study of powerful men, 50 per cent had been left by their women, compared to 15 per cent of men who were less concerned with acquiring power. When it is the men who move on it is sexual variety they seek. Their fantasies and dreams, according to one study, are full of the harm that a woman can do to a man, suggesting the old fairy-tale fear. Women are frightening, they gain control over a man and will reject or abandon him in some way.

Is this the motivation for heroes? It has been suggested that the drive for power is an exaggerated response to the drive for competence, and masks repressed anger. The power-seekers care more for public appearance than private contentment. These are the men who want bimbos, not brains. These extremes of domination and exploitation, pathological sadism and violence, are not the stuff of most relationships. Most struggle with equality, sometimes their confidence being undermined by the concentration of the power-seeker on the weaknesses and vulnerabilities of the partner. And sometimes the ridicule, insults, bullying and criticism being buried between the moments of emotional and sexual closeness.

The companionate marriage has been here since the 1940s, and there are now ideals of the therapeutic marriage. This is when each will put into a partnership what they can and take what they need, forming a totally equal partnership – where the husband can be emotional, upset and anxious over something, and the wife will try to put things right, go into battle on her husband's behalf, calm him down and generally take control. And then the next week the situation may be reversed; she may feel anxious over something and he will take on the protector role – while stirring the soup.

Many women see this as an ideal, although men are still a bit wary; at first glance they have much to lose (more housework, family involvement) but long term, the benefits of domestic equality transfer to a psychological equality. Cleaning out the cupboards also means time and opportunity for the man to discover how the children are growing and developing. It means being able to rely on his wife for real financial help, not just the pin money she brings in. Most of all it means better health for him. A life of differing tasks means variety and choice. He is less likely to suffer from 'burn-out' (stress brought on by the routine of a highly pressured job), heart attacks and emotional repression. He will be appreciated and respected more by his wife or girlfriend.

Most couples nowadays do start out on such an egalitarian dream. The 1960s flower-power movement spawned many such alliances, which are now volcanoes of anger, claims Bebe Campbell in her book *Successful Women, Angry Men*. The issue is over control. Some men feel their wives' success means their loss of control over her and if that control defined for them their masculinity there is a backlash. When men feel women's gains are their losses they throw in the towel and go back to what they know best – being a traditional male.

But there's no going back

The different stages of closeness are affected by the impact each seeks to have on the other. While a man's power was unquestioned, his impact on a woman's life was socially sanctioned. With technology producing surplus food, improving our health, cutting down on family size and lightening the daily grind, economic and social reforms for women culminated in the gradual evolution of the traditional into therapeutic relationships. But ideas still advance ahead of reality. The Economic and Social Research Council's 1990 report entitled *Who holds the purse strings?* concluded that the control of the family finances is crucial to the issue of equality between husbands and wives. The report commented on how little household money and organization had changed, with the majority of husbands controlling it, making the financial decisions and having more personal spending money than their wives, even if their wives worked. Some of the couples they looked at may be therapeutic relationships in the psychological sense, but optimism is not really justified. Emotional power has a habit of following financial power.

Relationship styles

Which type of relationship a couple forms depends on how close they prefer to be, and this preference is moulded by childhood attachments. But closeness is militated against by unequal power. Research reveals that couples can be fitted into one of three types of relationship; the traditional, the separate or the therapeutic.

The traditional relationship

Anyone who has watched romantic comedys on television has a good groundplan for understanding this type of relationship. The couple do most things together, even when one might not enjoy the activity. This is their way of creating the closeness, security and stability they feel is important. They value family life, even though such emotional fusion militates somewhat against spontaneity. Much emphasis is laid on appearances, what they achieve, what they look like, rather than on how they feel – which is the concern of the therapeutic relationship. The usual pattern is for the woman to be financially dependent on the man who is, in turn, covertly emotionally dependent on her.

The separate relationship

These are the people who do not want to 'live in each other's pockets'. While emotional closeness characterizes the traditional relationship, emotional distance is the keyword here. There is a shared intimacy, companionship and friendship, but each expects a degree of freedom. From the traditionalist's point of view this is an emotionally muted relationship – they might as well be good flat mates.

The therapeutic relationship

Vistas of the future – when we are all equal and androgynous. The relatively minor proportion of couples who fit into this category give evidence of the difficulty of the parallel development of psychological growth and committed love. It is not necessarily stable, in that couples don't automatically *expect* it to last as traditional couples do, but they are concerned about the feelings they personally experience in relation to their partner. These are not the usual standards of success in relationship. Being a good provider of financial, domestic or sexual 'services' is immaterial to the therapeutically minded couple, if they feel an emotional interdependence, trust and stimulation that the other provides. The new and interesting experiences, friends, and ways of looking at life bring much enhancement to their individual lives, as well as providing a safe haven from which to springboard onto new levels of psychological integration.

In order to maintain separate identities while feeling that there is a stable joint identity to rely on, the couple have to do a balancing act between behaviour that emphasises togetherness and stability and behaviour that allows each some freedom to be themselves – known by the clumsy phrase of 'identity-enhancing behaviour'.

Examples of failing to achieve this compromise are in every agony aunts column: 'I was just a cook and bottle washer'. Or, over the pub bar 'I was just the man who banked the cheque every month'. These are illustrations of feelings of being taken for granted that concentration on traditional roles and joint identity brings. Both feel devalued and their real identities ignored and denigrated. Each must feel they would still be valued for themselves if they stopped the domestic and financial roles.

The happier couples had an automatic counterbalance when they engaged in any stability-threatening behaviour, such as going out to a hobby group, or with a friend. They immediately followed it with a stability maintaining behaviour – like talking about future plans or memories of past times together.

Most relationships run in predictable grooves and become habitualized rather than changing or exchanging fresh views. A little regular injection of pleasant unpredictability is an art that must be cultivated, even though it may seem a contradiction in terms. In fact, many couples expressed dismay at the way circumstances had overtaken their ideals of intimacy. Work, domestic chores, children took so much time and energy there was no time to do something different to get out of the routine. Stability can become suffocation, just as uniqueness can become estrangement.

Jerry, a 41-year-old marketing manager, worked with his wife Susan. Although they were in separate departments, they met for lunch nearly every day and had done so ever since they met at work 12 years ago. While this was a happy marriage on the whole, Jerry did mention a disturbing feeling that had jolted him recently:

> This lunchtime there was the usual companionable silence between Susan and me, suddenly shattered by a burst of laughter from the office girls a few tables away. Just for a moment I felt it would be nice to break the routine and be part of that animated conversation. I looked at Susan who was quite scornful about 'empty cans making the most noise', and I had horrible visions of being chained to each other across the canteen table for the rest of our lives. It didn't last long, I've always been glad Susan and I could coordinate our lunch hours together. It gives us a chance to talk away from the children and other things besides domestic life. We're both a bit shy so it was also a relief not to have to strike up conversation with someone new every time you sat down in the canteen.

But those unbidden images did shake him, sufficiently to worry that there was something wrong with him or the relationship. They had reached a critical point in the I/we balancing act, allowing the stability forces to march on relentlessly, as we all do, until habit and routine threaten the sense of identity.

All that was necessary was to alter the balance. But without this understanding many couples take the unresolved balancing-act of stability and identity as evidence of relationship breakdown, and attempt to redress the imbalance by doing things that help them feel more 'themselves' – but in a way that damages the relationship: starting affairs, taking up with old pre-relationship friends, going on holiday alone or refusing to talk about intimate thoughts, as if this was one aspect of themselves they now wished to guard and not share. One of Jerry and Susan's problems was that they had so long been seen as permanent lunching couple that no one else ever joined them, which magnified Jerry's feelings of stultification. Susan had picked up his momentary disconcertion and done exactly the wrong thing. She had tightened her grip on their joint identity by denigrating the laughing girls, further reinforcing Jerry's feelings of being chained and trapped. A better move would have been to lean over to the girls and say 'That joke sounds good enough to be shared', or some such statement that led away from the emphasis on her and Jerry being a closed unit. Optimum psychological functioning is served by having the freedom to explore from a secure base, as anyone who has watched a toddler and its mother will have observed. Games are played when mother is in the room, but the minute she leaves all exploration is abandoned, in the effort to be reunited with her.

Recommendations for balanced relationships

1. Be alert to change of experience in your partner that might change their idea of themselves, and talk about it and change your reaction accordingly.

Tony's story is a typical example of how Mary, his wife, did not respond to change, to the detriment of the relationship. He had started working as an electronic technician, but rose fairly rapidly to buyer. Along with the usual problems of long hours at work or being away on business that Mary had to cope with, Tony would make veiled complaints about 'not being treated right'. While Mary was pleased about the promotion, for Tony's sake as well as for the extra money it brought in, she felt Tony was using it as a 'get-out' clause. He was buying more time away from home, which she resented, having given up her studies for a series of part-time dead-end jobs as the two children were born. When Tony described the lavish business entertainment that other firms would lay on for him as the buyer for a big firm, she would sometimes dismiss it as a waste of tax-payers' money – a clear contrast between her view of his worth and the firm's view. As his idea of his capabilities and his self-esteem was enlarged at work, it was belittled at home – so eventually he left home. Mary is still angry about what she gave up for him. She had been doing a business administration course before the children arrived and felt quite equal to Tony. They had talked a lot about business strategies and methods, but as Tony moved up the ladder he became the 'real' businessman while Mary's knowledge was 'only' theoretical and not even completed at that. What could she know of the business world as it was practised every day – the short-cuts and pressures and lack of structured rules to deal with situations that are not in any text books.

The main issue between Tony and Mary was her attempt to impose stability and prevent change. Reacting to Tony as the clever technician, while Tony now had staff who reacted to him as the successful buyer and up-and-coming manager/director precipitated the very thing that Mary feared most – that Tony would grow away from her as a result of his success. Her solution was to prevent change, to keep reminding him of his origins, but that was impossible, given his change of experience. Stability, in this case, was limiting. If one partner wants to impose an identity on the other it has to be one that the partner agrees with. This is the value of an agreed idealization of each other. It allows room for growth in a positive way and stops stability forces shaping us into routinized, dull individuals.

2. Have agreed periods of privacy, which can be interpreted as freedom.

Paul felt the need of this very much. He had been a merchant naval officer and was used to long periods away in exotic places. His favourite relaxation now that he had a desk job in the shipping company was building his ocean-going yacht in the garage. He conceded that it wasn't just the building of it – he knew it wouldn't be completed for years, maybe a decade. But that wasn't the point he said; even if it was never finished it allowed him his dreams. Tania was quite understanding, even if she did fume about the waste of space, the cost of the project and the fact that their two cars were outside on the road gathering dust and parking tickets. But she realized that that was the price of Paul's feeling of freedom, and preserving his only bit of unique identity that he had left from his sea-faring days. And if he did finish it and they could sail away into their retirement on Caribbean breezes, well that would be wonderful. She said she hadn't always been so understanding, in fact, after a whole weekend in the garage a few years ago they had had a confrontation. The upshot of it was that Tania had used family money, credit and the next ten years' Christmas gifts to fund an art course. It was a privately organized group that met every week, went to Italy every summer and was totally dedicated to improving their painting. They even owned a villa in Tuscany, and Tania's outlook on life changed considerably as a result of meeting others like Paul, others pursuing an ultimately impractical dream for the sake of expressing their creativity. This was an unexpected benefit, since her original idea had been only to have something for herself of equal value to Paul's obsession. Now Tania and Paul talk enthusiastically about sailing and painting along the Mediterranean coast, and Tania is designing murals for the yacht.

3. Actively seek new experience, for both: it's never too late!

One charming woman, Brenda, was experiencing the I/we conflict after forty years of happy marriage:

> When Jim retired he didn't know what to do. He started gardening and pulled out all my bulbs, thinking they were weeds! I used to go to my evening classes twice a week and he volunteered to do the evening meal. I arrived home once to find he'd used my crystal bowl for mixing the eggs. When he bleached my silver spoons I banned him from the kitchen. He destroyed my whole routine and I felt he was trying to take over my life. We had the worst quarrel we'd ever had in the whole of our married life. Ridiculous. He had always complained when he was working that he had never had enough time to listen to music so I bought him some new records, but he said he wanted more activity. Then when I went to my classes one week I just happened to see an announcement at the community centre about ballroom dancing classes. I'd never done it – but I thought, well, why not. Jim would like it – and he did. We joined up 4 years ago and are now dancing for the county championship award. It's just wonderful. I never thought we could have such fun again. Our children are thrilled with us and say they expect to see us on 'Come Dancing' on television one day. And we've made so many good new friends.

Encouraging new experience in the other gives new chances to talk about feelings and life experience. It's also a short cut to knowing what it's like to become involved in that particular experience. Many couples stop talking after their fifties; in order to talk you must have something to talk about. After twenty-odd years of living together most things have been 'talked out' it seems, and so new experience must be solicited in order to keep talking and keep intimacy.

4. Maintaining relationships with others.

We form new ideas of our partners by talking about them to others (as well as talking to them). Seeing them through others' eyes adds new dimensions. Says Carol:

> I never knew what Gary had gone through until I invited his service colleagues to dinner. They had all been together in the Falklands war, and his mates clearly thought of him as someone to be relied upon in danger. 'It made me feel good' Carol went on, 'to see that strong men had trust in my husband – I felt safe and protected.'

Deeper levels of understanding come from older relatives too – ones who remember childhood experiences and who can help trace connections. And new people bring new ways of interaction, stimulating long-forgotten possibilities and new experiences to reflect on and talk about to each other. Harriet told me:

> In my efforts to find something to talk about at dinner I embellished the poor old dog's behaviour, described his fights with the neighbour's cat and his imaginary thoughts and philosophy of the universe. It got to be an ongoing saga. Peter would ask as soon as we sat down what insights into life Gruff had had today. He thought it was so funny he made me write it down. Then a friend who illustrates books read it one day. He did some lovely witty drawings of Gruff and showed it to a children's comic publisher who is going to use it. I'll even get paid for it! Me, who couldn't get through A level English!!

5. Never, *never* think of your partner as 'the wife', 'the girlfriend', 'the boyfriend' or 'the husband'.

These identities heighten stability but are the death-knell to identity maintenance. Once the strait-jacket of the husband role is strapped on then men cease to exist as individuals, and what is or isn't appropriate to any husband becomes the norm, regardless of individual interests, needs or traits.

For instance, Abdul said that 'Elizabeth wasn't flirty like other girls', but she was his wife now and therefore he couldn't let her go on the week-long course away from home, where there would be men he couldn't protect her from. Elizabeth was amazed, and said she'd been going to these sales campaigns for 5 years before they'd been married – what was likely to be different now? The change was Abdul's transformation of Elizabeth into 'my wife'. This is the rather sad change of people who live together quite happily for several years and then decide to get married. It all falls apart after the wedding day because the individuals cease to exist in the other's perception and become instead a marital role. 'My wife' or 'my husband' has a whole new set of expected behaviours and reactions.

For a sense of stability, permanence and exclusivity – you should do just the opposite

1. Avoid new experience where interpretation might differ and lead to disagreement. Ideas of self might change so dramatically the 'new' person is not likely to be satisfied with the old partner.
2. Do everything together – so the partner doesn't get any idea of themselves as a separate person, with a separate destiny.
3. Discourage outside friends and influences, who may interfere with the stability of a relationship because they could affect the commitment of the partner by showing them alternatives, or beckon them on to exciting new experiences.
4. Don't talk to others about your relationship. It could be disloyal and you could find out things that may change your idea of them.
5. Emphasize joint identity. Refer to my husband/wife/boyfriend/ girlfriend. Display symbols of joint identity, like wedding certificate, rings, joint mortgage, and talk about 'we' more than 'I'.

Obviously the timing and choice of either stability or identity-enhancing behaviours is a matter of sensitive feedback from the other, of alertness to their non-verbal cues as well as the knowledge that there are stronger forces pushing us into stability than there are forces of change.

Traditional relationships are made by the homebirds, who emphasize stability; therapeutic relationships focus on identity-maintaining behaviours. Separate relationships also do this, but they don't start from the basis of closeness that the therapeutic couple does, so they have neither stability – or identity-reinforcement from their partners – they concentrate on their own identity.

In the romantic love stage the drive to certainty was the goal. With commitment (certainty), the psychological process of adaptation sets in. Once we are certain of each other we stop trying to be so fascinating, and fall into habit and routine with each other as we pick up the other areas of life, usually neglected in the falling-in-love stage. The dangers of this are the feelings of being taken over by the relationship, or losing control of one's freedom and one's life.

Part II
Balancing the Withdrawal–Closeness Cycles

By one of those paradoxes that only the universal creator could invent, two human beings, a man and a woman, blend into one another, becoming a suprapersonal unit by the fact that their relationship magnifies each to the point of greatest autonomy, to total and eternal self-centredness.

Lou Andreas-Salome, *EROS*

3

The scent of similarity

The marriage-market appears to be trading in the same way as any other market-place: best stock at the front, exchange price based on supply and demand. For example, for long, shapely legs and blonde hair you're going to need at least a good job and probably good evidence of generosity and humour. Everybody has a compatibility rating below which 'no sale' – they're not in the market.

But there is another specification in this exchange formula, and that is 'similarity = compatibility'. These are not just the social similarities, such as intelligence, education, attractiveness, class, race and religion; they also include similarity of biochemical make-up. We can hardly carry a DNA typing kit around with us to test prospective suitors, so we use the best index we know of – the sounds, sights, smells and feel of early experience with mother.

Because related individuals (like mother and child) are likely to have a similar biochemistry, the intimate encounter that can elicit the now grown-up child's social-bonding memories will also have a similar biochemical password. Different individuals will have different keys to unlock that genetic identity. Some say their interest was first aroused by their lover's voice, others fell in love when their eyes met across a crowded room (truly). Still more caught the realization of love when it was carried on the breeze; these are the good rememberers of odour – the mere wisp of freshly baked bread jetting them back to grandmother's kitchen.

Love is . . . a similar genetic make-up

All these enchanted meetings have something in common. Voice, chemical odour and facial features are unique to the person. No one else looks exactly alike, or has the same expression, and no one else can have the same odour profile or voice print. If you measure enough things about enough couples you end up with a global pattern, based on length of big toe, width of ear-lobe, colour of eyes, angle of nose and all sorts of physical traits, that defy a common-sense explanation. Beauty is in the eye of the beholder – it's not to do with being a good mate so much as being a good *match*; what biologists call 'phenotype matching'.

All these similarities are rolled into one global message that promises the solicitation, care and comfort of mother. The memory of mother's love is first laid down through the sense of smell within hours of birth. There *are* those who can ignore their senses and search for a conscious ideal, like 'practical and trustworthy', or, 'a swinger to have fun with' – these are the pragmatics and ludics described in Chapter 5. But the freedom-seekers eschew this, going for the challenge of difference. So do second marriages. The older person who perhaps married for comfort when young was attracted more by the pheromones saying 'same as mum' than more suitable qualities for them, which they are able to choose freely second time around.

The smell of comfort

Smell was probably our first means of selecting a mate, and still is in many other species. It triggers the powerful approach or avoidance responses, which are the basis of like and dislike, love and hate. Just as communicating non-verbally took a back seat to language once it evolved, pheromones which undoubtedly exist and influence people, nevertheless became less informative.

Although we may have other reasons now to like, love or hate someone, basic links of smell and emotion survive in humans today. People who smell almond (which is attractive to almost all of us) tend to remember pleasant events, and those whose nose gets stuck into horrible smells suddenly recall other unhappy situations, like being ill. Molecules of odour seem to stimulate the same brain centres that motivation to approach or avoid is stored. And that is our first basic emotion from which all others are refined.

When you realize that we each possess a unique 'chemical

signature' (a variation of lipids and fats in skin cells) which sends a distinctive odour message to potential suitors, some of the mysteries about who attracts whom become clearer. In animals, smell ignites deepest memories and drives and allows them to keep track of relatives.

Opinion is divided as far as human emotional response is concerned, but weight is swinging onto the 'pheromones do influence us' team. Of course, dog-owners knew all this long before the scientists took up the cudgels. The only individual dogs can't recognize by smell is an identical twin, and the day when a dog can sniff out a potential kidney donor is not impossible to visualize since similar chemical signatures will have similar immunological make-up. Postmen could also have told the researchers not to bother before they set up their massive electro-chemical experiments to find out that fear and stress give off odours quite different from normal chemical signatures. The smell of stress is recognized across species barriers, and different odours have different effects on our physiology, at a subliminal level. It may well be that related individuals all prefer certain odours and dislike others – on the basis of the family-related set of genes that recognize the odour. These genes also make antibodies to fend off foreign particles invading the bloodstream, which is why the same vulnerability to specific diseases runs in families.

Odour is important to babies too. One-week-old babies will turn towards breast pads their own mothers have worn and begin sucking – this is before they can recognize their mother by sight or discriminate her voice. It is the scent of the nipple pads that is the stimulation, and the odour releases opiates, which achieved their fame in connection with the 'joggers' high'.

Mother's chemical odour lays down a responsiveness in later life to that particular odour, which is why we like the smell of some people – those people whose chemical signature is similar to mother's and therefore triggers endorphin flow. In fact the part of the brain that does the analysis of what we smell is shared by all creatures that look after their offspring.

Researchers have had wonderful fun using sex hormones known to work on animals, dabbing it on human candidates for jobs and finding them rated more favourably than those who relied on qualifications. Male pheromone (androsentenol) alters mood – it makes women feel more submissive in the middle of the menstrual cycle and more irritable just after. Much other research has shown that pheromones are involved at least somewhat in sexual arousal;

it is the role of pheromones in mate selection and the degree to which mother's memory is included in the package that is the subject of newer research. The release of endorphins codes emotional memory as well as making us feel good, and ensures that we keep searching for the pleasurable events that rewarded us in the past. Like morphine and heroin, the opiates have a compulsive, addictive quality, which can be good or bad according to the circumstances. Insurance companies think it's good when a man kisses his wife every morning before leaving for work. They give him lower life premiums because he tends to live longer, and what the couple are doing is reimprinting themselves on their chemical signatures to update their memory about the rewards they give each other.

It is bad when the endorphins have formed a compulsive bond to a destructive behaviour, like drugs, crime, vandalism, eating disorders, gambling, drinking, smoking, workaholics who apparently enjoy their labours but with a 'driven' quality, neurotic and psychotic or sado-masochistic behaviour. Anything indulged in under stress is likely to be caught up in the pleasure/addictive cycle, and this has vastly different ramifications for treatment.

This is because the opiates are the body's pain relieving system, and physical and emotional pain sufficiently strong to release stress hormones will also trigger the comforting reward of beta-endorphin, at least initially. (There are other pathways and other receptors for different types of opiates but this is not a biochemistry book! References for the interested are fully listed in the back.) The endorphins are what allows the farmer to pick up his severed arm after a tractor accident and hike off 3 miles to the nearest hospital to have it sewn on again, all the while feeling no pain. This does not prove that farmers are stoical but that it was a survival trick in our past to suppress uncontrollable pain and conserve energy until help arrives or we get away from the 'lion's mouth', badly mauled, but moving. Alertness and the conservation of energy cycle underlie the intimacy and withdrawal cycles of relationships, and the balance of the molecules of euphoria and anxiety which regulate the degree of social confidence is the arbiter of intimacy. Any major upheaval of physiological balance – which can happen through either emotional or physical stress – will arouse the counteracting influences of the pain-relieving endorphins, and the feeling of needing to eat, drink, or getting close to someone, since these are the most likely to restore the relaxing feeling of balance and 'all's well' with the nervous system. When a memory is retained the cells in the nervous system alter, as if laying down a pathway for easier use next time. So when a baby sees its mother, molecules tag that image and all the sensory information associated with it, and store it away for the future. There are different hormones and different pathways for different types of memory, and they all become integrated at a higher level of brain functioning. We store away memory according to our present mood and emotions. And there are hormones influencing pleasant emotions, the euphoria molecules, made from the opiates. And there are different hormones underlying the unpleasantly arousing emotions. While it is too simple to say that there are hormones coding all the happy memories and other hormones coding all the unhappy memories, it is certainly true that a pleasant mood tends to evoke all the previous pleasant events of our lives and an anxious or sad mood will bring up all the depressing, negative, past events.

Endorphins are there to help us attach ourselves to our family. They give us the sense of comfort we get when we're with someone after a period of loneliness. Social emotions like that have been programmed into every social species, so we stick to each other and increase our survival chances and the attachment bonds they promote between us are lifelong, much like the 'bonds' people make to their morphine fix. A form of tolerance occurs in both, with more of it needed to get the same effect. The loss of a loved one and the passage of narcotics from the body lead to psychic pain, crying, irritability, insomnia and disturbed appetite. It is the socially uprooted, the first generation immigrants for example, who suffer the highest rate of drug addiction, and it is also those from 'parentally uprooted' family backgrounds who develop the psychological addiction of insecure attachment, with its anxious, dependent clinging.

Experiments done over many years by ethologists seem to say that whoever 'mothers' a baby serves as a beacon for the offspring's later search for a sexual partner. In fact, the best party trick I know is to innocently ask several people what they most liked about their opposite sex parent and write down or memorize the most outstanding attribute they come up with. Then go round again, being more subtle and ask them what attracts them most about a man (or a woman if talking to a man). The punch line is matching the two answers – you'd be surprised how often it's the same, and people are often astonished at a connection they had not previously made. It can be a physical trait, like dark, wavy hair or crinkly blue eyes; or a feeling like warmth or conscientiousness. But psychoanalysts would say that the physical trait stands for the feelings evoked, the feelings we associated with mother and father in childhood are the feelings that later draw us towards a mate. So neglecting, distant and cold fathers are exchanged for neglecting, distant and cold husbands or jealous, demanding, smothering mothers for identical wives.

Don't fence me in

Psychoanalysts claim that mothers who don't encourage their children's independent action set them on the road towards the love-crazy or love-blind extreme, but since it has been shown that the levels of endorphins in the mother's blood at birth affect the attachment bond, it seems likely that this is also what affects the degree of dependence and independence that the child insists on. The child who equates love with dependence will give up love for independence, and create a separate kind of relationship. Or he or she will associate independence with loss of love and become clinging and over-involved in the adult relationship. The view they take depends as much on their birth levels of endorphins as their later learning from mother, since the clingers are likely to suffer panic and anxiety at any hint of separation. Between 20 and 50 per cent of adults who get panic attacks had sufficient separation anxiety from mother that they developed a school phobia in childhood.

It is a speculation, although a reasonable one, that the different sex hormones in girls and boys which influence much later behaviour may also affect endorphin, which is a hormone too, so that one sex may make stronger social bonds than the other. *Guess which one!*

It is true that oestrogen, a female sex hormone, affects whether a rat will become addicted to morphine, and anecdotal accounts suggest that women who try narcotics are more likely to become addicted than men. Women are much more likely to become depressed than men, and recent research has uncovered a lack of endorphin production in depressives. In other words the higher level of endorphin functioning in men would mean that they have less need to make the social bonds that promote endorphin production; but, therefore, more need to develop the social skills of relationship.

Current conceptions of what is suitable for bringing up a boy baby (robust handling, encouragement of activity and independence) versus what's suitable for a girl (care, soft voices, fragile handling, restriction of movement etc.), suggest an overstimulation of boys' neural systems and an understimulation of girls', which would have effects on their preferred level of intimacy. Almost as if the shaping up of parasympathetic dominance for girls, and the fight/flight sympathetic reaction for boys, was a cultural command. There is some evidence that early stimulation alters hemispheric dominance, and hemispheric arousal results in change of emotion and cognitive functioning, so differences in the way baby boys and girls are treated could quite plausibly account for the differences in emotional, cognitive and activity levels of girls and boys.

It is important for later too, to remember that social bonding is *one* emotion – the one that gives us the desire to be with our own kind. It has little effect on the other emotions men and women feel – anxiety, fear, hope, optimism, sorrow, hate, anger. It is these that are heavily conditioned (easy expression of anger for boys and anxiety for girls). It is a mistake to give equal weight to all these different feelings, even to store them all under the same heading – emotions – without distinguishing between social emotions and the more individual psychological ones.

If, at the beginning of life, a male baby learns to respond to mother's features more than a female baby because of his presumed higher endorphin production, which would encode memory more indelibly, we would expect men to go for 'Gals just like the gal that married dear old Dad', more than women seek out replica fathers. Much psychoanalytic observation seems to support this notion. And then, once sought out and biological programme fulfilled, the endorphins adapt, and wife's image fades into mother's image. And he's ready for a new goal.

One inconvenient fact disturbs this cosy tale; more men kill themselves over the loss of a love relationship than women. But if we distinguish between social emotions and the individual/ psychological emotion of love, we can talk about women enjoying multiple attachments as well as single intimate ones, while men invest their all in that one intimate relationship. When it goes wrong they have no other attachments (or practice) to take its place, and some men at the vulnerable end of the spectrum will see no hope of ever replacing that lost relationship.

After a calamitous drop, when his attachment object is no longer there, a man has no other immediate means of stimulating it, whereas as a woman, who had lower levels in the first place, has been developing other sources all her life, and can find solace through them after loss or bereavement.

Personality and the happiness search

According to the radical thinkers of the medical world, it is endorphins that stimulate the body's natural healing mechanisms, and doctors are only catalysts which trigger the flow. Any caring, listening person can trigger the love-energy, which is why those in good relationships have better health than those alone or in emotionally distanced ones. There are hardy personalities who survive against all the medical odds such as those reported in Bernie Siegal's book *Love, Medicine and Miracles*.

Lack of love is a major contribution to illness. Emotional loneliness is a stress that generates biochemical changes which eventually exhaust the body's defensive capacity. Diseases of adaptation, like hypertension, arthritis, ulcers and so on, are the result of extended stress. Love is an immunological shield to ward off the stress of life.

Reports of those who can reduce massive tumours with positive belief have encouraged the ill and infuriated the conservatives of the medical profession. But whatever the veracity of these accounts, it is true that under hypnosis some people can visualize the activity in their immune system sufficiently well to boost its efficiency even after only two hypnotic sessions.

Many anecdotal accounts of patients who survive (pain-free) years longer than medical diagnosis would allow because of some project or family need they want to pursue, to die the day after the event they had been waiting for, suggest that personal happiness and confidence in the future is mediated by endorphin flow, and that there is a stability about our endorphin production that is linked to the optimistic and independent personality. That being so, the idea that endorphin production is one of the prizes we include in our unseen similarity search equation suggests itself.

In fact, the highest correlation in all the similarities tested in the 3,000 couples in my study was the degree of happiness with the relationship they shared. It is usual to believe that one *makes* the other happy and vice-versa, but other research suggests that in order to make a commitment which will entail emotional and financial risks if not honoured (as one out of three marriages are not), a bit of prior form-checking is sensible. And top rating goes to those who are happy now and therefore likely to be happy with the relationship in the future. Happy personalities make happy relationships.

So the *real* detection game is this: check the level of endorphins, using all the indices necessary to arrive at a good judgement, blending into the equation other clues like sexual arousal and how well they get on with mother. The synchrony established that leads a person to feel they know and trust this virtual stranger is enhanced by the individual's chemical signature, the signature of similarity.

Since similar arousal levels are so important to compatibility (even animals are attracted to mates whose activity level matches their own) it was at first a surprise to find that extroverts and introverts were quite happy with each other. Introverts both get up and go to bed earlier than extroverts, have a lower pain tolerance cycle, withdraw from stimulation much quicker, and have quieter, more passive and pessimistic cycles compared to the extrovert's talkative, active and optimistic cycles.

The explanation was that the optimistic extrovert has different criteria for happiness than the pessimistic introvert. Analysis of the 'happiness' questionnaire they completed revealed two different patterns: introverts were most happy when the relationship was calm and there was a high amount of agreement on most issues. When they had learnt to resolve conflict easily by give and take, the relationship was fairly free from quarrels and bickering. Extroverts may have had the same happiness score, but it was based on time spent together, the amount of activities they shared, the frequency of talking things over, and sex. So, for some, happiness is simply freedom from anxiety and for others sharing experience. The fear of introverts is conflict and chaos, and the fear of extroverts is being bored, ignored and isolated!

The oscillating nervous system

The nervous system is balanced between alert vigilance and relaxation. The molecules of activity and alertness carrying the message 'do something' interact with the molecules of euphoria which keep down the anxiety. These molecules of euphoria (the endorphins) help balance other chemicals that slow the heart and breathing rate, lower blood pressure, relax muscles, digestive processes and general restitution cycles. The logical extreme of the slowdown is inactivity, sadness and depression – or hibernation in animals. People who can relax, cope well with stress and have the energy to climb mountains to see what's on the other side have a constant supply of endorphins available.

The less lucky have to eat, listen to music, jog round miles of running track, laugh themselves silly or get massaged to produce them. But even for the lucky few, adaptation builds up and new experiences beckon. The urge to explore is as strong as the urge to conserve, and life goes on in these alternating cycles of relaxation and activation. Rhythmic cycles of mood, libido changes, sensitivity to pain, odour, all rise and fall with the tide of hormonal output.

Most of us balance the positive and negative events of life and their ensuing emotions and integrate yesterday's nostalgia with tomorrow's promise sufficiently well to keep happy and healthy most of the time. And we are greatly helped by a supportive relationship, which synchronizes our physiological cycles with comforting regularity.

Experiments on the anxiety/euphoria axis show that anything that stops the endorphin flow increases the anxiety levels. So, listening to music, eating, exercising, making love, being touched, smiling, all help to give the green light to the opiates and happiness and the red light to adrenalin and vigilant anxiety. The exact interaction of the stress chemicals and euphoria chemicals has generated much more speculation since the finding that they are both released in the nervous system in response to any life stress which feels uncontrollable. The feeling of control over the potential stress, whether it is an illusory one or not, alters the biochemical balance again and motivates us rather than tranquillizes us.

The sympathetic, or activating, branch of the nervous system is stimulated by adrenalin which can rapidly convert a reaction to novelty into a full blown alarm – to fight or flee. When the new and novel thing or situation turns out to be safe, the nervous system quietens down and becomes habituated and restored to balance by parasympathetic calming chemicals.

Temporary or permanent imbalance can result in many stress-related diseases, irritation, fatigue and depression. Depressed people will remember all the humiliating failures that make their lives hopeless. When their friends try to remind them of past success it's forgotten or downgraded as a one-off piece of luck, never to be repeated. All the 'if onlys' overwhelm their present perception with guilt and what they should have done. Resentment and hopelessness and negative emotions block present potential and endorphin flow. We move from contentment to sadness.

Only anticipation of change can get the flow going again – or stress. Diversity and change create stress and when positive anticipation and goal-planning accompany it, the consequent endorphin flow creates an exhilarating 'eustress' (a combination of euphoria and stress which the anxiety expert Hans Selye used to denote beneficial stress, since it was motivating, energizing and life enhancing). It is opposite in meaning and biochemistry to distress. The difference between the two states is the amount of control we feel we have over the potential stress. Memories of past successes in coping, conflicts resolved, and compromises maintained influence the attitude to perceived control, and therefore what is stressful for one person can be exhilarating for another.

These memories and mind-control tell us that whatever happens we can cope – the best psychological gift any fairy godmother could give a baby, and it is a gift of understanding that most of us struggle through life to find out. The magic wand is positive expectancy. This is why attitude influences happiness, health and relationships. Positive attitudes towards disease have been shown to halt the progression of the illness, and heightened suggestibility under special conditions like hypnosis and the healing power of shamans can allow people to undergo the most amazing feats of endurance and healing.

It is the euphoria of endorphin release that underlies the caring, love and bonding between human beings, and it is increased by a sense of control in the relationship. The partner that feels a lack of control is the partner who is likely to feel distress rather than eustress, and since it is women in relationships who are more often without control (physically and financially, if not emotionally) it is no surprise that it is women who are more likely to suffer the blocked frustration and depression that go with underproduction of the molecules of euphoria.

Endorphins underlie the chemistry of goal-directed behaviour, and through an interaction with other chemicals give us a feeling of purpose and energy that keep us going on with plans – life plans, relationship plans, career plans, as well as minor short-term plans – against all obstacles. The achievement of the goal often quite inexplicably brings a demotivated, depressed state. Consider a student working for a degree over three years. Everything else in life has been subsumed by the goal and at last – success. A good degree. Is there a triumphal parade, a wild ecstatic partying? No, more often there is a feeling of 'Is this it? Have I really worked this hard just for this. Where is the fanfare?' At best there is a sense of relief, safety and contentment. The achievement of the goal coincides with the drop in the endorphin flow. Truly, it is better to travel than arrive!

The only cure for the achievement of a goal is the replacement of it with another goal – our student can now embark on a PhD. By the time they have that they might be wise enough to remember the post-degree crash and already have other plans on the back-burner, ready to regenerate the endorphin flow.

We put together past experience and project that into the present to make future predictions about our happiness and our partner's likely continued support. These predictions affect our quality of life. It is the confidence generated by these predictions that keeps a relationship together. To contemplate the next ten, twenty or fifty years together, confident in the response and trust of the other, knowing one can face and work out future problems, brings visions of harmony and happiness that make today's washing-up and concrete-laying take on a rosy glow.

At the end of Chapter 9, there are six relationship planning stages which happy couples have found carried them through a life's relationship. Making, revising and carrying out plans, is like looking only at the next upward step on the long elevator, when you're carrying all the shopping and the push chair too. To look at the top immediately overwhelms motivation. Specific, next-stage-only plans which can be visualized trigger the motivational effects necessary to weather the conflict and withdrawal cycles which are the inevitable consequence and downside of the intimacy and approach upswings.

If happy people make happy relationships because of their positive expectancy based on past good memories – what about unhappy people and unhappy relationships? The major difference between happy and unhappy couples is how they respond to each other's criticism or negative remarks. Unhappy couples respond in cross-complaining cycles, their unpleasant feelings escalating, all the while affecting their heart-rate, muscle tension and skin temperature. Often they are unaware of it, they experience only a rising tension. But in simulated conditions when a couple are rigged up with electrodes each verbal complaint goes with several non-verbal 'intensifiers' – the voice and breathing cues and facial musculature and mouth and eye patterns; as well as the physiological reactions. So negative physiological messages are returned and escalated as well as the verbal conscious ones and their associated body-language.

Even before a word is spoken these negative messages can be going on. The feelings of irritation, annoyance, boredom, anger, anxiety have a physiological basis that is conveyed by subtle body language to the other. This 'physiological linkage' means the other starts feeling vaguely tense, wonders what's wrong, but can't put their finger on it.

Enter: All the prior bad memories of times past to fill the gap of vagueness and next thing the couple are rowing about what happened twenty years ago.

Exit: Trust, emotional support, intimate communication and happiness! Happy couples have their cycles but they are validating ones, criticism is voiced but responded to in a deactivating way as far as the nervous system is concerned. Negative statements are acknowledged and either agreed with or challenged but in such a way that the unpleasant physiological cycles are *unlinked*. It seems happy couples are more responsive to body language and meta-language (the *way* the words are spoken) and they act quicker to short-circuit a negative, escalating cycle.

Each time a person feels they have lost something, an argument, the love or regard of their partner, endorphins falter, their sense of control is diminished and motivation to try harder is dissipated. As eustress turns to distress the adrenal glands manufacture more of the stress hormones which increase their action on the fight/flight nervous system. The endorphins which would normally be released on stress and which would regulate the nervous system's proper functioning are swamped, as the conflict and unhappiness escalate. Eventually this can lead to hypertension and heart disease, or, if the pendulum swings the other way, depression.

Where survival and pleasure interact, the opiates run the traffic flow. The red, green and amber of the nervous system shuffles the endorphin molecules through the brain and the master gland, the pituitary and the hypothalamus (the emotional centres) and the gonads (the sex-stimulators) to ensure that a species can reproduce when times are good and not when overcrowding, famine or other hostile events are paramount. In fact, the body's ability to produce endorphins goes with the onset of puberty and correlates with the growth of sexual maturity and the associated sex hormones.

If the worry and anxiety of stress triggers endorphins along with the stress chemicals, then we can get to enjoy stress, because of the relief associated with it when the endorphins kick-in. We literally become addicted to it and the experiences that elicited the stress. Even remembering or going back to the place it happened stimulates the body to increase the endorphin manufacture. Sociologists who study the way people learn to become drug-takers or drinkers have always noticed how much the 'role' of an addict is learned, suspecting that addiction is learned and not biochemical. It's a shared set of rules that gives them a feeling of social participation, they say. But both influences have the same bio-chemical basis, the context is slotted in with the addiction so the sociologist and biochemist are both right. Stress-seeking can be seen as a healing device for disturbed balance, the endorphins that come from stress promote physiological balance.

This explanation can be stretched to cover the stress of inadequate relationships to any behaviour entered into under stress – and so, too, conflict in relationships. Especially if they are using it as a replay of a painful past – which is now a rehearsal. *This* time they will have more control and make it come out better. Some experts on evolution believe we are programmed to get reward for wandering, which would have increased the likelihood of finding new habitats. The psychological equivalent is to be found in the mental rolling stones of this world, who feel rejuvenated on picking up their kit bag and moving on to the horizon of positive expectations. They may gather no moss, but they *will* get an endorphin kick!

To some extent, change is youth-orientated; the young seek experience, test their powers, find out what they like and don't like, can and can't do, develop their abilities, and then settle into what they like best. But failure to change at all after that leads to monotony and habituation, trudging through life with a mind-numbing invariance which atrophies the brain. Even when old rats and monkeys are put in a cage with daily changes of toys and running wheels their brains grow – the parts of the nerve cells responding to new information stretch and make more connections with each other. Experiments giving old-age home residents the opportunity to change and control their lives find they live longer. Those who limit life's experience fail to enrich their nervous system, which is stunted by psychological and physical *inactivity*, not age.

It is endorphins that promote the continuous cycle of energy exchange, endorphins that give us the energy to respond to change in a positive way. Endorphins do drop off with age, but can be boosted with anticipation, plans and goals, exercise, laughter, touch, talk, smell, music and art, and continuing social interaction. When that becomes predictable it becomes ritualized and stereotyped, and the relationship loses its vitality. The 'now we are settled' response leads to taking each other for granted, boredom and estrangement. This is not to say that one should not expect a lifelong trusting, supportive relationship – but it doesn't come with relaxing.

Creative, interesting relationships that improve life are ones that climb through conflict and its resolution to new perceptions. It is the type of emotional conflict with the ever-present possibility of separation that creates stress, but the feeling of control over the resolution (we've worked it out before and we will do again) restores the biochemical balance, which gives renewed energy, promotes new goals, re-establishes bonding and understanding and moves us on to new levels of intimacy.

Through the ongoing balance of the active nervous system and the resting nervous system we adapt to life, connecting emotional events from the brain as well as current sensory impressions to approach or avoid the next conflict. Avoiding it decreases both the endorphin flow and future intimate involvement.

A final heartening word here. A very recent study found that most of the happiness in marriages was explained by one thing and one thing only – the amount of humour the couple engaged in between themselves. Telling jokes, flippant remarks, reinterpreting things in a ridiculous way, playing practical jokes, pleasant teasing, all the things we mean when we talk about a sense of humour.

When we remember that laughter releases endorphins you can see why – the feeling of love, care and bonding that flows with the endorphins is attributed to the other person and changes arousal levels. And it is not impossible that the motivation to change and heal a stressful relationship can be accomplished by the same means. After all, if Norman Cousins can laugh himself out of a terminal illness why can't we laugh ourselves out of a terminal relationship? Anyway, The National Council for Laughter Therapy sounds more inviting than the serious-minded National Council for Marriage Guidance!

Anxiety

Every individual is born into a world over which they have no control. Survival is dependent on adults, at first mother, who provides food and protection. The well-being and security of the baby are totally in her hands, and its growth and development involve a continual struggle for greater independence and control over the things and people in its life.

The infant's world is one of perpetual chaos in which it has no concept of self or identity. By several months it has realized that the mobile overhead and the teddy bear at the end of the cot are not part of itself, and the beginnings of an identity emerge. The baby becomes gradually aware that it can manipulate some of its environment as it pleases. These magical powers, though, are opposed by the power of others, and the first conflict we all have to resolve is assertion or independence, while still being approved of and loved by the very ones the baby is trying to become independent of. This conflict is the basis of the later joint-versus-unique identity, in relationships. For some the struggle of autonomy versus independence can go on for a lifetime.

A very credible psychoanalytic view is that there are inherent, constructive forces that urge the child to realize its given potentials, like maturation, walking and talking, none of which can be suppressed unless conditions are really extremely deprived for the child. You can't teach an acorn to grow into an oak tree but given soil, water and air its intrinsic potentials will unfold – just as the human develops the discrimination and refinement of emotions within and learns to communicate thoughts, feelings and needs. The human equivalent of soil, water and air is parental warmth, which develops inner security and releases the forces of affiliation, and parental allowance of independence which develops inner freedom to have different thoughts, feelings and expression and releases the forces of expansiveness. So the child with the right parental nutrients grows up in accordance with his or her 'real self', the innate temperament which is characteristic of his or her physiological 'mix', and the particular blend of affiliation and expansiveness that temperament unfolds to. But when parental warmth and freedom are lacking, the child's needs are neglected and the energy that would have gone into elaborating its identity – mixing and matching its present day learning with its genetic pattern – is redirected. The aspect of itself which the child feels is disapproved of remains frozen, immature, undeveloped and encapsulated. In severe cases, the whole self is rejected and the child's energy goes into creating a new 'false' self that it imagines is more acceptable.

When the child grows up with a sense of not belonging it leaves him or her feeling isolated and helpless in a hostile world, coping with mounting insecurity, anxiety and helplessness. When this anxiety state reaches panic levels the child reacts to this psychological threat just as a biological creature would react to a physical threat. There are only three possible responses: to flee, to fight or to submit to the danger. These translate into a psychology of trying to be invisible, to be bad or to be good. The physiology of the child predisposes them towards one or other of these defences.

Differences in the way neurochemicals are metabolized affect the reward and punishment pathways in the brain, making it more likely that the child frightened of punishment will be the fleer and the one motivated more by reward will be the fighter.

The 'invisible' child tries to be just that, to flee or withdraw from relationships. If you can't become invisible you can at least be silent and aloof! This child grows up responding rather ambivalently, a curious mixture of compliance and defiance, and is very sensitive to the expectations of others, moving away from relationship involvement. Even though they may not be able to define it they will later insist on being 'themselves' and will idealize wise self-sufficiency; their heroes are often the modern-day gurus or cults and academia.

The 'bad' child is aggressive and competitive (although this may be in an unobvious way, like being quietly perfect and better at things than everyone else). Valuing strength and the capacity to endure, this child idealizes winners, power and success against the odds and in general moves against people and will try to dominate in relationships.

The 'good' child who has taken the submitting defence is a predominantly complying child who tends to subordinate themselves to others, who needs to lean on them, tries to be useful, unselfish and good, and in general moves towards relationships. This child will grow up with an idealized version of themselves as a saint or a martyr.

These vignettes are stereotypes of trends we all have under attachment stress to become 'self-alienated' and move away from expressing unique potential. The more we feel a lack of identity, the more life feels meaningless, and the more we search for the elusive 'buzz'. Not relating to others spontaneously means clinging to the strongest person or withdrawing emotionally and shutting others out; or even fighting and competing with others, attempting to control them, or rise above them by being superior in some way.

Becoming an emotionally mature adult is a lifelong process. None of us escapes totally from the conflicts of childhood, and although some are neurotically full of revenge and want vindictive triumph over others for the humiliations suffered in childhood, most of us want only to avoid loneliness and rejection. The point about neurotic trends is that they are so compulsive and are practised against the best interests of the self. Bowlby noticed what ethologists had also observed in the wild – when a primate infant is separated from its mother it goes through a predictable series of emotional reactions:

- *PROTEST:* crying piteously, actively searching for mother and resisting other people's efforts to soothe it;
- *DESPAIR:* quiet desperation, sadness, passivity, ignoring others.
- *DETACHMENT:* (more in humans, but known to dog-owners who go away on holiday leaving their dog behind) an active, angry, defensive disregard for mother, even avoiding her when she returns.

The parallels of fight (protest), submit (despair) and flight (detachment) are fairly obvious, and in a study of over 1,000 people's romantic styles, researchers discovered 'mental models' of relationships that were, in essence, the relationships of the fighters, fleers and submitters. These mental models matched the description of their early relationship with their mother and father: 56 per cent reported warm, loving parental relationships and had secure, trusting attachments to their present partner. But the others who had cold and rejecting mothers (as they perceived it) unfair fathers or intrusive and demanding mothers, were split between the 'avoidant', 'anxious' and 'ambivalent' present relationships.

The fighter

The child who labels itself bad and sets out to prove it, got early attention, but was pressured to keep rigid standards and was exploited. Will take the aggressive stance, believing attack to be the best method of defence.

BELIEVES IN: strength and the capacity to endure, self-aggrandizing.

TAKES: a competitive stance against others, needs to triumph over them to feel good.

DOWNGRADES: affiliative emotions to enhance expansive drives and moves against people. Takes an active mastery approach to life to conquer anxiety.

FANTASIZES: about being the best, a hero, achieving anything.

MEASURES WORTH BY: the amount of power and control over others.

NEEDS: the respect and attention of others, and can be driven by a need for vindication, revenge and triumph.

FEARS: being exploited or controlled by others.

IN RELATIONSHIPS: Their needs stem from an unfortunate childhood and the handling of feeling, originally a necessity for survival, allows unhampered growth of the drive towards a triumphant mastery of life. Love, companionship and consider-ation are felt as restraints on the road to mastery. Optimistic and cheerful, the fighter takes on too much because they overrate their capacities. Promises much, can be generous, but often unreliable. The arrogance concealed behind a generally friendly exterior is revealed as perfectionism, obsessively demanding of themselves and their families a superiority which they believe is the way to control life. They expect success and fortune because of the assumed superiority, whether professional, sporting, mothering or any endeavour of life. Some fighters let vin-dictiveness rule their relationships, striving compulsively to beat anyone who has more power, of whom they are suspicious and contemptuous. Anyone else's achievement is infuriating to them, and they will do all they can to frustrate others. Heavily criticizing others is another favourite pastime although they can't stand being criticized themselves. When the fighter doesn't get his own way, reactions range from irritability and sulking and stirring up guilt in the other to explosive, violent, open rages.

The elusive fleer

Their label is *uninterested*, 'I don't care about anything'. In essence, they 'resign' from life, expecting nothing, demanding nothing. In opting for a life without pain and friction caused by wanting things the parents couldn't or wouldn't supply they also resign themselves to a life without zest. Therefore they are constantly searching for meaning and interest in life.

ATTITUDE: to life is detachment, avoidance, pessimism, futility, passivity.

BELIEVES: that it is better *not* to wish or expect anything and then they won't be disappointed. Life should be easy, painless, effortless. Won't get involved in anything that is going to arouse emotions or in striving for achievement.

TAKES: an emotionally distant attitude to others, withdraws from involvement, moves away from people, becoming elusive and aloof.

DOWNGRADES: both affiliative and expansive drives, to become merely an interested intellectual observer of their own emotions.

MEASURES WORTH BY: self-sufficiency, independence, stoicism, freedom from desire and passion.

FANTASIZES: about being a wise guru on the road to serenity, ego-rejection, and all-encompassing enlightenment.

NEEDS: privacy, freedom, will know what they *don't* want but rarely what they do want.

FEARS: that others will expect things.

IN RELATIONSHIPS: The child who decides to remove itself psychologically and as much as it can physically, won't do anything to have attention drawn to itself. Even as an adult will speak softly, eat little, sit in out of the way corners doing anything to make itself invisible. Parental pressures have usually been such that the child couldn't speak openly, the family influences were either too strong or too intangible. Often a closed, intense, family atmosphere that cramped all individuality and therefore the fleer fears the emotions of others. If anything does come to matter – job, promotion, people, possessions – it is experienced as a burden, and dropped. The adult fleer will be quietly rebellious and can at extremes be a shallow liver, unambitious, never trying, throwing the towel in under frustration. Will keep strong feelings towards impersonal things only – art, music, literature, nature, ideas, all potentially controllable. Even at the first romantic meeting the fleer will worry about lasting ties and how he can extricate himself. Often willing to give all sorts of help – so long as it doesn't involve him emotionally. Hypersensitive to pressure and the expectations of others to the point of resenting being expected to give birthday presents. Will inwardly rebel and 'forget'. Can enjoy distant relationships or short-term ones so long as there is not much emotional involvement. When the fleer does have a long-term relationship it is opposite to the submitters, with their need to merge with the other. The fleer maintains distance by various means according to the particular circumstances; this could be excluding sex, or subscribing to the madonna versus whore complex (wife seen as too good for sex and can only enjoy sex with emotionally uninvolved strangers), or the fleer could restrict the relationship merely to sexual contact and not share emotional experience. May be attentive to the partner's needs but never talk about himself. Will usually have an area exclusively for his use to escape to: a computer room, garden shed, study.

The submitter

The exemplary 'good' child who subordinates themselves to others for approval, appeasement and love feels inferior and guilty, quite opposite to the fighter, who feels superior and proud. The submissive child idealizes others and has often grown up in the shadow of someone who was stronger or preferred or somehow perceived as better, maybe a beautiful, successful mother or older, cleverer brother or sister.

ATTITUDE TO LIFE: helplessness, anxiety, self-minimizing, a Pollyanna who idealizes people.

BELIEVES IN: winning over of others in order to gain acceptance, and the submitter credits any success to luck and any failure to their own worthlessness. Can't stand up for legal rights but can use their skill in attaining something for others – in the guise of social worker, victim supporter or neighbourhood helper for example.

ATTITUDE TO OTHERS: apologetic, attracted toward the powerful.

DOWNGRADES: all expansive drives to emphasize the affiliative ones, moves towards people.

MEASURES WORTH BY: the amount of love they can get from others, their unselfishness, generosity, goodness, forgiveness; tends to overrate what they do for others, who may not need help!

FANTASIZES: about being a saint or martyr – a noble victim suffering in a cruel world.

FEARS: winning, being selfish, taking undue advantage, being presumptuous, fighting and friction, not being needed or appreciated, being left alone.

NEEDS: to be accepted and loved, liked, needed, wanted and is therefore dependent, compliant, appeasing, seeking help and protection from someone they can look up to.

IN RELATIONSHIPS: dramatizes love, is defenceless against exploiters like a fighter, but accepts suffering through love. Is dependent, clinging, tender, affectionate, giving. Lacking in ambition and achievement since all the expansive drives have been inhibited, and therefore needs to be allied with someone whose ambition can substitute for their own.

So again, three types of troubled love according to what we learn about love at mother's breast and father's knee, and also to the time at which any separation or emotional disturbance (like the birth of a new baby) occurred. There are also differences in innate temperament and physiology that influence attachment style and intimacy model, and whether we end up with avoidant, anxious or ambivalence attachments and how we proceed to secure attachments is taken up in Chapter 5, where couples have elaborated their ideas of what love is. Life's experience, media and literature have all had their influence and those who are more similar in their attitude towards the love they develop are happier together.

A summary of this chapter, which is the basis of the micro-cycles of attachment, is that people are attracted to each other on the basis of unconscious similarities, which indicates at bottom similarity of nervous system and neurochemical functioning. This means they will find it easy to modulate the other's arousal levels to optimum functioning, sometimes calming, sometimes motivating, according to the amount of stress or stagnation each is experiencing from everyday life. They build up between them intimacy and withdrawal cycles; we all need to achieve a balance between merging self and maintaining self. Emergent properties like trust, warmth and positive regard of the other shape us all towards socially desirable traits and connections with other people, outside the relationship. It protects us against stress, which is physically and mentally debilitating. We literally become what we couldn't become alone. To empathize with another develops intelligence, a sense of justice, and maturity.

Intimacy happens as a function of human emotions programmed by evolution; it can't be short-circuited. The permanent and exclusive bonds that form when the relationship follows its natural cycle, from initial interest, assessment of the other's qualities, and physical contact to full commitment of sexual and emotional needs to each other is reinforced daily by repeated touching, kissing, making love or talking. This releases the 'social-pleasure' chemicals which maintain the circadian rhythms of internal physiology as well as keeping the couple feeling good about each other.

4

The molecules of anxiety and euphoria

The universe is rhythmic, and we respond to those rhythms, from the cycles of the seasons and their hot and cold temperatures, to the day/night changeover. These signals come from the spinning of the Earth on its axis as it progresses round its celestial orbit every 24 hours, submitting plants and animals to highly predictable daily rhythms.

From the growth of a tree to the flight of a bird, the steps of life are centred on repetitive, rhythmical acts. Human life is patterned by layer upon layer of biological and social rhythms. Sunrise, heartbeats and musical notes are some of the billions and billions of rhythms of life. Each has its own beat, from the rhythms of cells that last milli-seconds, to climatic changes of maybe 100,000 years.

The behaviour and metabolism of most living things follows a 24-hour cycle, even when removed from this circadian rhythm of light and temperature. It has become built into life, which now has the ability to measure time. Birds, bees and fleas have a memory for these 24-hour cycles, it avoids wasting energy in the daily round of finding food, shelter and mate.

Synchronizing the beat of the important activities of life, such as reproduction, communication and defence, has helped animals to survive. Using the cosmic signals and gradually developing an internal biological time sense, species manage to hibernate, migrate, sleep and wake, feed and drink, grow and mate at the same time. And that time will be the time that species history has told them is best to exploit food and shelter resources. This timekeeping ability became built into early plants and animals through genetic memory, and has been passed on over millions of years to the human species. So birds sing in chorus at dawn, deer all give birth together at spring, crabs all hide under stones before the low tide exposes them to the air, and humans living together match their biological rhythms of energy, courtship and sex, movements, eating, speech – even diseases and death. Underlying these behavioural cycles are biochemical oscillations of cell division, cell membrane permeability and neurotransmitter synthesis – all rhythms with their own frequency.

Rhythmicity is also a universal attribute of our biochemical pathways which have seasonal and light/night fluctuations that interact to make millions of cyclical physiological events that regulate all our functions. If you could reduce your 24-hour day onto a 2-hour video, you would notice some basic rhythms in your life. Some lasting fractions of a second, others for minutes and hours. Blood pressure, for example, shows a 20 per cent fluctuation during the day. Testosterone, the male sex hormone, is highest in the early morning and lowest in the evening. The efficiency of drugs also depends on cellular rhythms. Behaviour oscillates between activity and quietness. The natural rhythm of energy dictates moods, which have biological functions, and so there is a genetic basis to these rhythms of alertness and optimism, withdrawal, passivity and pessimism. Moods influence everything from social and sexual activity to the type of food we eat (soft foods when we're happy and hard, crunchy food when angry and liquids when we're lonely according to one study).

Who is the timekeeper of all these cycles? How are they coordinated, so we get them humming together energetically? Imagine standing in a room with hundreds of clocks all ticking independently of each other. It would be like the orchestra warming up before the conductor arrives. All rhythm systems in the body have relaxation oscillators, whether the rhythm comes from the 20 cycles per second of the muscle fibres or the 16 per minute of the breathing cycle.

Rhythms of relationships

The timing and activity of the micro-cycles alters according to whatever else is going on in life at the time. And the physiology that drives our rhythms swings between movement and rest, a reciprocity of conservation and expenditure that suggests and sustains the other. A satisfactory life has to involve a balance between these opposites – a cycle of reaching out to horizons new, counterbalanced with one of security, comfort and relaxation, an 'at homeness' versus an adventure. And between the upswings and downswings of our daily round there are several states of physical and psychological functioning, all of different intensities – a continuum of awareness between oblivious, habitual response and vivid mind-blowing reality. Restful retreat swings to watchful advance and back to matter-of-fact familiarity.

Dreams of the day and terrors of the night

Actually, there are two major mood systems. One is generated from the cosmic circadian rhythm and affects body temperature, neurohormonal rhythms, sensuality cycles and our general *joie de vivre*. It is a diurnal energy curve, rising from its trough in the early morning to a peak before midday, then another trough, not quite back to early morning sluggishness. Then another rise to a second peak at around 6-8pm, followed by a slow shut-down to a midnight low.

The other mood system comes from within – the autonomic nervous system that gears us up to fight or flee from dangerous situations and people. When at rest, the parasympathetic division of the nervous system is dominating, and when that coincides with a circadian high of energy we feel great – energetic and vigorous, yet relaxed. But, with a low it's drowsiness and 'can't be bothered'. When armoured against danger (and it's not man-eating tigers these days, it's other threats to our well-being – things like relationships going sour, the fleeting glimpse of disapproval from someone important or vague hint of dissatisfaction that put us on edge), muscles tense and mood becomes agitated and unpleasantly aroused as the sympathetic nervous system hormones of stress and fear get the upper hand.

Our two mood systems are orchestrated at the physiological and biochemical level, creating cycles of interweaving waveforms, which are coordinated into a rhythm by two oscillators, affected by light and social interaction – the features of our environment that now structure our well-being.

Social interaction can even help jet lag: when rhythms are lost due to the circadian oscillator getting confused over the abnormal day/night cycle of jet travel round the world, interaction with the locals can overcome the worst effects of jet lag. In an experiment

where half the travellers went to the hotel and the other half went
out with the locals, the latter recovered more quickly.

Circadian rhythms of compatibility

Interaction rhythms are the results of the interplay of the nervous
system with all other systems of the body, the somatic (skeletal and
muscle), the endocrine system, and even the atomic systems of
cellular division and DNA metabolism. In the first chapter, Julie
described how she started a synchronous rhythm with Sam. As they
sat talking, facing each other, the muscle systems of their heads,
faces and mouths were signalling and echoing back to each other.
Their hand and arm gestures and shoulder movements combined
in this rhythm, their individual rhythms started to mesh. The
perturbations occurred until there was a stability of frequency
between them, and that was the point at which they were
synchronized. It was also the point where this conversation of
gestures became a conversation of feeling. Feelings between people
are time bound. We like someone we can harmonize rhythms to,
and feel uncomfortable with those who mismatch our rhythms,
those we are not 'in tune' with. Getting it together can be measured
both electrophysiologically and, by asking someone how much they
like the other. It comes to the same thing! So, rhythm is a prime
mover in social relationships. The synchrony of the rhythmic
sensori-motor cycles of all our internal systems is dependent on our
daily round with other people – other people that mean something
to us. It doesn't have to be the great love of the century – just a friend
who cares and with whom one can become emotionally involved.
Even events that stand for social interaction (church bells,
telephone conversations, photographs of loved ones) can help, as
well as knowing that the separation is temporary and predictable.
Social chemistry sparks off optimum arousal and energy in times
of routine, and calms when anxiety sets off unpleasant arousal.

Relationships as regulators

We are dependent on the pattern of stimulation our partner
provides in everyday life for maintaining our complex rhythms,
originally set to mother's tune. We don't notice our need of other
people until our concentration, memory, sleep pattern, attention,
perception, appetite and tolerance to pain becomes altered, and
periodic fatigue sets in. All this coincides with an impending sense

of loss of control. This can happen slowly, as emotional alienation increases between a couple, or suddenly, as unexpected separation rips asunder the timing and synchrony of our rhythms and cycles.

We use symbolic events to hang on a bit longer, like keeping the possessions of the lost one in the same place, setting the table for the missing one and so on to remind and retrain our rhythms. Permanent loss, like death, alters expectations. That person will never entrain our rhythms again. But re-experiencing multiple expectancies, for example the repeated returning of a temporarily separated partner, elicits fresh waves of distress that are the consequence of arhythmic cycles reattaching and disengaging.

The beat of love

Each of us acts like a radio transmitter, putting out a weak signal of electrical currents and magnetic forces. And each of us can amplify a weak signal by sensitive tuning of the meta-messages of voice and breathing, the body ballet of movement, pattern and flow that becomes a rhythm; all these are linked to the biochemistry of brain reactions. The length of a gaze, the duration of a touch, the interval of a smile, the pause between words, all are measured by the brain's internal clock. Brain time is harmonized with the inner pulse, which itself is a preset echo of mother's heart beat, imprinted in the last 6 weeks before birth. This is when the auditory nerve in the unborn baby is myelinated and it can hear. Even music played in pregnancy has been shown to affect the baby's memory and later preference for that music. One mother always did her prenatal breathing exercises while watching videos of M.A.S.H., and the introductory tune had become a signal for her to relax. Years after her child would go into a near trance every time he heard the M.A.S.H. signature tune! Studies attempting to investigate the effect of quarrelling between parents and anxiety of the pregnant mother have long claimed deleterious effects on the child's personality, due to the effect of stress hormones in the mother's blood being passed to the unborn baby's blood supply.

Rhythmicity in mother and child continues, with bouts of baby activity matching mother's activity, nappy changing, feeding, crying, arm-waving. Babies and mothers are so sensitive to all the nuances of each other's behaviour that they establish shared rhythms – an imprinted emotional pattern which will form the basis of communication, even in some babies who went to foster parents at 11 days old.

The function of attachment is not merely to provide protection for the baby, it promotes the synchrony of the two branches of the nervous system. Mother, like a drug, is a physiological regulating agent. Mother's particular combination of gaze, talk and touch sets the baby's attention to inattention cycles. She will change her beat from one episode to the next to maintain a pleasant arousal and attention level in the baby. Mothers have an intuitive realization of the importance of repetition in their rhythms of talking, touching, gazing and playing. Any mother and baby game has a subtle coordination of facial expression, eye contact and movement. The mother reflects the baby's movements, and the whole game is one of repetitive movements and intonations. They know that these micro-rhythms of rapport and synchrony affect the quality of their bond by the baby's reactions.

The function of matching rhythms is social bonding, but it is less likely that she realizes that her orchestration of the baby's excitement is the chief means by which it comes to like a certain level of arousal and to develop expectancies about the world. Playing, making faces, talking, gurgling and so on are all lessons in entrainment – the process by which we coordinate to each other socially and emotionally. Cultures where baby is passed around several adults often result in the mismatch of adult/baby patterns, the tendency is for that baby, when adult, to have many friends but not at a very deep level of intimacy. Because of our social conceptions of gender differences, mother and daughter relationships are more enmeshed than mother-son ones (a crying baby will elicit explanations of anger if it's a boy and fear if it's a girl!). This is proposed by some to be the basis of later male lack of intimacy, but even mother rats lick their baby sons more than their baby daughters, and it has been shown that this affects their later sexual behaviour. Another interesting study of baby rats showed that handling them affected the size of the bundle of fibres connecting the two brain hemispheres. But while handling 100-day-old male rats increased the amount of these fibres, in the 100-day-old female rats it decreased – a sex difference in the way the brain fibres (called the *corpus callosum*) responded to handling. So there seems to be an ethological basis to our social stereotypes.

In our society father tends to be the super charger of the baby's arousal. His voice is louder, his movements more vigorous, and babies come to expect more excitement, even though it's for a shorter time, than they get from their more solicitous mother. To be a good pace-setter for the baby, adults must just exceed the baby's rhythm. This is just like the piano player who is technically perfect, but unexciting and unexpressive unless deviating ever so slightly from the beat. But to be unpredictable in rhythmic sequences makes a bad piano player and a turned-off baby, who gives up trying to predict when mother's next peek-a-boo is going to happen.

Initially then, the mother regulates the baby's cycles of activity with her own body rhythms. The pattern of optimal stimulation sets the level of alertness, relaxation, spontaneity and positive feeling that the baby gets used to and which he or she later comes to manipulate with the microflow of behaviour. These are all the apparently purposeless, useless things we do in a day which are interspersed with the more serious, purposeful things like work. The reading of newspapers, horoscope columns and agony pages, talking to plants, pets and gossiping over the back fence, drinking coffee/tea, yawning, watching of television, smoking etc.

Microflow profiles

The ways a person builds up a unique microflow profile based on their physiology and uses it to match their skills against the opportunities for action in the environment needs a good nervous system balancing act. Variations in individual arousal level due to differences in this homoeostatic balance account for the different levels of placidity, excitement, optimism, anxiety and boredom characteristic of a particular person.

We tend to have a favourite physiological function behind our preferred level of arousal. For some it's a particular level of heart rate, for others a particular skin temperature, and still others a characteristic blood pressure. In a study of gamblers, treatment was trying to widen that arousal preference so the gambler could find other things that gave him that same physiological reward, and this strategy could hold good in relationships. So, try new behaviours together that give you the same level of pleasant arousal but which will have a different physiological basis to take the place of your established one – and prevent later boredom.

Regulating the amount of stimulation increases attention and involvement and some people deprived of stimulation for long enough have hallucinations and psychotic breakdowns. An experiment requiring people not to do any of their enjoyable microflow activities for 48 hours (only the serious work related 'deep-flow' activities) disrupted those people enough for the researchers to conclude that the microflow of behaviour serves to compensate for insufficient stimulation. Disruption of it leads to thought and perceptual disturbances which looked much like symptoms of mental illness. The extreme symptoms were a bit like schizophrenic thought and emotional disorders.

Actually the multitude of microflow of behaviour, from everyday trivia to artistic creation, can be put into six categories, although the common structure still underlies all categories, the feeling of control the right patterning brings. The six categories cover what most people do spontaneously in a normal day in our culture and historical time, excluding perhaps the very young and very old. People pattern their lives differently according to these categories. Some depend on physical activities like walking, dancing, sports, while others occupy themselves with the social category, talking, visiting friends, going to social events and so on.

Excitement and tranquillity cycles have even been established according to the material we read. Light fiction or heavy factual information is read at faster or slower speeds to maintain optimum arousal. Eye fixation rates vary from 100 to 500 milliseconds for a single passage as well as other physiological measures such as heart rate, skin response and muscle activity. A book is a conversationalist able to engage us in pleasant chatter that takes us out of ourselves – we become absorbed to the point of a reading trance.

Conversation between couples has a predictable cycle too. Every 92 to 94 minutes, according to research, the urge to talk to each other comes on, as does activity and rest cycling. Much work has been done trying to relate the various psychological cycles with physiological underpinning like fluctuation of hormone levels in the blood, neural activation and so on, and the search goes ever deeper into the internalized time script each is adhering to, syncopated by mother. The raw data of perception reaches us in vibrations of the nerve fibres, pulsing as the cells fire off their neural codes for us to interpret as something we have already seen and named or something new to categorize and store away in labelled rhythms, of which we have billions.

At a comfortable level of arousal a person's cardiovascular and neuroendocrine systems are ticking over with no strain. The average energy level used in alertness, attention, and becoming committed to some task or social interaction is characteristic of the person. They have invested themselves to a level which is sufficient for meeting daily work and relationship demands, not under- or over-involved, inwardly or outwardly – just hanging on in!

The intimacy–conflict cycle

Everyday we go through several cycles of involvement and withdrawal, and, between couples, cycles of intimacy and conflict. For every state an equal opposite. It is here that action and reaction are triggered off. The feelings of closeness, pleasure and attraction are predictably balanced by turning away, turning out to others, getting on with work and then the coming back together again.

There is a relationship rhythm of intimacy and withdrawal similar to the energy and conservation cycles of daily life and the protest and despair cycles of lost attachment. These are mediated by the same brain mechanisms as the drug tolerance and dependency cycle. The highest manufacture of the brain's euphoria molecules is in the part of the brain that is responsible for the way we pay attention and the way we synchronize all our biological rhythms. When circumstances in our lives push us too much one way we slide easily into a confused, demotivated state or, conversely a tense, agitated state. When someone who lives with us matches our optimum arousal point they can show the way, physiologically speaking, and help to de-escalate the tension or energize the demotivation. Chronic mismatchers are also chronic desynchronizers. Even partners who normally spark off energy or calm down tension and anxiety can, due to extreme circumstances, get out of synchrony. Melanie, a trainer for the Civil Service, described her relationship as happy, enjoyable and interesting. 'But,' she said, 'there are predictable times when I can't stand Don in the same room. I'm only away one night a week but that's the end of a hectic two-day training session, and I don't get home until about 11 p.m. on Friday night. I come in and unpack all the day's papers and overnight things, separate it from the shopping I've usually done on the way home and then I just want to relax. After two days with fifty strange people and then a strange hotel room I really don't feel like talking and doing the "home at last darling" bit. I just want to shut the door on the world, lie on the bed and turn off. If I hear him coming up the stairs I feel like screaming, but I've never been able to tell him that. It used to worry me until I realized that that was the only time I felt like crawling into a shell so it must be more to do with me and the job than Don or our relationship. It takes me an hour and a half every time, and then I'm ready to go to bed properly.'

Melanie is voicing the frustration of being further aroused when she was already on the verge of unpleasantly high arousal, and just wanted to de-escalate. Being alone was avoiding more stimulation.

The micro-cycles of attachment

The base level of arousal, activity and involvement that is a person's preferred and comfortable state (not to say addicted state) is the point where their circadian energy rhythm peaks and coincides with their nervous system arousal low – or calm point. This interaction of energy and arousal gives us the whole spectrum of mood states, but much research suggests there are four recognizable clusters. From calm energy that goes with sustained work, thought and social activity to fatigue and indolence and, depending on the circumstances, a hyperactive arousal which can be pushed still further into an extremely unpleasant high level.

In Figure 4.1 the top quadrants are characterized by more self-centred thought and behaviour. People who have had their arousal increased experimentally by all sorts of worrying (untrue) suggestions start referring to 'me' and 'I' more often than usual. The bottom half is other-centred. Empathetic emotional arousal is the state of intimacy which circles along the energy dimension, interacting with the arousal dimension and motivating us to seek active involvement with the other every 90 minutes or so.

The experience of empathetic interest from another leads to a higher degree of self-awareness. It increases our capacity to evaluate ourselves and makes us more 'pro-social' and able to stretch out our time in the intimate and social quadrants. The quadrants work like emotional machinery – a fair increase in arousal will decrease energy and vice-versa, which is why exercise is so beneficial. It is a therapy – better than tranquillizers for reducing the anxiety of arousal.

All these states have different physiological back-ups, which are measurable by machine as well as an intimate partner who senses the withdrawal from intimacy with as much acuity as a micro-electrode.

Reality changes with circadian rhythm

There are, of course, personality differences so that one person's minimum arousal point can coincide with another's maximum arousal point. These two would *not* make good partners or mutual

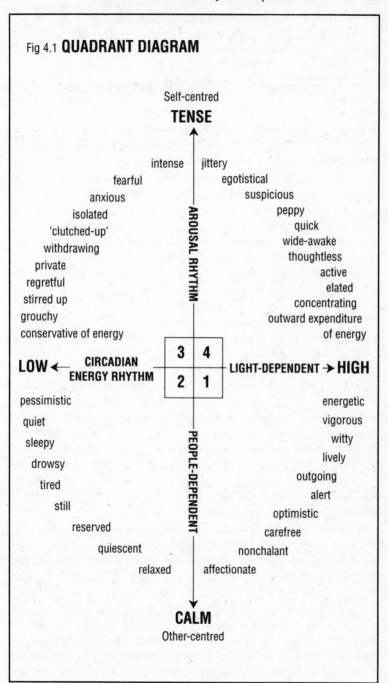

Fig 4.1 **QUADRANT DIAGRAM**

Self-centred
TENSE

intense | jittery
fearful | egotistical
anxious | suspicious
isolated | peppy
'clutched-up' | quick
withdrawing | wide-awake
private | thoughtless
regretful | active
stirred up | elated
grouchy | concentrating
conservative of energy | outward expenditure
| of energy

AROUSAL RHYTHM

3	4
2	1

LOW ← CIRCADIAN ENERGY RHYTHM   LIGHT-DEPENDENT → **HIGH**

pessimistic | energetic
quiet | vigorous
sleepy | witty
drowsy | lively
tired | outgoing
still | alert
reserved | optimistic
quiescent | carefree
relaxed | nonchalant
relaxed | affectionate

PEOPLE-DEPENDENT

CALM
Other-centred

mood adjusters. For at least some time in the 24-hour cycle, couples must feel in tune with each other and be able to match and amplify the intimacy cycles while toning down the withdrawal cycles of potential conflict. A couple discussing a problem can remain rational in their calm-energetic period (mid-morning and early afternoon if they both share the same circadian rhythm) but that same problem may provoke tension and slammed doors if their discussion is in their tired, withdrawal period – late at night. Their energy low contributes to their tenseness which pushes their arousal levels into the high and unpleasant level, like Melanie's.

To someone whose characteristic level of engagement in their surroundings is higher, the lower style of involvement is, to them, unresponsive, flat and socially inadequate. Conversations lag, hesitancies in planning and doing things abound, non-verbal signals are not echoed or reflected, there are lengthy pauses between words, all of which have consequences for compatibility outside the couple's awareness (much more of this in Chapter 9). The chronic unresponsiveness of the low level aroused person makes the higher level person feel like getting behind and pushing them. But to the low engager, the enthusiasm and hyperactivity of the higher engager, their involvement, emotional investment and commitment to anything they do is too pressurizing. Playing hard and working hard brings no benefits to the lower engager. The cost is counted in chronic overarousal and lowered health and vitality. The patterns of cost at both brain and behaviour level are the same patterns of cost in relationships. Adapting to another takes emotional and physical energy and not to be able to fit into the arousal pattern of another is a bit like being chronically jet-lagged. It is critical that a couple is matched in their excitement to security cycles to give the arousal and relaxation cycles a synonym. Or at least that they are not too differently pitched to keep in harmony, and act as arousal manipulators for each other. They needn't go for exactly the same thrills and experience. Skiing down a mountain-side for one might be as exhilarating as the discovery of a new idea for the other. Or making new friends equal to scuba diving. The degree to which a couple need a similar challenge and novelty from life was a major finding making for compatibility in the couples I surveyed. Whether it was high or low was immaterial, whether it was the same was not. Similarity went with happiness, causally.

When a couple's need for challenge and activity is not met by opportunities for it, boredom, restriction and even illness will follow. Studies on risk show that however safe we make the environment –

rubber-padded playgrounds, reinforced cars and seat belts, or underground passes, the recipients of these safety measures alter their optimum arousal accordingly. The kids foresake the safe playgrounds for the adventure playground or dangerous old deserted houses, the belted reinforced steel car drivers drive faster (injuring more pedestrians) and pedestrians still nip across the six lane roundabout weaving between the traffic precariously. Why? . . . the thrill of it! We need a degree of risk to maintain the balance between the euphoria molecules and the arousal molecules.

Complete self-regulation of all our biological cycles may not be possible. It was mother from whom we increasingly gained physiological autonomy, but such is the social nature of our species that social interaction continues to play an important role in the everyday regulation of our physiology. Significant partners entrain and adapt to each other's cycles which gives new meaning to the Biblical phrase 'to be joined as one flesh'.

Like fireflies, who flash erratically until mutual entrainment develops when they flash in synchrony, we are all populations of uncoupled oscillators until we form a bond with someone. When mutually coupled the peaks and troughs of intimacy and withdrawal generate a very narrow frequency band; in other words our electrophysical vibrations are matched and can be seen on a computer screen if the couple are hooked up to electrodes. The micro-cycles are the low challenge counterpart to the macro-cycles of the relationship.

Moments of intense intimacy will be followed by moments of withdrawal and involvement in other things than the relationship. If your intimacy cycling doesn't match, then at least it helps to be aware of it. It prevents the faster withdrawal of the other being interpreted as boredom, being turned-off, or having lost interest. It's a natural oscillation of the rhythms of energy and arousal. The powerful impulses that push us together are matched by the equally powerful forces that pull us apart.

Keep a record of your individual activity/arousal peaks and quiescent lows and relaxed cycles. Note how long each up and down swing lasts, the feelings and bodily sensations that go with them and how pleasant/unpleasant the feeling was. Use a rating scale like Figure 4.2 (overleaf).

1. Make a list of the adjectives in the quadrant diagram. Put them in the right quadrant list i.e. overaroused tiredness/overaroused energy/calm tiredness/calm energy. Look back over the day

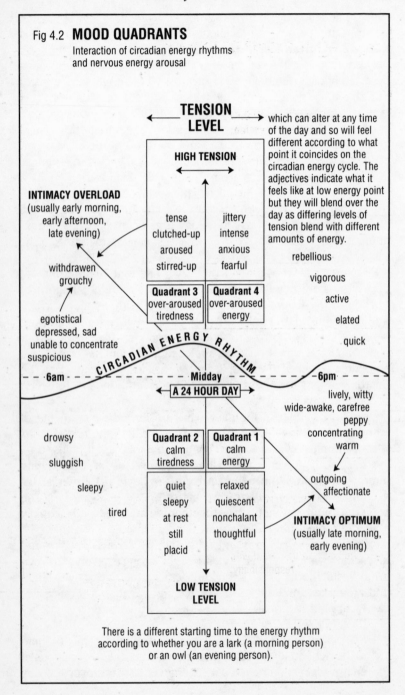

Fig 4.2 MOOD QUADRANTS

Interaction of circadian energy rhythms and nervous energy arousal

TENSION LEVEL

HIGH TENSION

which can alter at any time of the day and so will feel different according to what point it coincides on the circadian energy cycle. The adjectives indicate what it feels like at low energy point but they will blend over the day as differing levels of tension blend with different amounts of energy.

INTIMACY OVERLOAD
(usually early morning, early afternoon, late evening)

tense
clutched-up
aroused
stirred-up

jittery
intense
anxious
fearful

rebellious

vigorous

active

elated

quick

withdrawen
grouchy

Quadrant 3
over-aroused
tiredness

Quadrant 4
over-aroused
energy

egotistical
depressed, sad
unable to concentrate
suspicious

CIRCADIAN ENERGY RHYTHM

- - 6am - - - - - - - - - - Midday - - - - - - -6pm - - - -

◄ A 24 HOUR DAY ►

lively, witty
wide-awake, carefree
peppy
concentrating
warm

drowsy

sluggish

sleepy

tired

Quadrant 2
calm
tiredness

Quadrant 1
calm
energy

outgoing
affectionate

quiet
sleepy
at rest
still
placid

relaxed
quiescent
nonchalant
thoughtful

INTIMACY OPTIMUM
(usually late morning, early evening)

LOW TENSION LEVEL

There is a different starting time to the energy rhythm according to whether you are a lark (a morning person) or an owl (an evening person).

Fig 4.3 **RELATIONSHIP QUADRANTS**

INTIMACY OVERLOAD
(subjective tension)

Felt like withdrawing into my shell, rushing home, bolting the door and disconnecting the telephone, cleaning up, escaping into fiction, computer games or day-dreams.

Felt as if my partner was deliberately trying to rub me up the wrong way, be rejecting, critical, or losing interest in me.

Wonder if I have much to offer anyway . . .

CIRCADIAN LOW
AROUSAL HIGH 3

Felt like dancing all night, turning up the stereo, going out, having fun, getting on with work or other ongoing plans.

Felt assertive, felt like taking control, taking the lead, having my say, dominating my partner.

CIRCADIAN HIGH
4 AROUSAL HIGH

CIRCADIAN LOW 2
AROUSAL LOW

Felt like flaking out, just watching television, reading a paper, definitely not like talking seriously.

Felt I needed reassurance, wanted to rely on my partner, felt like giving in, shunning responsibility.

1 CIRCADIAN HIGH
AROUSAL LOW

Felt like relaxing, chatting, talking about us, staying home and cooking for two, making love, sharing a joke.

Felt affectionate, warm, caring and optimistic about our future together.

INTIMACY OPTIMUM
(subjective energy)

when your mood changed and tick the adjectives you felt. You will find that one list predominates every one and a half hours or so. You should be able over time to plot a predictable cycling of your moods and how long they last. This is your base line and you should pick a normal few days in which to do this profile, no long lost relatives turning up, holidays, accidents etc. Establishing a reliable profile might take about a week.

2. Now establish an 'intimacy mood-match'. List some intimate behaviours you like and also some turn-offs to match against the quadrants to see what's going on in your relationship when you are in certain moods. Of course your common sense will tell you your quarrels will appear more often in the over-aroused/tiredness quadrant, but you may be surprised at the regularity of timing. When irritability and bickering does happen at a naturally high energy point look for what ever else caused that unpleasantly high arousal.

3. Depending on the mood quadrant we're in, circling between energy, alertness, optimism and withdrawal, pessimism and passivity, we evoke memories of past events to fit. Long-term repeatedly occurring patterns are misinterpreted and mis-matched so that you really can say that reality changes with circadian rhythm. At its low point, past memories of failure and fatigue push us into unpleasant arousal, uncertainty, anxiety and depression. But at the upswing the same ponderous insolubles are transformed from things we wonder what on earth to do about into things we are confident of coping with. The upswing is further fuelled by memories of past successes.

    Having counted the time and duration of your cyclic intimacy/withdrawal cycles, compare with your partner your cycles. Include working hours but compare differences for times you are together. Try to use other activities to fill in mismatches. If you predominate in quadrant 4 for example use exercise to manipulate your arousal and to bring your 4s down to your partner's 1s quicker. If quadrants 3 predominates cut down unnecessary stimulation to match your partner's stage 1 more often.

Understanding the inevitability of at least occasional physiological mismatch in the intimacy/withdrawal cycles and possibility of conflict makes couples more motivated to match and modulate the other's arousal, and synchronize with them. Withdrawal is then less an occasion for conflict than for secure replenishment of nervous energy.

Long-established happy couples are automatically adjusting all the time. They are attuned to the signs of over and under-stimulation. His slightly tense irritability that means he needs to be left alone with the paper or her grim, slow over-concentration on a household task that means an evening out is the order of the nervous system. One that will alter the tension and relaxation balance of the rhythms of energy. A music concert which manipulates emotional arousal, a dinner-dance, a comedy show.

Inability to match rhythms leaves couples feeling as if the relationship is out of their control – they are pushed into spending more time in the tense and irritable quadrant, depleting their natural energy resources and rhythms. Synchronizing interpersonal cycles and continually entraining them to reflect to each other any change from the environment enhances health, physical and emotional well-being, fertility, even our intellectual capacity. Breaking the rhythm disrupts learning, and the making and breaking of the hormonal concomitants of health and energy.

The micro-cycles of the nervous system feed into larger psychological cycles; the need for love and the fear of rejection. Fighting, fleeing or passively submitting are defences that deplete energy and block homoeostatic balance. Thus the separate and traditional relationships can become closer and happier by moving towards interdependence, which means a better balance of the 'I versus we' conflict.

Shelly couldn't have been more wrong when he wrote:

> Fate, time, occasion, chance and change?
> To these all things are subject, but eternal love

Love, *more* than all things is subject – it must be to survive. Shelley and the romantic poets have hindered relationships for hundreds of years!

5

Matching love-styles

The love-crazy to love-oblivious spectrum

There are natural rules to anything humans organize – including relationships. To keep going, the relationship has to have some pleasure and avoid too much conflict. There is probably some precise mathematical equation to describe it. If the balance isn't right then humans feel uncomfortable in the relationship, as if it doesn't 'fit' them, they become indifferent towards each other, demotivated and unwilling to put themselves out for each other. This is as true for pubs, clubs and multinational corporations. These reward rules and conflict rules obligate us to return favours, support, interest . . . all unspoken, unwritten but *known*.

However, because we aren't all the same, the rules of relationship likewise differ, or at least are elastic. In spite of the unified version of love and intimacy that poets, novelists, singers, religious authorities and the media propagate, men and women live together quite happily in a lesser state of grace than the celluloid ideal. Continual closeness, constant companionship and frank self-disclosure are the modern day formulae prescribed for a life-enhancing intimacy. But too much intensity doesn't suit some whose style is more reserved, thoughtful and cautious. On the other hand, neither does too much distance suit those who like to react spontaneously, embrace wholeheartedly and share themselves unreservedly. What makes for happiness is being oneself and being able to pursue one's own interests and needs, not performing for the sake of the approval or expectations of others. And being able to count on the support of a partner and feel able to reciprocate. This means sharing the same 'relationship-code'. Relationships fail when the intensity or distance preferences of one is not matched by the other. Too much distance means not enough sharing of the self and too much intensity means a stifling overfocusing, but there are many healthy positions in between these two extremes. Both distancing and intense closeness are useful ways to manage anything frightening – including intimacy, until permanent trust is established and most couples ease themselves into a relationship this way, taking years to creep nearer to the balance of intimacy and selves that makes them feel happy, healthy and 'authentic'. So these are the ways humans relate, and have done since at least the Greeks because they had different words for the intensity and distance of ways of relating. These words (*Eros, Ludus, Agape, Mania, Storge, Pragma*) all fitted someone's experience of love and intimacy and sum up the different but equally valid rules of avoiding conflict and getting pleasure. The love-crazy (*mania*) throw themselves headlong into the relationship, for them anxiety comes from distance, while the opposite end of the dimension, love-oblivious (*ludus*) experience anxiety from closeness that threatens to restrict their freedom.

Emphasizing distance and guarding closeness are short-term solutions to the pleasure and conflict problem and are only maladaptive when they become rigid stances dedicated to ignoring unresolved issues and used to exit emotionally or physically from any involvement or responsibility in the relationship.

The four couples whose relationship stories unfold throughout the rest of this book illustrate one or other of these positions regarding the relationship rules of closeness/pleasure versus distance/ avoiding conflict, from the crude physical to the minutest symbolic manipulation of approach and avoidance.

A ludic love story
with a space dimension

It was late afternoon, as the sun was setting over the charming garden square with its rickety wrought-iron railings and garden shed. It was an up-and-coming area of London with skips outside three-storey regency houses, the odd BMW parked between Hondas and tatty minis. Rushing out with the rubbish she had forgotten was a mini-skirted woman with bobbed hair.

Barbara and Edward's front door was faded black but the hinges and bolts looked solid enough as it opened into a long hallway, which dispelled the shabby atmosphere of the square. Lemon and grey striped Victorian wallpaper and ruffled curtains, through which there was a view of a leafy green and geranium studded patio. A slightly bizarre note was played by a huge telescope mounted between seedling boxes which held test tubes, especially when most of the furniture was genuine good quality antique.

Barbara had just arrived home from school, and is now on the phone in the kitchen, which is lined with books and files as well as saucepans and herbs; Ed is upstairs in his study putting data into the computer for one of his business clients. A tall, thin man with receding hairline and horn-rimmed glasses, he looks the epitome of the computer boffin. He has heard Barbara come in, but he knows she will be on the phone as usual or going through the vast amount of papers she has brought home to organize for tomorrow, so he waits for the call, 'Cup of Tea, Ed?'

Barbara and Edward have been living together six years. Edward doesn't want children, and at the moment Barbara agrees, she's too busy. Sometimes, however, she wonders if she will regret it; she still has a few years to make up her mind finally, but it would mean finding someone else, since she is sure Ed wouldn't agree. Barbara had several boyfriends before Ed; she was a vivacious, attractive woman with a yen for travel and art. Her job was the only anchor in her life; her parents had divorced when she was a baby and there hadn't been much family life. Her mother had spent much time complaining about her father and warning Barbara against unreliable men. Money had been short, and only the generosity of her uncle had allowed them to live above social security standards. Compared to her friends she felt she lived an unconnected sort of life. It was quite easy to see the school at which she now worked so enthusiastically and conscientiously as a surrogate family. She had been made a head of department at 32, although she wasn't an ambitious person at all.

Edward was almost her opposite: introverted personality to her sociability, retreat to her involvement, passive to her active approach to life and its problems. But they shared the same interests in art, philosophy, psychology, music and books – and they spent much time discussing these subjects. They always found something of interest to say. They also enjoyed the long walks together at the weekend. The only thing Barbara did without Ed was go on foreign holidays with her colleagues or class. Ed wouldn't go on aeroplanes and didn't like the idea of foreign food, friends or hotels sufficiently to overcome his fear of flying. When they did go on holiday together, they had wonderful times camping around England's coastline or in the Scottish highlands.

Edward now comes down to tea and complains jokingly about the sticky buns Barbara bought on impulse on the way home. Bad for his health and bad for her figure he mumbles, as they munch away contentedly. He is going to cook tonight, but not until after she gets back from the meeting, so they can enjoy the buns without guilt they tell themselves.

Ed's family was much more traditional than Barbara's but he always felt weak in the face of his two older brothers and a mother, who, disappointed in her husband's continual illness and inconsistent work-record, took over the role as the head of household. Ed had wanted to be a teacher, which meant further training, but his mother had wanted him to take up the full-time job offered to bright school-leavers by the local firm he'd worked for during school holidays. There had been a row about it, and he'd moved out vowing never to ask for anything again. He never did get to do teacher-training, but taught himself computing and had set up a small business designing computer systems for small firms. He liked this because he could work from home and come and go when he wanted. He felt that he and Barbara had a very good relationship, they agreed on so much: both were vegetarian, animal rights campaigners, and they had similar views on almost all aspects of love, sex and life. And both spent most of their energy at work that they liked. So life was as good as he could expect, even if the routine made the future look a bit heavy if he thought about it too much. The 'buzz' of new ideas was important to him – and he felt it was a bit lacking in the business world. But now and then he would get clients setting up innovative business schemes, which were a challenge to him. Some of them he did follow-up work for, for no charge, just to get involved in the heady atmosphere of invention and novelty again. He would sometimes stay up all night finishing a programme he was excited about. For this reason business was a bit chaotic – and even the well-done jobs were sometimes not paid for by unscrupulous firms.

Barbara considered their relationship good too. No real arguments. They had planned to marry when they first met, but Ed had panicked at the last moment and thought he hadn't loved

Barbara enough to go ahead with it and asked her to wait. She was shocked and upset, but knew that forcing him would end in resentment and him feeling suffocated. She knew too that he wouldn't leave her, but was insulted to think that he felt pressured when she was the last person to be possessive and demanding. In fact, she was so involved with school life, her pupils, parents, colleagues, and so on, that she felt she hardly noticed Ed during term-time. She could never find out why he felt as he did, marriage had become a taboo subject with them. It was one area where his normal calm reserve deserted him, and he would shut himself away in his study for hours at the first hint of any conversation about it.

Barbara imagined she would go on working at school and had a favourite image of herself, grey-haired in her rocking chair with all her former students visiting and telling her about world famous exploits for which her teaching was the catalyst. Ed's fantasies were no less grandiose. He was fascinated with languages and communication. Not only computer languages but extra-terrestrial communication and parapsychology, and he practised astral projection. His friends were mostly confined to the people he met through present concerns and his only long-term friend was an old university mate, who now lived abroad and had probably lost contact, for the present anyway. Barbara was different in this respect, often inviting people round for coffee or dinner and having a long list of Christmas card regulars from years back, her foreign country exchange visits, old school and college friends. She enjoyed the annual, cryptic, life-progress reports.

So their lives ran along predictable tracks, even if the stops were unpatterned. Barbara had been a courier once, and still liked the idea of herself as a free spirit, travelling carelessly through life. She thought it was Ed's stability that had enabled her to stay at her present school and make something of it. It was nice to know he would usually be in the house when she got home – even if he was up in his study. She actually preferred it that way while she was reorganizing herself, since she rushed around so much in the day and got all her papers and plans jumbled up. Ed disliked meetings, or sorting out the teamwork he would have to be involved in. A year's stint as the residents' association secretary had cured him of that for ever. He had only volunteered because he was trying to change his passive response to life's opportunities. He wanted to be more of an initiator like Barbara; he felt she had a command over the community while he was just an adjunct. But most social groups overwhelmed him. He felt disconnected from others, even day-today business life was a struggle, with his sense of estrangement from the wheeler-dealers he met, and he wanted to withdraw most of the time from the pressure of profit-justification. People and their vagaries were not Ed's forte – Barbara's company was all he needed. As a team, he felt, they were quite unique.

Edward and Barbara had achieved a space in their living arrangements which separated them psychologically as physically. Although they shared a bedroom they often got up and went to bed at different times according to their particular schedule. The most reliable time together was the cup of tea they shared when Barbara came in from school, and breakfast – though this was a rushed affair, hardly the vehicle for intimacy. If Ed had been up late Barbara would eat alone anyway.

They were happy enough, their separate identities suited them but their space cycles were not close enough to withstand any stress, and when it came along it forced them further and further apart. The idea they had of their relationship was that they were two independent individuals who were able to master the world by themselves. Their feelings of dis-connectedness fed into their fragmented relationship. On the surface life was fairly predictable, but they both used space to decrease intimacy, out of a basic mistrust of the reciprocity and endurance of the affection. They did help each other, but solving problems was more a demonstration of their individual independence and decisiveness than a joint solution. Ed especially felt that accepting Barbara's suggestions was a sign of his weakness. On the whole they believed their separate experience led to different realities, and that therefore the other's observations were of less help than getting to grips with it alone.

These feelings of hanging on precariously in an uncaring, unforgiving, world were expressed in many aspects of their life. Work and leisure activities overlapped, as did the places they were done in – the second computer in the bedroom, syllabuses, timetables and reports crammed into box files that took over the sitting room, piano in the bathroom. A middle-class mess they called it fondly; and it couldn't have been more different to Pauline and Bob's household.

A manic love story
with a time structure

From the imposing colonnaded and chained front door, deep pile of the stair carpet and gilt framed mirrors on the hall, Pauline and Bob's flat screamed mini stately-home. Sunk into deep leather chairs and drinking dry white wine from heavy crystal glasses, it was hard to believe that this was actually a town-flat. Resting her glass on an antique rosewood occasional table, Pauline anxiously turns to Bob and asks what he thinks of her dress. She is a slim, fair, 35 year old and looks wonderful in a smart two piece. Tonight's guests are Bob's senior partners in the law centre, and Pauline is eager to make a good impression. She organized the pre-theatre drinks party which was convenient to the partners since Pauline and Bob's flat was between the practice and the theatre.

Bob's relaxed reply hadn't been enthusiastic enough for Pauline, who immediately wondered if she was a bit overdressed. The outfit had cost a fortune but it was better to change it if it was wrong, so she dashed upstairs to exchange it for a simple black frock before everyone arrived. She was terribly anxious to have everyone like her. Bob's family and partners were all so confident and knew the right things to say and do so easily, she couldn't bear to be out of step in any way.

Pauline and Bob had met when she was a probationary social worker and had to go to court for a client who had broken the conditions of a court order. Bob was everything she had ever wanted in a man; respectable, knowledgeable, professional, earning well and likely to do even better in the future. He was kind to her, even indulgent, and made her feel like the 'daddy's little girl' she had never been. Her father had died before she was two, and Pauline had grown up helping her mother with her younger twin sisters. These twins were the apples of her mother's eye, and Pauline herself was proud of them too. A talented singing and dancing duo, they had carried off all the dancing school prizes and were now models, earning a lot of money in advertising. It was very nice in conversation with important people to be able to refer to her modelling twin sisters. They had generously repaid all Pauline's early sacrifices when she had worked in Woolworths during school holidays to help pay for their dancing lessons: they had paid for her wedding to Bob, which had been the happiest day of her life. Everything had been perfect; her dress, the church, the reception, the presents, the guests and most of all, the bridegroom. She felt 'settled' in life as she had never done before.

Bob was flabbergasted when she reappeared in black velvet, and there was another expression on his face which Pauline couldn't quite fathom, although she was usually very quick at picking up what other people were thinking and feeling. It seemed to be a sort of resigned exasperation, but there was no time to say anything, as the doorbell rang. As he let in the noisy guests, the room filled with sounds of tinkling glass and ice, classical music and convivial laughs. Pauline busied herself with the task she liked most, serving the champagne cocktails and canapes. She knew they hadn't expected anything quite so elaborate and she was pleased with their appreciation. She was a little less pleased with the way they treated the flat though. Her carefully chosen curtains pushed aside with drinks dangerously in hand, as the balcony was admired. (She had spent everything that hadn't gone on her outfit on exotic plants, orchids and palms that Bob had said wouldn't last through the English winter.) A still burning cigarette tipped out of an ashtray onto French polished antique wood: how could these people be so careless – they all came from good homes, Pauline thought.

Bob asked for a lager and Pauline was further chagrined – she hadn't imagined anyone would want beer when she was providing champagne. 'Very nice darling,' Bob had said, 'but I'm a plain old working-man at heart – beer and salt 'n vinegar crisps will do me.' Pauline hated him saying things like that. His father had been an executive in a national industry. In fact, his origins constituted one of their favourite arguments, with him downplaying a respectable middle-class family life. He had got through his law exams by working at a local solicitor's office and doing a part-time law degree, which he was proud of because it was hard work that way and showed tenacity and ability. Pauline would rather he gloss over that, and always referred to his law-student days. As she dashed upstairs with the beer from the corner shop, pandemonium hit her. Bob had tried to work the soda machine with the orange squash, which was now all over the cheesecake she had planned to serve next. 'Never mind darling,' he laughed in his characteristic, cheery way – 'we've all eaten too much anyway'. Pauline knew that it was going to ruin the theatre for her, but she put a brave face on it and finally got everyone the right coats and they went off to the theatre. She felt like sneaking out during the interval and dashing home to clean all the cheesecake and squash off her once perfect linen tablecloths, but the best she could do was to plan to leave work early tomorrow and get it all cleaned up before Bob got home.

Bob was very happy with his marriage too. Pauline was an attentive, beautiful, sympathetic, sexually responsive wife – always on his side, even if she did go a bit over the top sometimes. They usually had a crisis if he had to be away overnight, that didn't happen often. He hoped her concentration on him would dilute a bit when they had children; they had been married 5 years and were ready. Pauline at first had wanted to wait until they had enough money so they could afford everything the baby would need; he'd been amazed that she was already thinking about school-fees. However, they had been trying with no results for the past two years.

They both wanted children, and the doctor had said come back in another year, no need to worry yet. But of course Pauline did worry, and he could foresee a big problem if she didn't become pregnant in that year. She was actually the last person he would turn to in a crisis, since she exaggerated everything and made it seem worse. He remembered with horror the hysterical scene over the client who blamed Bob for his lost court hearing and tried to break into their house. Nothing would satisfy Pauline until they moved to a safer area, and their present flat was the result. Mid-terraced, no garden, alarmed windows and only one, triple-locked, entrance.

Bob had only one joking complaint about Pauline. She loved him too much! So much that it frightened him sometimes – he felt he could never let her down. Not that he wanted to, but it did feel like a responsibility. He had had more fun with other girlfriends, but Pauline made him feel protective and 'right', and they agreed on family values. Self-discipline, self-sufficiency, duty to others, commitment to each other were their watchwords, family before individual interest. Family solidarity had been Bob's model and Pauline's ideal. Any surrender of individuality was worth the sense of 'ownership' each had of the other. They both felt they had created together a physical, tangible, rooted entity – a relationship which now had a life of its own.

Pauline had had only one love affair before Bob – one which caused her long periods of pain, agony, yearning and depression, with moments of ecstasy in between. Her jealousy over his previous affairs had wrecked it. He had said he couldn't go on being made to feel responsible every time he inadvertently looked disinterested or wanted to do something else other than dance attendance on Pauline. She had been obsessed by him in the classic Romeo and Juliet way. As he withdrew from her emotional onslaught (as he put it), Pauline felt more for him, not less. She couldn't believe that deep down he didn't feel about her as she did about him. She believed he was being pressurized by his mother, and interpreted his anger as an indication of real feelings towards her that he couldn't hold down, no matter what he said. He must care to show so much feeling, she reasoned. When he left her in no doubt by literally shutting the door in her face when she came to his flat, she would sit outside, leaning on the door, crying and wailing – for hours! He had to resort to climbing out of his window and along the fire escape to try to avoid her, just to go to work. His neighbours would initially invite her in, but got fed up with her recital of how cruelly wronged she had been, and eventually they clubbed together to tell her they would be making an official complaint if she didn't stop sitting and howling outside her ex-lover's door. She never knew whether he was in on the plot or not, he moved shortly afterwards so she couldn't find out. She remembers the whole affair with an embarrassed defiance still; she hopes she would never be so obsessed again, but she couldn't imagine what she would do if Bob left her. 'I just lose all rationality when I think I'm going to lose someone,' she admits. A truly manic lover.

Pauline's one and only complaint about Bob is that he doesn't spend enough time with her. It is the only issue she is prepared to make a stand over, but it's not just the amount of time, it's what they do with it when they have it. Bob wants to read or watch television, and Pauline inevitably wants to go out, to friends, or a film or concert. She resents Bob taking on so much work that he is too tired to spend time with her.

When people don't give enough time to each other it harks back to days of infancy, when the length of time it took mother to respond to cries of the baby was an indication to the baby of how much it was cared about.

How time is spent and what is done with it influences the ability of a couple to get in phase with one another. Dual career couples, for example, may pass each other on the doorstep for several days at a time, which inevitably leads to drifting away from each other. When a couple feels a day has been well spent together, their daily time cycles have been well matched.

Bob and Pauline always had different ideas about the proper way to spend leisure time: Bob watched television, or read newspapers and magazines as relaxation; Pauline was bored by television and reading. She felt her life was regulated by Bob's hours of inactivity in front of the television, much like at home when her grandfather had lived with them for several years.

Household life had slowed down to accommodate his pace. His conversation was limited because he didn't experience as much in a day as the three girls did, so they would be sitting at the dining table having a completely different conversation between themselves, in terms of pace and speed of question, and answer to grandfather's conversation with them, which was going on at the same time. Grandfather could never catch up on all that was said, and mother would sometimes intervene, making them slow down when she could see him getting upset. The house seemed to be ruled by how fast he could move, talk or walk. Bob was similarly slower-paced than her, and she always seemed to be waiting for a response from him.

With Bob she didn't want a separate space; she wanted them to arrange their time together doing things they both liked. The television news droning on every night was a signal of stultifying boredom to Pauline. She was aware of their different perception of time as far as planning went. She was all for planning ahead and had their whole future mapped out. She was willing to forgo many things, like holidays, now, for future benefits. Bob's joke was to ask her when they would have the school fees invested, so they could go away on a romantic weekend and start the baby. She was exasperated with his belief that everything would come out all right in the end, and pointed to past experience to prove her point. As a solicitor he should know better than to use *ad hoc* arguments she said.

Looking back was one of Bob's favourite pastimes. He liked family reunions, old photographs, old friends, had saved all his old love letters – things Pauline found difficult to join in with because it was a past history that didn't include her. It was worrying too that Bob had different ideas, she felt that they should think, act and feel in concert. She relegated to the past anyone and anything that didn't fit into and enhance their relationship. Gradually, she replaced Bob's family rituals (except the country cottage holiday) with rituals of their own, and in many ways demarcated an 'outside world' and 'our world', which eventually overcame their time-orientation difference.

Differences in time reference are one of the things that stops a smooth synchronization of cycles. Bob's past orientation suggested to Pauline that he wanted to go back to something that was better, before her. It didn't give her much confidence or trust in his continued commitment. Whereas Bob felt the opposite, that she was glorifying the future at the expense of the present, as if she was saying things aren't good enough now – and giving directions for a future achievement he should make before she would be happy with him.

Their metaphorical 'relationship clock' had become out of synchronization, as well as their daily time-structuring, from getting up in the morning, meals, leisure activities to going to bed. Pauline was trying to make things better by forward planning – daily, annually and life-plans. Consistency and regularity in time-structuring, she realized, made for smooth functioning, and on the whole Bob agreed. The household ran perfectly, Pauline doing the domestics superbly and Bob good at anything that needed a screwdriver or monkeywrench. As they lived together they created new rituals and ceremonies that helped keep their time perception in step.

A pragmatic love story
with an energy rhythm

In the large, leafy garden of a high-ceilinged Edwardian ground floor flat, Jeanne is trying to persuade one of the stray cats she cares for to eat the food she has put deworming tablets into. There are several cats ranging round the vegetable patch where Jeanne grows lettuces, tomatoes, chives and carrots, all organically. She has cared for these neglected moggies for years now, and the word has got around the feline world. That was how she met Simon, who was working at the local animal welfare centre. On handing over one of the sick cats, she looked into his eyes and just knew this was the man she was going to marry.

But she didn't. Simon, although passionate, romantic and intense, felt he wasn't ready. He was only 27 to Jeanne's 33, and Jeanne felt his hesitation was quite reasonable. She wanted his love, not his legal bondage anyway. Simon moved from his bedsit to Jeanne's flat.

Jeanne was a sitting-tenant of the ground-floor in Hampstead. The low rent enabled her to work part-time at the local health shop, spending the rest of her time looking after the stray cats, the garden, doing her psychic readings, her singing lessons and counselling sessions.

The flat was bright, colourful and informal – 'ethnic' tapestries, woven rugs on polished floors, Chinese lamps, stripped pine furniture . . . you could almost smell the apple pie baking! Jeanne's family had been political liberals. Her father had once written speeches for Liberal politicians, and she had grown up in the

Quaker/pacifist tradition. Her mother, who needed constant help because of a wasting disease and died early, had encouraged independent thought, and reflection upon one's own actions and the consequences of them. Jeanne was a compassionate, gentle woman with a strong desire to help others. Her dream would have been to have had some participation in creating a better world. She was unworldly, not in a naive or unsophisticated way, but in the sense of not calculating her financial advantage before all else.

Simon was very attracted by such idealism, and also by her connection to politics, a submerged desire of his. Although from a fairly impoverished working-class background, he had gone to a direct-grant grammar school, due to his good exam results and had some political knowledge, in that his uncle had been a shop steward and grandfather a trade union official. The family ideology had been one of confrontation and aggressive negotiation, and the three boys had been brought up as achievers. Veterinary training is highly competitive, but against the odds Simon had managed it. Work, in his family was dignified, noble and the way to attain prestige and self-esteem. His father's whole meaning in life had collapsed when he'd become unemployed, and he had turned bitter, angry and resentful, which had probably contributed to his fatal heart attack at an early age.

With a rather ambivalent attitude to women, helped by his mother's alternate looking after and raging at his father, Simon had had no contact with girls at his single sex school; he didn't know any women very well. He had joined various sporting organizations, but these had a high proportion of male members. He had worked hard to get through college and had not wanted to threaten his exams with uncontrollable love affairs, so had only ever got as far as the 'having a drink' stage with a few girls. The busy practice, combined with his weekend trips home or out with the club left him little time actively to search. He had always imagined he would eventually move back to his home town, start his own practice and find a suitable woman there. His brothers both lived in his home town and were quite successful, and his mother was still quite important to him. He wanted to justify his education and enjoyed his old school reunions. It would be nice to have some extra success to report every year.

But then Jeanne had come along and blown this plan apart. He wasn't sure what his mother would think of her, even though she would be impressed by Jeanne's family pedigree. He felt she was too lacking in common sense to be left alone to spend her windfalls (from wealthy relatives) on stray cats, and although he was not ready for marriage, he felt it his responsibility to help her get the best deal she could out of her sitting-tenant's rights. So he moved in, and with one of Jeanne's windfalls as a deposit, they took on a joint mortgage to purchase the freehold of the flat.

Jeanne says:

> Simon was so romantic, so intense – he bombarded me. He would ring every ten minutes to tell me how happy I made him and how I'd changed his life. He swept me off my feet and made me feel special, as if I was the only woman who could satisfy him. When one of my old boyfriends turned up just to say hello, Simon was beside himself, and terrified I would go off with Tim again. He was so sweet then and I was so flattered.

Jeanne broke off, sadly savouring those long-past days:

> We spent hours and hours talking about how we would change the world if we were politicians, and I thought we were going to change a little bit of the world around us anyway. We were so close I was surprised when he wanted to keep going to his sports club every weekend, and evenings and started playing snooker with a friend I hadn't heard about before. I had hoped we could do some more for the environmental recycling programme the health shop was running – they needed volunteers to keep it going.

Jeanne's first real shock and intimation of the future was when she attempted to do something about the increasing chaos of rising housework, now that she was working full-time to increase her ability to pay half the mortgage, *and* there were two sets of laundry/dishes/cleaning and so on. She had less time and she had expected help from Simon. He had managed to keep his bedsit clean and tidy, so she wasn't prepared for his utter rejection of the rota of housework she drew up. At first he laughed, then tore it up saying she was better at looking after the house, and now he was paying half the mortgage that was the full extent of his involvement. Jeanne couldn't believe this was the egalitarian philosopher she had fallen in love with.

The rota had been based on the time and amount of energy needed to do a chore. The rubbish had to go down a long path so had a score of 7 units compared to something that took more time but less energy, like ironing. A week's ironing equalled 9 points. Energy was important to Jeanne now she was working full-time, and on her feet all day for the first time in her life. She even gave him two hours a day off for his driving to work, since it only took her five minutes to walk to the health shop.

How could Simon claim that she was 'draining him' and 'controlling him', with her domestic demands – when he would come in, throw his coat and bag on the floor and immediately get down to 40 minutes hard exercise on his rowing machine? Then he would have a shower, leaving his old clothes strewn round the bathroom, wander into the kitchen and ask 'What's for dinner?' This was not Jeanne's idea of a joint partnership and she patiently explained to Simon that he must take more responsibility for himself. Doing necessary housework was more important than exercising. His laughter turned to contempt and fury. How did she ever think he might marry her if she couldn't do the dishes without his help? She realized that he had expected to be able to give up all domestic work now he was living with her, and every attempt of hers to challenge his attitude led to angry accusations of not being woman enough to run a house and do an undemanding job like adding up a few pence. It wasn't as if she had living beings under her care and control like he did. However did she expect him to get into local politics if she couldn't provide him with a clean shirt now and then?

Jeanne was so shocked that she gave in, but the repressed anger every time she did a task she'd designated as his fatigued her. They were still in love, but didn't seem to be able to live together easily. She used to have time for so much, tending her stray cats, running the nutritional counselling at the shop, and the allergenic sessions, and psychic readings, and the gardening; but all these had to go by the wayside with her full-time hours and tiredness the rest of the time. Television was about all she had the energy left for.

Simon was the same. Even though they'd met over the cats, he resented having them around when he got home after a stint of patching up north London's pets. He found his future pressing quite heavily on him. Instead of developing and publishing new techniques which might take him to a private practice, or instigating a pet-companionship scheme with the local social services, he spent his days patching up scruffy animals for down-at-heel owners, and Jeanne's strays were a perfect symbol of his fears.

Their big difference, they both said, was their attitude to money. Jeanne found it a necessary evil to survive, while Simon felt it was a measure of his worth. He was annoyed at Jeanne's involvement in voluntary, unpaid community projects, and all the free counselling she gave her friends. Their kitchen was literally papered with charts of vitamin classifications, dietary precursors to enzyme reactions, pH balances and energy fields, as well as being 'knee deep in her parasitical friends', as he once blurted out in a fit of pique.

The little differences should have been manageable – he went to bed later and got up earlier, and whenever they did a task together Jeanne was always slower. Patient and methodical she called it, while Simon was impulsive and erratic. They were both appalled at how difficult they found living together, but wanted to understand and change whatever was wrong between them. They were still deeply committed to each other.

So, after a crisis which built up because they were both just too demotivated and tired to do anything about it, even though they could see it coming, they went to a marriage counsellor. The advice was concentrated on their stated problem, both feeling so drained and exhausted. He (and the fact the counsellor was a man was significant to Jeanne) advised Jeanne to do as little housework as she could stand seeing not done, and gave them relaxation exercises to cope with their frustrations.

They went to another counsellor, who did probe for underlying patterns related to childhood fears, but even she was unconvinced that the minor disturbances of their respective childhoods accounted for their problems now. This time the advice was addressed to Simon, to try to change his competitive attitude. To see every life-situation as a challenge was bound to use much of his energy. But that didn't explain Jeanne's fatigue.

The next solution was to go on holiday, to an idyllic Greek island where there was nothing more strenuous to do than lift a full wine glass. This period of isolation from their daily lives did give them clues that they were mismatched in their energy expenditure. Simon was always off to see what was over the horizon and pulling Jeanne along. She would become unsettled and keep trying to pull back or slow him down. On the other hand it was Jeanne who had the tenacity to spend two and a half hours patiently and quietly explaining to every official at the airport that she was not leaving until their missing suitcase was located. Simon and Jeanne considered explanations, like Jeanne's slowness and calmness being some sort of metaphor for Simon's fears of being held down by a relationship with her; but he said, on the contrary, that she gave him a base from which to launch his new endeavours. So back to England they came, and the slide into chronic chaos. Simon did attempt to do more, but gradually started getting involved outside the home again, Friday nights at the gym, Saturday at football and the evening in the pub after playing snooker. Jeanne alternated between not doing anything and then launching into action like an overwound clockwork robot.

Simon and Jeanne had violated each other's energy rhythms. The proper flow of energy is vital to life, and this is the principle behind much ancient eastern wisdom. When people's rhythmic patterns get out of synchronization, they generally try to compensate and re-establish properly interlocking energy cycles. But different people have different ideas about how to use energy.

A successful relationship monitors and balances energies, so that there is a similar level in each. None is wasted on unproductive psychological, emotional or physical work, and there is enough left over to mobilize for crisis or change. Simon's exercising was a physical drain far exceeding doing the laundry or dishes, but the latter were emotionally draining to him, far in excess of the exercising – which actually generated new energy in him if he kept at it long enough (the old endorphin flow!). Housework brought images of being trapped, which drained his emotional energy. Generating new emotional energy means finding new sources of it. Jeanne's life was in balance before she met Simon – selling in the shop balanced with the counselling, tending and growing the garden balanced with the routine, time-consuming household tasks, and her stray cat unofficial rescue service keeping her compassionate ideals energized.

But for Simon, new energy was generated from novelty and triumph – thinking up new ideas for the animal centre to get involved in, the companionship of sporting friends over a beer, winning at snooker or a shared win on the football team. There is a biochemical basis to this, similar to the balance described in Chapter 3. Anticipation, curiosity and novelty spark off the energy and drive to explore as anyone who sees an unfamiliar object, event or person on their horizon knows. This is why reciprocating each other's optimum arousal levels is so important. A little pleasant unpredictability maintains expectation and generates the energy change. A relationship needs more than the routine maintenance of status quo to allow the couple to seek new options and explore new patterns of development.

Simon thought Jeanne was trying to control his energy-generating sources (although he wouldn't put it in those terms), which were different to hers. One of his sources was making love: he could work for hours after that, but she preferred talking about romantic times past. For Jeanne those revived memories gave her new impetus to cope with the conflict and chaos she felt they were sliding into.

Their energy mismatch turned previously single, interesting lives into a drain on each other's energy expenditure. Even that would have been surmountable had they had common goals to put their energy into, but different arousal levels combined with different ideologies of relationship created an incompatibility that proved to be insurmountable.

A storgic love story

Ann and John live in a cottage in the Essex countryside, and if you could see the tracks worn over time by human, canine, feline, avian, equine and feral feet, you would see that although it's outside the village, it's really at the village centre. The outside world seemed to flow into it as if Ann and John were the transducers of the community energy, giving a sense of continuity to everyone around them.

Ann's brother Paul had introduced her to John. The three of them would meet for motor rallies for years, and it was to Ann's great surprise that while they were celebrating Paul's engagement to a woman in the village, John said, 'Paul thinks you and I ought to get married.' It did make sense, when Paul married she would be alone with mother. Her father had died when she was 20 but her mother, although unable to walk more than a few steps, was likely to live another twenty years.

Ann had been born in the cottage, and when she married John he had moved into this thatched roof sanctuary to help her look after her mother, who couldn't be left too long on her own. This he did with good cheer and stoicism all through the old woman's long and increasingly disabling illness. Ann had wanted to be a nurse in the local hospital but, training had been impossible, with its awkward shifts, until John came along and proved trustworthy enough to take over looking after Ann's mother.

They saw a lot of Paul and his wife Mary, who now lived in the village. So, Ann and her mother exchanged a brother and a son for a husband and son-in-law. It seemed the only difference was that John and Ann now shared the big bedroom, and that Ann changed her name. Ann said:

> We're not old-fashioned, but during our engagement we didn't sleep together. We knew we would eventually and we wanted it to be a proper experience rather than some car backseat between rallies. We wanted to look at each other with different eyes I think, it took time for me to change my thinking from John, Paul's friend to John, my husband. As I got to know him as my fiancé, I realized how different he was in little ways to Paul – yet the same as me. Sometimes when I'd listen to him it was as if it was me talking, we agreed so much about everything.
>
>   We have always felt comfortable with one another, in fact I can't imagine going anywhere for long without John. And I know he hates me to go away, as I do very occasionally to visit my sick brother. We are really each other's best friend and want each other to get whatever we want out of life. I'm quite prepared to give up my nursing if he needs me for his business. As things are at the moment he really needs me to answer the telephone, after all it's for us both and I can always go back to nursing. Neither of us could imagine life without the other you know, but if it ever happened it would be for a good reason and I know we'd stay friends.

Trust, empathy and harmony characterize the storgic love stories. This spreads outwards to those around them – Ann and John always seemed to be helping someone else and were involved in many village projects, between their own activities. No story was too long or sad or shocking for Ann to listen to and comment sensibly on. Boundaries in the cottage were flexible and really only guidelines – both physically and emotionally. This is not to say life was chaotic or disordered – only that it was also negotiable. There were events of importance they would never miss, but they tended (in contrast to Pauline and Bob) to be ones other people could join in on.

Relationship styles

All these couples fell in love, and all say they still love each other, but clearly they all have different ideas of what love is. At the beginning, the biological idealization described in Chapter 1, is the same for all – only the intensity is different, and the lengths we will go to keep it.

   The ancient Greeks had a word for it – Eros. Love was best characterized by Cupid, with his arrow of erotic love, ready to strike like lightning, at random. But a randomness guided by socioeconomic channels. It is rarer for us to fall in love with someone from a different class and financial bracket, not while parents are around to grease the channels anyway. So, love is not the mystery that all romantics believe. But that doesn't mean to say it's not uncontrollable once elicited – people do all sorts of things in the name of love. Chocolates and cars are sold through it, women persist in violent marriages for the sake of it. So we have to conclude there is some element of inevitability about it.

The ludic relationship

Barbara and Edward (p.113-17) both characterize a degree of emotional disconnection while Pauline (p.118-23) would go to the extreme, an emotional fusion, if she could get Bob to agree. On the traditional to therapeutic scale described in Chapter 2, all relationships fit into one of three types, and again the ancient Greeks come to our rescue with names to describe these three types of relationship.

Barbara and Edward have a *ludic* relationship – that is they have fairly emotionally separate lives. They have the financial and social benefits of living together, they are great companions, sharing much, but there is a psychological withdrawal. Edward, more than Barbara, withdraws from all relationships. She cultivates many but they are easy to manage, she is always in the role of teacher or mentor.

Before living together, Barbara and Edward had both enjoyed other sexual and romantic relationships, but with no real emotional involvement. Edward had made very sure of that with all his girlfriends – as soon as he perceived them 'making demands', he decided he was bored with them and went on expertly to woo and win another.

Sometimes they mistook his romantic gallantry. One young lady, who was determined to take him home to meet her parents after a weekend in an idyllic country hotel, found herself driverless. To his eternal mortification, Edward remembers seeing through the open door of the hotel restaurant they had been eating in, an inviting vista: a stream undulating through conifers just inviting someone to hike off on the road to freedom. As her 'laden-with-future associations' conversation went on, the tension built up. When she left him for a moment, he couldn't resist the invitation to the open road, walked through the door and to a phone box, telephoned the hotel to pass a message on that he'd been called away unexpectedly, and never contacted her again! 'The feeling I got when I turned my back on all that family scene and hiked off alone was indescribable, as good as a cocaine snort, I imagine', said Ed.

Barbara and Edward avoid stress and conflict by the simple expedient of just not talking about emotionally charged events. Edward disappears moodily into his temple (the study), and Barbara just invites more people round for coffee and talks about their lives instead. They did try to get their own way over various things, but it was by very subtle means. Extended discussions when some meaningful clue would be dropped, part disagreement rather than outright challenges, alternative ideas suggested instead of preferences clearly stated – and in the end nothing finalized. In avoiding conflict they didn't learn anything about each other. It sounded a good communication plan, but they weren't able to coordinate an active, sustained discussion about any problem long enough to resolve anything. They negotiated a joint pattern of avoidance rather than a joint solution. Even in common problems, each would make up their mind what to do without reference to the other – so that they could maintain their sense of continuity, and not disturb it with emotional discussion. But it was an isolated continuity, each was 'fortifying' themselves so the other couldn't intrude.

It worked well enough for 6 years, but it was a potentially dangerous solution. Many couples like this eventually trust enough to move towards each other, developing a closer and more intimate relationship. In Barbara and Edward's case, to the amazement of all, they did split up. Barbara, as she got nearer the end of her safe childbearing years, did try to talk to Ed about having a child and getting married. The result was a three-month silent struggle, with Barbara left to wonder whether it was marriage, children or her being not good enough that was the stumbling block: 'I knew every time the conversation turned to something to do with dissatisfaction we were talking about it again, but in a disguised way', said Ed. Barbara said:

> I felt a wave of blackness descend over me every time I couldn't talk about what really bothered me, that we had to talk in red herrings instead of spades. I literally got a headache every time Ed started off with some roundabout dialogue I knew was never going to reach any conclusion.

In the middle of all this Edward fell in love with the secretary of one of his clients. It was a passion like he had never felt before, he told Barbara as he moved out to set up home with Fiona. They also had business plans, since Fiona was sure Ed was working below his potential and she was bored with her job, had the contacts in the computing world Ed needed, and persuaded him to set up a company with her. He was gone within a week of telling Barbara, who, although pretty shell-shocked, had many friends to rally round to stop her being lonely. They spent every night into the small hours going over the details and deciding she was better off without him.

Ed generously signed over the house to Barbara and did well with Fiona in business. Initially he hadn't wanted Barbara to know where he lived, but after six months he started telephoning her and it was apparent all was not well. Fiona had been accurate in assessing Edward's potential, but not his nature. He could set up many complicated programming systems, but he had a resistance to putting all his life's creative endeavour into profit-and-loss systems. Fiona did not anticipate how much he needed novelty, and she wasn't the person to be able to stimulate him, or he her. She was a conformer, money was a means to a comfortable secure life, whereas to Edward money was a pleasant bonus to the intellectual challenge of systems management.

The traditional relationship

Simon was also on the emotionally distancing end of the attachment spectrum, but instead of moving away from people, like Edward did, he tended to move against them. In many ways you could see Simon and Pauline (Bob's wife) in a perfect partnership, pathological though it may be, she the giver, he the pragmatic taker.

But Simon was living with Jeanne. There was a similarity in the two relationships though – they were both traditional. Pauline, the traditional woman, deferred to Bob, was conciliatory, and he turned a blind eye to potential conflict. So did Jeanne, she let Simon be the traditional man, lay down the rules, take the lead (and the money) and by doing so she didn't see how Simon was changing.

Both these couples knew less about each other's feelings than John and Ann, and even Barbara and Edward. They maintained their relationships initially partly by colluding with each other (less so in the case of Bob), helping each other believe in illusions about each other, and exaggerating their similarity. They believed in the love of the other without checking reality. Pauline had felt she had the best man in the world, Bob was a bit uneasy about this epithet and did sometimes try to point to his clay feet. Simon needed to believe that Jeanne was an utterly perfect woman, and while she was indeed beautiful and talented she had to hide her inadequacies, fatigue and emotional needs in order to avoid his displeasure. It was two or three years before she recognized what she was doing and what effect keeping up the perfect façade had on her psychology. She started to eat sugary and chocolate things, which had once been of no interest to her, and as she put on weight Simon's exercising increased, as if to try and exercise some of her excess pounds off by proxy.

Then the sugary delights turned to alcoholic delights, but much of this Jeanne put down to the stress of full-time work, and planned to cut down on the daily wine anyway. As Simon's idealization of her turned to blame, he turned her patience into slowness, her calmness into passivity, and he also turned her love for him into bitterness.

Although Pauline was seeking emotional fusion to overcome her anxiety and separateness, and Simon was putting emotional distance between him and Jeanne, he was still using a pseudo-traditional relationship to cover his emotional disconnectedness. He was ambivalent about Jeanne, needing her, yet resenting her. Wanting a 'better' woman to be the ideal wife he had in mind, one that he knew his mother would admire, he still took from Jeanne what he felt to be his due. One of those things, eventually, was the flat which he felt was half his, since she couldn't have got a mortgage without his extra income. The considerable deposit he also felt was half his – if he hadn't forced her to use it for the flat, it would have gone on the potty cats. And even getting it for two thirds of the market value due to her sitting tenancy rights he felt to be his work – she would never have done it on her own, so of course he was due for half the benefits of that.

The traditional woman gives too much and the traditional man takes too much. The traditional woman tends to the manic love style and the traditional man to the pragmatic.

The storgic relationship

Happiness doesn't come with the declaration of human rights, or with the conscious intention to pursue it or automatically with a relationship. The insights of psychologists lead us to believe that happiness comes with active commitment to some pursuit outside the self. Further failure to seek such goals leads to boredom and failure to develop potentials within. Commitment to another is the start.

Ann and John's commitment was so automatic they had no idea that it was a problem for anyone else. But they went much further. They were committed to a democratic stance towards each other, both seeking energetically to find out what made the other happy. Much of their conversation was trying to understand the other's position, so they asked questions a lot, went over things again, asked for clarification about statements and so on. They fully understood one another and shared problems equally. Even when they didn't agree they supported each other to the outside world. Because problems were experienced as 'out there', and not the fault of either, the solution was merely to work out logical connections and arrive at a solution.

Those who start out on the storgic route may be those that value the familiarity of childhood security. Why wouldn't they when that experience was good? The pheromones of pleasant familiarity with the promise of life like with mother may account for the extraordinary physical similarity between these couples. Very often it was like looking at brother and sister, Tweedledum and Tweedledee!

Those who grow into a storgic relationship were attracted by the qualities that matched their previous psychological state of exaggerated capacity for relatedness – or the opposite, a fear of it. If they didn't work that out together, then the only alternative was separation. When one partner distances themselves from the assumptions embodied in the other's love map, or realizes that the other doesn't wholly share them, a process of alienation starts.

The traditional to therapeutic dimension and how the different attachment styles map onto it

Those whose attachment styles are either manic or pragmatically orientated tend to make *traditional* relationships. Those whose attachment styles veer towards the ludic make *separate* relationships, those who are secure in their attachments form interdependent and *therapeutic* unions.

Although most relationships move along the traditional to therapeutic dimension, with time, it doesn't mean that everyone should be the same. Different degrees of closeness suit different people with different lifestyles, interests and abilities. The creative artist may get their satisfaction through involvement with their craft rather than their partner. And the sociable nurturer may be totally fulfilled by a traditional relationship in which they are dependent on their partner for financial support. To thine own self be true. But there does seem to be a state of loose interdependence with another that fulfils the attachment needs of most of us, which could be different at different stages in life and psychological development. The only question is, to what degree?

Strongly ludic, manic and pragmatic relationships could take more than fifteen years to move into the storgic pattern of relating, communicating cooperatively, negotiating control and power equitably; the move to the therapeutic relationship for the less extreme manics, ludics and pragmatics was much faster. There was a tiny minority who never moved, and stayed locked into their fight or flight for the whole of the relationship. A few couples who had been together for more than thirty years were heartbreakingly miserable, but fear of being alone and poor kept them together.

We all make loving relationships with differing ideas of what love is, ideas culled from the society around us, mixed up with the intimacy and attachment we experienced with our parents. Societal ideas have ranged from pluralistic, semi-religious, universal, altruistic notions of what love is to the dominant fantasy of modern western world – exclusive romantic love as an institutionalized irrationality, and a temporary period of insanity everyone should go through for their moral good!

So we construct a love-code which guides the development of our relationships, fashions our assumptions and expectations of the way conflict and disagreement should be handled, of our mutual obligations and benefits, gives us life objectives and a shared view of the world.

Babies experience anything from emotional fusion to emotional distance, which affects their future ability to be close, distant or interdependent. But they are not passive blackboards waiting to have mother's trademark stamped on them. They protest if neglected and shape mother's responses as much as she impinges on them. Babies are born with innate tendencies to be attracted to novelty or a fearful preference for familiarity. At birth, the baby is wrenched from the biochemical exchange with its mother; just prior to and during birth her levels of the social bonding chemical endorphin will be high, to help with the pain of birth.

It is speculated by Professor Panksepp that some children may not make the transition so easily (perhaps due to irregular birth or nutritional deficiencies during pregnancy which affect the hormonal balance in the mother's milk). If this is the case, the baby may be left with an excessive level of brain endorphin which, while necessary before birth, now hinders the assimilation of the child into the social world. It must exchange the high endorphin level with weaker neurochemicals of the same type, and there is some evidence that autistic children do not. They have excessively high endorphin levels, which means they don't get the comfort from mother's touching, talking and attention to them, and find it difficult to respond to normal social interaction. A recent report even claims that painkilling drugs at delivery can increase the likelihood of the baby growing up to be an addict.

When mother's endorphin protective shield is removed too quickly, as perhaps in premature birth or stressful pregnancies, the child may be left with too few social neurochemical necessities, and be born with an innate lack of confidence and trust which will lead to a persistent social hunger. It is undeniable by all who observe new-born babies, researchers included, that there are differences between them in the comfort they derive from being picked up. Some love it and go to sleep immediately, others squirm and cry joylessly. Later, they also differ in their interest in new objects that hover onto their horizon – some reaching out with curiosity while others withdraw fearfully. They differ in innate rhythms of sleep, hunger and thirst, activity and quiescence. All these differing degrees of contentment have been summarized by researchers into three main categories: the difficult child (arhythmic, unpredictable); the easy baby (predictable in its needs and content); and the slow to warm up child (like the easy child but slower at reacting).

Babies shape their mother's responses as much as she impinges on them. The easy child, born to a 'good enough' mother, to use a famous psychoanalyst's term, is likely to be a pleasing, contented, heart-warming baby who will make a secure attachment in later life. The difficult baby will need a highly empathetic, willing and attentive mother with plenty of time on her hands to manage a satisfactory relationship with her and grow up to make a secure attachment. The slow to warm up child will need just that little bit of extra understanding and patience.

A mother mirrors her baby in a synchronous way – the essence of the courtship synchrony of Sam and Julie in the first chapter, and the basis of later intimate communication. Mother 'attunes' with it in a largely unconscious way, stimulating it when it's bored or passive and calming it down when it's too excited or upset. As she matches the child's actions, she is showing it that she understands what it *feels,* and this aids the baby's developing knowledge of itself. She is using a symbolic way to tell the baby 'Yes, I understand' by matching or nearly matching the baby's moving parts of the body. For example, she mirrors the baby's excitement at waving a rattle by raising her voice and using the same rhythm as the rattle. This awakens the baby's sense of 'I'. As it connects its emotions with mother's body language and voice, it achieves a stable self and a secure attachment.

In these alternating periods of stimulation and quiet, it discovers it has a separate awareness. As it develops a sense of self it moves on to adulthood and develops a synchronous smooth relationship with another adult. Problems of misattunement are either overstimulation or understimulation, which lead to avoiding withdrawal for the overstimulated baby or anxious attention-seeking for the understimulated baby.

In the romantic adult, ideology, experience and innate temperament combine to draw a person to a particular ideal of love which reflects their combination, and motivates them. Those who are handicapped by insecure and ambivalent prior attachments can, with time, become more secure. Each new shared experience and intimate exchange with another liberates endorphin manufacture. Psychologists like Sydney Jourard have always maintained that a person who does not exchange confidences with anyone else does not know themselves. He regards each new social contact as an opportunity for self-clarification and self-knowledge, and social contact, endorphin release and psychological development are all correlated. The unstable, unpredictable, potentially dangerous world becomes ordered, predictable, trustworthy and masterable. Love choice is not so random and illogical as the mystics would have it.

There are two aspects of innate functioning that are important to us all in relationships. One underlies the attachment style we form in infancy, and the other is the degree of attraction we feel towards this new, exciting person.

Attraction

While nearly all of us are attracted enough to someone to call it 'love' at least once in our lives, there are a few people who, having once discovered that attention and admiration of another is an antidote to emotional loneliness and despondency, get hooked on it. Their need for approval is insatiable, and when the usual tolerance builds up in the other this attention-seeker is off to greener pastures. The biological idealization lenses are readjusted every time so that as each new potential life's partner comes along, they are *the* one, the one that will transform life. Everything is interpreted unrealistically and inaccurately – an outright rejection can be brushed off as evidence of really deep feelings underneath, so deep they can't be expressed! The fear of rejection arouses tension, vigilance, sleeplessness and anxiety in all of us, but most of us read the cues quickly enough to shut down our attraction mechanisms and avoid unrequited love. Extreme sensitivity to rejection and clinging dependency go together.

Then there are the sensation-seekers who are either so sensitive to rejection they get in first and dump their partner before it happens to them, or are 'attraction-addicts', who love being in love. Whatever the reason, the effect is the same, they come on strong with the candlelit romance and promise is high – but involvement is low. The excitement of new encounters is more important than commitment and attachment, particularly for men who still believe their ideal sex fantasies will come true one day. For some men the chase and newness are the only way they can keep performing sexually – the boredom of certainty and fear of attachment are both sexual turn-offs. These are the men who cultivate charisma, charm and deviousness, which is, to some inhibited and guilt-ridden women, very attractive.

Guiltless, ruthless men and guilty, low-esteem women go together like snap-fasteners – they are an echo of the stereotypes about the proper nature of men and women. Both agree that the man is worth more, and the woman will happily help further his interests at the expense of her own. She accepts his philandering as something that doesn't harm their relationship, but sustained intimacy is never possible when sex-role characteristics swamp individuality. Women too can be sensation-seekers, but usually not placing such a high priority on sex without commitment. In fact deep involvement may be a type of sensation-seeking, with getting to know another person intimately the excitement that the sensation-seeker is looking for. Thus these relationships tend to be of the emotionally inter-dependent therapeutic, storgic kind.

Who are the attention-addicts and the attraction-addicts?

Of course, there are men who love too much, men who cling desperately, threaten suicide, and men who ceaselessly buttonhole anyone who will listen to their tormented outpourings about lack of response from the love-object. The relationship, unlike the pairings of most men, is not one of support for his other roles; it is like Byron once claimed of women's relationships, not a thing apart, but her whole existence. Such men who love too much are at variance with our ideas of a 'real man', and their yearning for their loved one, agitation at her absence, and overwhelming possessiveness and need are usually hidden away and referred to by those who know such a man and want to protect him as a bout of depression, or overwork – anything except excessive love.

However, the exaggerated idealism which sweeps away any sensible scan of what is in one's best interests does appear to be more a woman's problem. Research is scanty on the subject, but medical departments that treat patients with hormonal imbalances report that the 'instant bonding' of the people who love too much is more likely to be a problem for women than men.

Being able to control the intensity of erotic passion does allow the early distortions of perception and misinterpretation of emotional cues to lose their compelling quality. Emotional maturity aids this, as does emotional cynicism. At this realistic end, the pragmatist can hold out for the best bargain they can get.

Attachment

Attachment is based on the balance of endorphin functioning, which was described in Chapter 3. Social animals are programmed to increase the production of endorphins in situations of social comfort; sitting round the tree, grooming your mates; or round the camp fire, singing in harmony. Some can do it more easily than others, and this is why some people feel more comfortable with a degree of closeness that another couple would find too intrusive. Endorphin levels are rising and falling all the time, and for some unlucky people, a calamitous drop can send them into a panic state akin to phobia.

A threat to end the relationship can precipitate panic, and therefore alter the progress of the relationship. Separation-anxiety sufferers are vigilant clingers, and tend to be at the love-crazy end of the love spectrum. Being with others lessens vulnerability to panic: what's the first thing you do on hearing some worrying news? Phone up your friends, dash over to the neighbours, pick up the cat? People who are exposed to dangerous situations will prefer to see it out with someone else rather than alone. It appears that we have a sort of 'isolation alarm', that is triggered to go into endorphin stall by the threat of social or emotional loneliness. The threshold is raised by anxiety-provoking situations. For a minority, not having an intimate relationship is anxiety-provoking in itself, and will trigger the alarm when an established relationship looks a bit wobbly. These love-crazy people are then of course less choosy about who will be the intimate other – any oasis in an endorphin drought. So, it is likely the choice isn't as wise as it could be, and that the relationship is stressful. But once established, the production of stress hormones elicited by the negative events in the relationship is linked to endorphin release, which the love-crazy can't do without. They are in a sense 'hooked' on the relationship.

The interaction: the love-crazy to love-oblivious spectrum

We are all somewhere on the endorphin-production range and we are all somewhere on the spectrum of how excited we are by a new, sexually attractive potential partner. All of us can be located on the love-crazy to love-oblivious spectrum according to the particular blend of social stimulation and social security we prefer. That means balancing emotional and sexual opportunities with the need for intimate secure attachment.

Those who need attachment to another emphasize exclusivity and commitment, while the attention-addicts, admiration-junkies and sensation-seekers are uncommitted games players, ludic swingers or serial monogamists. Those who have strong attraction needs (excitement, novelty) at the same time as strong attachment needs (security, togetherness) are the love-crazy, and those who don't need either very strongly are the altruistic saints of this world, dispensing love to all with no hope of reciprocation.

The graph (Figure 5.1) illustrates that *Eros* is common to us all, and in two thirds of the couples I surveyed, it combines with a moderately strong need for intimate involvement to eventually produce an emotionally interdependent and balanced relationship.

Another way to look at this love-crazy to love-oblivious

dimension is to see it as a disturbance of self: the love-crazy are too concentrated on self, and the love-oblivious not concentrated enough. The storgic, emotionally interdependent love-style balances self against other in a harmonic equilibrium. Each love style denotes a particular degree of closeness that each prefers – and if that were all, the course of love would run much smoother. But the differences between men and women complicate each type of relationship further.

These relationship styles are an explanatory system that guides the couple towards someone who shares their view, and is likely to act according to a shared relationship code which incorporates the couple's beliefs about the world, their relationship, their response to stress, their approach to problems, childrearing, sex, making decisions, and just about anything that affects relationships.

Their explanatory system carries the history of the past, interprets the experience of the present and guides the expectations of the future.

Traditional couples erect a joint barricade against unpredictability and danger.

A cooperative close knit, self-protective family living a patterned routine where collective tasks are done effortlessly, with unruffled assignment of marital roles, like him emptying the rubbish while she does the cooking and cleaning.

Cracks are pasted over very quickly and the couple are highly mutually involved, excluding many of their previous interests and friends. The actions, thoughts and behaviour of one are held to reflect on the other. Consensus is valued above all else, so that they tend to have 'joint views' and shared realities. They grab at solutions and explanations of problems very quickly as they strive for coherence and continuity, hoping problems will just go away if they ignore them. For this reason they don't see larger problems, like affairs or addictions, until disintegration is upon them. The traditional family best matches society's ideal of the family, especially when there are no major problems to deal with, but they are vulnerable to blame and breakdown when one member can't or won't play the game.

Separate couples seem to have come together haphazardly and don't see themselves as an entity, just two people who 'happen' to be together. The truly separate couple didn't have much social involvement anyway and have even less, once living together, since

Fig 5.1 **Love-Crazy to Love Oblivious Dimension**

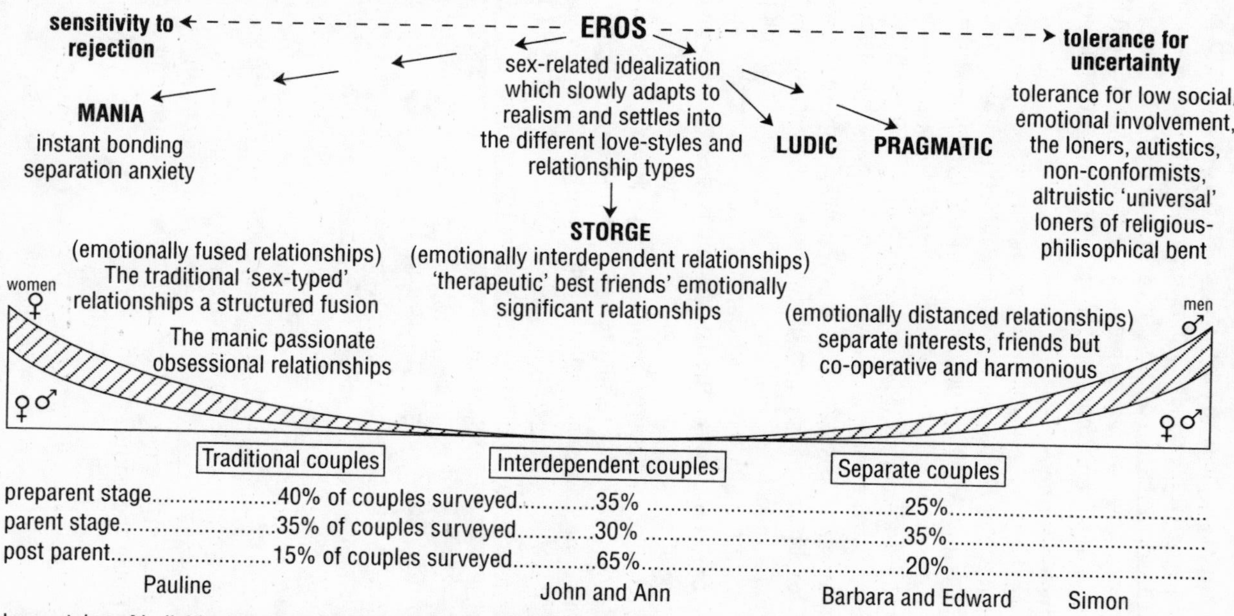

sensitivity to ◄ — — — — — — — — — — — — — — — — — ► **tolerance for**
rejection **uncertainty**

EROS

sex-related idealization
which slowly adapts to
realism and settles into
the different love-styles and
relationship types

tolerance for low social/
emotional involvement,
the loners, autistics,
non-conformists,
altruistic 'universal'
loners of religious-
philisophical bent

MANIA

LUDIC   **PRAGMATIC**

instant bonding
separation anxiety

STORGE

(emotionally fused relationships)
The traditional 'sex-typed'
relationships a structured fusion
The manic passionate
obsessional relationships

(emotionally interdependent relationships)
'therapeutic' best friends' emotionally
significant relationships

(emotionally distanced relationships)
separate interests, friends but
co-operative and harmonious

	Traditional couples	Interdependent couples	Separate couples
preparent stage	40% of couples surveyed	35%	25%
parent stage	35% of couples surveyed	30%	35%
post parent	15% of couples surveyed	65%	20%
	Pauline	John and Ann	Barbara and Edward Simon

Love-styles of individuals = **MANIA, STORGE, LUDIC, PRAGMATIC.**
Relationship types of couples = **traditional, interdependent/theraputic, separate.**

they now have each other for the minimal social contact they prefer. But their lives are still fairly independent of each other – typified by the dual career couple who pass each other on the doorstep, going different ways. Problems are not solved jointly, often not even mentioned, so the other doesn't have to be involved. They each value independent action and freedom, so they reject the idea that either could be a 'representative' of the other – totally opposite to the traditionals.

Therapeutic couples trust each other just like they trust the world to be stable and reliable. They keep up their friends and families and even increase their contacts. Roles are seen as constricting individuality, and each does what seems best to them, which may mean him doing the domestics while she runs up a tonne of cement for the garage floor. Because they are individuals, they don't assume that the experience of one is a useful guide for the other, or that their actions reflect on each other. Their flexibility gives them a tolerance for ambiguity which allows them to grasp subtler problems and come to complex decisions based on all the evidence.

Not everyone gets together with their same relationship style match, there are ludics with manics, or storgics with pragmatics, but these 'mixed' relationships tend to be less happy than those based on a shared view of relationship reality.

6

Regulating intimacy cycles

The same mechanisms that regulate the microcycles of love also operate over longer time periods. The intimacy shifts which match couples changing circumstances are clearly illustrated by the four relationships types that Barbara and Edward, John and Ann, Pauline and Bob, Jeanne and Simon typify: the separate, therapeutic and traditional.

Space, time and energy are intimacy-modulating mechanisms that these couples used for trading off the tension of involvement with the isolation of independence. Couples mark out their comfortable distance from each other with them, and maintain it by modulating the use of the space they live in, the time spent together and the amount of energy they are prepared to put into the relationship. Space, time and energy are used in conjunction to regulate the emotional distance between them; none is separable, but due to the attachment styles, one or other means tends to be more marked.

The function of daily, weekly, monthly or annual cycles is to assess the state of the relationship. Each cycle provides order, continuity and a sense of permanence within a framework for updating and matching ideas about the relationship.

Five years later
Barbara, Edward, John, Ann,
Bob, Pauline and Jeanne
reviewed their relationship

Edward had been terribly unhappy, feeling that he and Barbara had got further and further apart. He couldn't catch her interest or attention and often felt he might as well not be there. This account of his was a surprise, since 5 years before he had felt threatened and confused by what he perceived as Barbara's demands for emotional honesty and closeness: 'But it was always about *me* and my deficiencies we talked. Never her, her attitude, the things she needed.'

I wanted her to understand me – she had a false idea of a super-cool human being who didn't need anything. Everyone and everything else seemed more important than me. So I made up my mind I'd be better off by myself. I didn't mean to meet Fiona. But she'd just broken up with a long-term relationship and was very cut up. We just found ourselves in a pub one lunch time during one of my jobs and we talked about our common experiences and how we didn't believe in love anymore and then found we were in love! I know now it was just a mutual prop, we were both so anxious and wondering what was wrong with us that we couldn't stick relationships. We thought we had found someone who understood at last, but actually we're very different. Fiona is a kind, attractive girl and will go places, but not with me. She's not at all interested in anything intellectual, more the sporty type, which bores me. And she does have traditional ideas, like it's men's job to look after women. So we separated amicably – she's much better off without me.

When Ed moved out, letting Barbara keep the house, she had covered the mortgage by letting out his room, and her life had not changed radically. She appreciated Ed not demanding that the house be sold, and at first did hope it was a temporary situation and that he would eventually move back. She went through long soul-searching, remembering how Ed had started to change and come towards her a little – but by then she was too busy to notice. Perhaps a bit of revenge as well . . . you didn't want to talk before so why now. Now when it's too late for her to have a baby. Ed had been horrified, 'How can we have a baby when we can't even get on with each other well,' and so on. He had, a year before meeting Fiona, suggested he might move out during the week to be nearer a big client he was doing a lengthy contract for, but didn't. Barbara had not attached much significance to the incident at the time, but remembered it now.

Although Ed said his unhappiness had been building up for several months, Barbara had no inkling. It had been the start of the school year and there was much organization to cope with. It was a shock when Ed told her he was leaving, and she remembered how the lack of physical closeness seemed to parallel their growing emotional distance. They always seemed to be in different rooms even when they were at home together. They had stopped going for walks over the winter and even in bed didn't touch much. Barbara waited for Ed to make the first move, which hardly ever came, so she turned over to plan the next busy day. But one moment stood out. After making love, actually as it turned out for the last time, she saw Ed's eyelids slightly hooded and drooped, with the pupils smaller than usual. It flashed into her mind that he was bored – although she had no idea why. But that expression she had seen before, and it meant boredom:

To this day, Barbara said, I can remember every facial muscle that goes into it; and all the things I'd only been half-aware of sprang into focus. In that moment I knew everything, even though I don't think he'd met Fiona then. But I *still* didn't think of him leaving. I didn't handle it right though. I accused him of not fancying me anymore so he was on the defensive from then on. It was blame and counterblame, demand and withdrawal for weeks, until he told me about Fiona. I did change then, and wanted to work it out and I told him I was glad he wanted to live differently. I had enjoyed our life together but the few moments of really deep intimacy we had had always came and went very quickly. It was my fault that I hadn't done anything to prolong them. Actually I didn't know you had to, it always seemed to me that if the basic chemistry was there then things would work themselves out. Because we'd been so in love at the beginning I took it that it would just come back, if you had to strain it then it wasn't the real thing or worth pursuing. I used to spend a lot of my time at home feeling hurt, certainly at the beginning of our relationship, and when I got fed up with that I'd go out with a friend instead of trying to talk to Ed. I realize now we never really talked about our feelings, we talked about everything else, but not about the most important thing. Well, one day last winter, after nearly five years' separation, Ed rang up. When he said he'd like to come over and talk I thought he was going to tell me he wanted the house sold, or was going to marry Fiona. So I didn't bother about dressing up, I went on doing the gardening actually. And there I was, geranium pottings in one hand weeds in the other, no make up, dirty jeans and he just walked across the patio and said, 'Will you marry me?' You can imagine the rest. It was amazing how quickly the old feeling came back and we had a wonderful afternoon, and night, and he never left again. But I think we needed that five years apart. We're not different people, but wiser people, with different emotions. I realize Ed did want to talk about his feelings. Or at least he wanted me to understand his feelings without having to tell me. And I kept giving him the poker-faced cool dude view of himself – so of course he couldn't be anything less. We went amazingly wrong from such initial promise and good will. If we had got back together one, two or three or even four years apart, the same old resentments would have come back. But now it's long enough for them to have faded away. I can remember them, all the disappointments, attempts to talk, Ed's chickening out of getting married and having a baby, but I can't *feel* them like before. I can now see them from his point of view as well, and we can laugh, or at least learn why we reacted like we did.

And we regard Fiona as a symptom, one that warned us about the disease before it got terminal. I was amazed at how jealous I was initially, but now I understand I can only feel pity for us all, and I know now that if we could survive that there can't be *anything* that could split us up now. It's a wonderful optimistic feeling that we have, a warm, happy future in front of us. I only felt like that in the first few months that we met. In fact it was the murderous jealousy that made me realize how we'd fooled ourselves about having a perfect relationship. All the books I read about creating good relationships meant something then.

No one can be as free and independent in a relationship as we'd imagined. Human beings have emotions, and the longer you live together the more you become attached, and the more you have to be careful of the other's feelings. We both placed too much emphasis on being rational, and downplayed emotional feeling, which then had all the more effect on us. All we had to do was to say to each other: 'We are going to be a *couple* and face the world together, instead of thinking about ourselves as two separate people who just happen to enjoy each other's company.' We still talk about art and philosophy and bicycle parts, but we also talk about the little things as well – our feelings and things that we considered trivial before. Nothing has changed outwardly, but everything has inwardly. I don't think either of us realized how hurt the other was by all that careful distancing.

All that negative emotional charge that built up in the last few months blew us apart, but in the end we realized that we were more compatible than anyone else either of us had ever met, and now we have the old tenderness between us again I for one am going to make sure we never lose it again. It might mean giving up a few interests but so what? Ed's more important.

Ed said 'I'm going to get to know Barbara's friends and not let myself feel pushed out again.' They feel the years away allowed them to build up respect for each other, Edward admired Barbara going off to Israel for 9 months by herself during their 5-year separation, and Barbara appreciated being able to keep the house, when so many break-ups she knew about lost their homes as well as the relationship. By 5 years, pride didn't come into it, they could both see and admit how wrong they'd been. Barbara tried to sum up the two different relationships, before and after (they call it 'the introduction' and 'the sequel'):

I used to think that we were different to each other, and different to everyone else's relationship too. I wasn't interested in swapping notes, I thought everyone had to work out life's meaning for themselves. But we're all the same when it comes to emotional nature. I'm amazed at the different ways we saw things, but also amazed at the similarities we had underneath, which we *didn't* talk about – only the differences, which of course separated us.

I thought of us as two people living together, not a couple: it is different, although I don't know quite how. Just doing things together seems to create a bond when you think of it as permanent. And when you know you will be doing other things together too, there is a feeling you don't get with work colleagues with whom you also do things together, sometimes for years too. I suppose it is the amount of private things you do together that's critical, things you would never do or talk about with anyone else. This is really the first time I've felt as if we're a family, even though we're unlikely to have children now. And with all the reading I did about breaking up, getting on and so on, thinking I was really locking the stable door after the horse is gone, I have become quite psychologically sophisticated. Not only do I know the jargon, but I understand the meaning of books I'd have just glanced at without really grasping before. You have to have the experience before you can read about it, which seems sad! Because the house has a big kitchen, with this second desk in the corner overlooking the patio, and Ed had the spare bedroom and we each had a separate storeroom for our books and projects, we did tend to stay away from each other physically. I realize this rambling house attracted us because we could set up our own private space, but we overdid it! Ed realized before me, I think. In 'the introduction', he used to say we're moving away from each other but he never said *emotionally*. I didn't really understand him. We could stay a day in the house and only see each other at dinner and in bed. I thought we were giving each other freedom when we were actually pushing each other away, into loneliness for Ed and a busy sort of emotional emptiness for me.

**Space is a distance regulator we all use, and it does affect
communication. Rhythms get out of synchronization, and that
affects emotional sympathy between the two. It's interesting
that emotions in families living in cold countries, where people
are forced to stay inside together, are different to the emotional
intensity expressed in hot countries, where people are outside
and have more physical space between them. As if they need
to make up for the space between them that the climate
dictates.**

Ed remembers the beginning of the end for him.

> We were having dinner, we started together, but Barbara finished first
> and just picked up her plate, dropped it in the dishwasher and went back
> to her work at the desk without a word. I realized she just hadn't noticed
> that I was there too, and we were having dinner together! She did
> nothing different to what she would have done when she was alone. I
> wondered if I'd accidentally eaten some magic potion that made me
> invisible.

Now he says he realizes what a tremendous leap of faith it is for
one individual to say to another 'Let us plan a life together.' It had
frightened him, but a life alone or a series of luke-warm
relationships frightened him still more. At 42, he was ready to make
the commitment. He had been at 35 in fact, after the pleasant initial
years with Barbara, but she had got out of touch with his way of
expressing meaning and didn't notice. He had never been able to
find a time and place where they could nurture emotional closeness
long enough for him to get up his courage and say it. That made
him feel increasingly insignificant, and when unhappy Fiona came
along, he had found a reflection of his isolation in her feelings of
rejection from her previous relationship.

Barbara and Edward find the biggest difference is how much more
they monitor each other's feelings now. Communication is not
easier, but it's richer, more subtle and conveys more ambiguity –
which keeps them on their toes.

As they understand each other, those horrid vague wonderings
about what the other is *really* thinking have stopped. They *know*
it, they talk about it and they can sense it more accurately now.
There have been a few occasions when the emotional skeleton
came out of the cupboard – but they have evolved a response, like
the animal submission ritual. When one feels the other is harking
back on the 'introduction' relationship faults, they say, 'That

previous incarnation didn't lift your karma did it?' It's their code for 'don't let it happen again'. And then the other cancels out the criticism/complaint or whatever they had started off with and changes the emotional tone. They still talk about that subject, but take time-out to calm down, both agreeing nothing is worth getting het up about. This was harder for Barbara, who had by now a lot more authority at school, but she felt it was good for her – to know she was in the right, but not push home her point so efficiently and assertively that it came across negatively.

From the free lifestyle that had turned into unplanned loneliness – nothing could be counted on, life increasingly irregular, not knowing whether they would be together for the next 50 years or next 5 months – they resurrected a strong relationship. Ed was amazed remembering how they became more silently alienated and routinized and how he felt everything he was doing was meaningless, and random. He is developing a computer programme for marital counselling now! Both think they are lucky to have a second chance to repair all that emotional hurt, and they are determined not to drift apart again. They wonder if they should plan an epilogue to follow their introduction and sequel!

The pragmatic trend of attachment that Simon illustrated doesn't mean that pragmatic relationships are unhappy, in fact they are amongst the happiest – but the criteria for happiness are based more on the relationship being a socially acceptable and respectable way to live rather than pleasure in each other's idiosyncracies. For a true pragmatist, almost anyone who matches the attributes on the shopping list (right accent, occupation, family background and so on) is 'the one'. These attributes are not determined by meeting eyes across a crowded room. The practical lover is too sensible to turn down the compatible boss's daughter just because he fleetingly fancies the blonde secretary. The pragmatists are in for the long haul, and make sensible alliances based on long-term compatibility. One highly pragmatic woman's (typical) view was: 'I don't understand why there's so much drama about marriage. It's the proper way to live; convenient, orderly, provides security for the children. It's a damn sight better than hanging round the single bars. But there are other things in life'.

The relationship is the valued thing, and the mate only so far as they fit into the framework. If Simon is a true example, he will likely marry, with appropriate ritual, a girl from his home town who comes from a family that his mother would respect and, if possible someone who brings him some advantage in terms of his career or social status. This hypothetical woman will see in Simon an ambitious, hardworking man, obviously destined for civic office, who will uphold ideals of respectability and stability. The traditional good husband and father. All she will have to do to complete this perfect picture is to keep a comfortable, tasteful house, produce well-disciplined children and develop hostess capabilities. Perhaps a bit of voluntary work when the children are at school, counselling for marriage guidance or the bereavement agencies. Inner drives towards enlarging psychological experiences are not planned parts of the pragmatic relationship. The Simons of this world find their fulfillment in the respect of others and public service – and where would society be without them?

At five years, Jeanne was the only one left to review the relationship. She had left, in the middle of a terrible night, after Simon had raped her, in her nightdress, or what was left of it, and gone to a friend. Her injuries were serious enough to warrant legal action, but she couldn't bear the thought of concentrating on the worst experience she had had in her life and refused to let her friend take her to the police. Simon moved in with a young woman from the animal centre and insisted on selling the flat to release his half of the equity. That had been, if possible, worse than their breaking up. It had been her windfall that had provided the deposit, and her tenancy that had secured the cheap freehold offer. He took 50 per cent of the sale profit and Jeanne, homeless and bruised, couldn't believe he could be so selfish. As she re-evaluated his 'love', her hurt and disillusion turned her previously quietly confident personality into a hyperactive, frenetic searcher for solace. In contrast to Simon, she talked to anyone who would listen and took up new philosophies, new therapies, new diets – when she should have been talking to her solicitor.

She lost her home – Simon had seen the end of the property boom coming and instructed the agent to reduce the price to sell it quickly. She had less than two months to remove her broken life from her home of eight years standing. She could have fought, she could have opposed the reduction, but somehow thought that Simon would relent – when he didn't she felt hopeless, demotivated, even a bit reckless. Perhaps she wanted her plight to be noticed by a good fairy, who would wave the magic wand and make it all better. She had not been equipped to deal with a pragmatic lover's philosophy. Fighting generalized injustice is one thing, fighting personal injustice from someone who was supposed to have loved you was another.

She believed now that she had acted as a sort of whipping-boy for the hurt and rejection Simon felt he had experienced from his mother. She wondered what was in her that had allowed him to behave so destructively to her. She questionned her love, or rather her psychoanalyst did, suggesting that she was attempting to atone for her feelings of helplessness and worthlessness over her mother's periodic illness and her subsequent inability to mother Jeanne properly. To regard herself as a masochist or martyr only increased her upset. She remains in a vulnerable state, an idealist who had the misfortune to trust a cynical pragmatist, whose conflict-intimacy cycling could never have synchronized with hers.

While the degree of commitment which affects the conflict-intimacy cycles is undoubtedly influenced by early attachments, the breakdown in communication is much better explained by the simple mismatching of cycles. When the couple are able to synchronize they can overcome the doubts and fears of early attachment wrongs, and move towards an emotionally interdependent relationship which then feeds back to increase their self-esteem and confidence in the world. Which is what fosters a secure attachment in the first place. So, in a sense, the anxious avoiders and fighters are learning to become the secure attachers, who then become the storgic emotional interdependents. And, it can work the other way around. Jeanne was a secure individual who became less so after her trust had been violated by Simon. Her next relationship will be critical. In her distress she is not in a good position to judge her own best interests. On the rebound two things can happen: either the grieving lover looks for a like replacement, jumps at the first hint of similarity and completes the emotional portrait erroneously – the more like the old person the new one is, the more the loss of the previous partner can be forgotten.

The other possibility is more likely for Jeanne. She will look for someone opposite to Simon. Any hint of competitive control or hostility will send her running away at the speed of light. She could easily mistake genuine offers of help for coercion, and may mistake passivity and weakness for gentleness and caring. Possibly, however, she can work out the anger, depression and bitterness stored inside. In talking so volubly to all and sundry

about it she is acknowledging it – so these negative emotions will lose their grip eventually, just as Barbara described. Jeanne moved back with her father temporarily, who was wise enough and kind enough to allow her to drag along the nine stray cats, and she is considering using the money she did get from the flat to finance a course on nutritional therapy, and become a professional, rather than a half-engaged worker. Many problems remain; her father, getting frail, hopes she will stay, so does her cat family, but she knows she mustn't retire from life. Pragmatists and idealists don't mix well.

Pauline and Bob, in their new house, had had their time asynchrony solved for them by the arrival of two children. They had already made a joint agreement about spending more time together, and had noticed how they were becoming more alike anyway – Pauline calmer, more rational and prepared to enjoy family gatherings, while Bob developed broader interests and curiosity in art and culture (although Pauline's thirst for cultural experience had diminished with the arrival of the children). Pauline's previous insecurity had disappeared for the most part, and she had moved from the love-crazy 'manic' mode of relating to the give-and-take, friendly affection of the storgic partner Bob had always been.

The insistence on rules and appropriate means of expressing their couple-identity was more rigid than John and Ann's style, nevertheless it was a relationship of great stability which enhanced their lives. The children completed their family and life plans. Bob was just as keen as Pauline to plan for the future. Pauline had given up work and was happy and busy with the children, local nursery activities and neighbourhood groups, but planned to go back at least part-time when the children were at school. Perhaps she would train to be a school teacher to fit in with their holidays. Bob was still working towards a more lucrative partnership in a private firm so he could give up the dogsbody work of the legal executive in a cooperative law centre.

What about the television watching? Pauline laughed that she was grateful for that now, it gave her a chance to get the children to bed and she liked to have their story finished at the exact time she heard the television theme music announce the end of Bob's news programme. Then she would start dinner as Bob took over the story-telling, after which the gap between the last 'Three Little Pigs' and dinner was filled with a cup of tea or drink with Bob and a run-down on the day's events. Bob's work was quite routine, preparing cases for court, basing everything on the results of past cases, and this left him little room for creativity and self-direction. This seemed to have bred a high degree of order and predictability which pervaded the family life. Rituals such as the bedtime story, the evening drink, family holidays at Bob's parents' country cottage, anniversary lunches at the restaurant round the corner from the court where they had first met . . . a settled family with a time and a place for everything.

This happy family now kept their emotional lives well harnessed. They seemed much less interested in explaining their motivations and emotions either to themselves or anyone else. Emotional expression had been worked out in the prior five years, and they were happy, busy and had become the traditional family. They both placed a heavy emphasis on conformity, and in childrearing practices voiced clear-cut standards of expectations, with violations punished. Law and order in all ways was upheld. When Bob related some of his more gory cases to Pauline, it connected with her beliefs about dangerous, uncontrollable forces lurking outside the family. Bob too was less laissez-faire, he saw how vulnerable the unprepared could be, and he acquiesced to Pauline's increasing control of their social contacts, especially in regard to the children. Only their family and a few trusted friends got into the inner sanctum, both physically and psychologically speaking. The cohesion of the family came close to a self-preoccupation which cut them off from most aspects of their community outside the school and PTA, but they were perfectly happy, and life ran in well-oiled grooves for the benefit of them all.

Space, Time and Energy: the three graces

Pauline and Bob's timing, Barbara and Edward's spacing, Jeanne and Simon's energy mismatches were the result of the some-times unequal balance between approach forces and avoidance influences. Edward, for instance, defined freedom by the amount of space he could call his own where he knew nothing would be tidied, rearranged, thumbed over, dusted or borrowed. He could lock the door if he wanted, and remain detached from social interaction. Pauline's idea of distance-regulation was *not* to; she wanted more closeness, physically and time-wise. She was happy enough with Bob's physical closeness when he was there, but she wanted more of his time; merely being there, watching television, was, to her, being unavailable. They could even be sitting together, her sewing or reading and him watching television, and that was still more emotional distance than she felt comfortable with. Simon saw a couple in traditional male terms, which at times seemed more like a combative unit. Either you were on his side, or you were the enemy. When Jeanne didn't see a woman's role the way he did, he took it as attack on himself – which he must justify. Their problem centred round who was going to do what, and Simon saw this as a competition to get the most reward for the least effort.

Time, space and energy are used by couples to regulate the degree of independence they are going to have in a relationship. The more space they put between them, the less time they spend together and the less energy they invest in the relationship; this reduces the impact they have on each other's lives. And, vice-versa, the more time and less space between them, the more impact. Space and time can be used to balance a sense of connection and togetherness with autonomy and independence.

The intimacy and withdrawal micro-cycles are matched to what is going on in the social surroundings. They can be stretched or shortened, according to the way a couple uses time and space, but there is a limit to the compatibility of these cycles. The couple can excite or calm each other much easier when their micro-cycles are evenly matched.

Humour, relaxation, productive help, spontaneity and variety come with synchronicity of energy levels. Uninhibited energy that sparks each other off can lead to things getting a bit out of hand, but more often fun and excitement and interest are the consequences of matching energy rhythms. Energy levels affect the patterning of conversation, conflict and cooperation, the expression of affection, and eventually feed back into the way space and time are used, thus reinforcing closeness or else distance.

Relationships are built on the synchrony of the intimacy/ withdrawal cycles because the successful resolution of differences before conflict arises depends on the cycling of give and take. As Ann says:

We don't avoid talking it out, but we wait until we both feel like it, it's not as if anything gets us into such a white hot rage that we can't wait. It's usually me that will hint a bit to see if he's ready and I just bide my time. For instance, he knew I was going to have my say over his mother deciding to stay over New Year when we'd previously agreed on just Christmas – but we didn't get round to it until the 6th January, when she'd gone, and we had Saturday afternoon alone for the first time in two weeks. I put lunch on the table and had just opened my mouth to say my piece and before I'd uttered a sound John said 'I know you want to talk about Mother, can it wait till after lunch?' So I did and then we said O.K. 2pm, let battle commence! It turned out she'd had a bad diagnosis from her doctor and twisted John's arm by saying this will be the last New Year I'm here, I'd like to spend it with my son. So he gave in, the trouble is you have to agree that at 86, it could very well be her last New Year, but he should have asked me first and he knew it. But she hadn't wanted anyone to know about the cancer, she has this old-fashioned idea that people won't come near you if they know, for fear of catching it or something.

Ann was describing a cooperative way of resolving conflicts. Like a team game, each participant waits in sporting fashion for the other side to have an equal chance. This is made easier by matching each other's periods of intimacy, when goodwill and cooperative-ness are more likely. You can only wait for those periods when you're sure they're coming. Barbara described them as fleeting, and the periods when they came unpredictable to her and ever more further apart. After they got together again she kept a diary of their time together and apart, and was amazed to find she could correlate the length of time spent together in some joint activity with an increasing amount of both feeling that wonderful closeness more often, several times a day and not just fleetingly. Once they rectified their space modulation they were almost back to five or six daily cycles of feeling happy and close, interspersed with the same amount of time doing some intellectual task which needed concentration and solitude.

To feel so upset about something that it has to be discussed immediately runs the risk of confronting the other in their withdrawal cycle. Conflict guaranteed. Either they will withdraw further, both psychologically and physically, or feel very disrupted by the unanticipated arousal. The particular modulating mechanism a couple uses most constantly does appear to relate to their position on the traditional to therapeutic dimension.

The *manic* lovers are sensitive to time. Pauline, for example, had only one complaint about Bob – it was how little time he spent with her. It used to be that way when they were courting and the complaint was only varied to how little time he spent at home. Bob's willingness to spend time with her was her yardstick of emotional intimacy.

Ludic relationships are spatial ones. Time is spent together, but it will be pursuing activities that still separate them, at an intimate level – entertaining, playing with the children, joint community, sports or family activities. Where there was once candlelight and champagne, now there is the PTA and the tennis club. They may once have had a close relationship, but it could have become devitalized and unhooked because it wasn't fostered. Ludic lovers grow apart, not together, though not necessarily unhappily – the division of responsibilities clearly suits some couples who have become heavily involved in career or other outside influences.

The *Pragmatic* couples are the energy modulators. When they share common interests they emphasize joint lives. Children, property, professional and career obligations are cooperated over and life is arranged conveniently, without untidy passion. Their life's activities, though, are for themselves, whether they are done jointly or not. Life's energy goes into dreams and activities that further the self.

The *Storgics* are bound by invisible, emotional ties – ties to which time, space and energy are inextricably linked. Privacy is a foreign idea. They have shared so much that it is often hard for them to know which things they want for themselves and which for their partners. Even if the activity turns out to be less fun than anticipated, being together was sufficient justification to salvage interest and fun out of the venture.

John and Ann managed such an equilibrium of the three modulating mechanisms. They had areas of tradition and stability as well as being open to spontaneous change. They constantly monitored each other and could withdraw any or all of the mechanisms, or even stop them, if necessary. They talked everything over – didn't flinch from conflicts and were often in a state of temporary disequilibrium and doubt until they were both satisfied that each was happy. They were quite creative and innovative in the way they solved problems and conflicts. Who would have thought of going to the local library to look up all the great celibates of history and their contributions to literature, art and society in general before broaching the subject of boredom with sex? Ann did this, and it turned out that John had been thinking the same. Their greatest pleasure was sleeping together, naked and massaging each other, but their eroticism was a generalized one. 'Lying together,' said Ann 'makes my skin tingle softly all over', but focusing on genital sex destroyed the lovely, lazy contentment of skin to skin contact. By mutual consent their lovemaking had dropped off from weekly to monthly quite quickly. In the last year it was more like alternate months and they were both quite happy with that. 'It amazes me how different our night life is to our day life', said Ann. 'In the day we're always busy, surrounded by other people, and at night we're entwined like one person, and concentrating on each other's pleasure feelings.'

They had noticed the intimacy/withdrawal cycles, although they hadn't put it in those terms. They just knew there was a time to hold your peace, keep out of the way and leave each other alone and a regularly reoccuring time when affection would be gladly or lightheartedly reciprocated, they could share a joke or serious observation about the world, or discuss some joint plan and go on their way, restored. They still had enough energy left over to give to others, even though their days were hardworking and full. Ann cooked once a day for an elderly neighbour and John did voluntary, unofficial driving instruction for villagers who couldn't afford or get up courage to start a course of driving lessons. The local bus service was always threatening to close down, so half the village was in a panic about transport.

The optimal distance-intimacy equilibrium is when neither is constrained; they can trust the other to support them and still pursue their own goals unfettered by guilt or other pressures. A balance between variety and security. It comes down to how adaptable the couple are at marrying their differences. Barbara and Edward made no attempt to adjust to each other, they just got out of each other's way. Pauline was too dependent on Bob's approval to do anything much except add to his life, although he did try mildly to encourage her to branch out. Simon was the opposite, too selfish to put more into his relationship and ending it with advantage to himself and disaster to Jeanne.

Relationship style differences in control of life

The power a person feels they have to affect another shows in the way they communicate. After commitment, when the couple are living together, there is often a power struggle (typically for about six months, as described in Chapter 2). Simon became domineering. Like many other women, Jeanne allowed him to get away with things. Things that no other man would have got away with. He was a man she loved, after all.

But turning the other cheek for the sake of peace has never been a good policy. Belief in an ideology of love can alter other beliefs. Jeanne started to believe that her friends weren't as important as Simon's friends, she allowed him, in her hurt, to make fun of her psychic readings, and so she lost belief in her own ability and eventually stopped doing them.

Slowly and softly, by criticizing, commanding and all the non-verbal ways he had of showing displeasure, he communicated, 'You won't be happy until you do what I want.' This is the best kind of dominance, when you can get the other side to do it for you! Simon had started up his old defence against intimacy and its fears – he started moving against Jeanne, frustrating her, competing with her, putting her down in the same proportion that she aroused frightening emotions in him.

'I never had the energy to stand up to Simon,' said Jeanne, 'he was so determined to have his way. The fight just wasn't worth it.' Often when Simon denied something that Jeanne knew was true she wouldn't challenge him, and just accepted it. But his pattern was the opposite with her, examining her reasoning closely to show her she was wrong. As he controlled and criticized, Jeanne lost her sexual feelings. This had already started happening when they visited the counsellor, but it hadn't been that serious, it was just that she was a little more reluctant to have sex as frequently as Simon wanted. But sometimes towards the end there was a brief few seconds when Simon's advances repelled her. She would fight the feeling down and manage to enjoy sex later. But the feelings, although fleeting, did worry her and got too much to control once, when she started hysterically pushing Simon off her. In that moment it felt like she was being murdered, and she could not bear him to touch her anywhere, let alone in a sexual sense. The revulsion she felt frightened her. She also felt ashamed of her reaction, and in tears and tension told Simon she was going to sleep on the lounge settee. But that night Simon raped her, violently – and thought he was justified. When a man comes to a relationship with a fixed idea about a woman and her relationship to him, any real life deviation from it seems like insubordination and a direct challenge to the authority he feels is his due.

Very often (probably in about 80 per cent of heterosexual relationships) the man will use physical violence to back up his point. It ranges from isolated pushings, slapping and kicking to nothing less than full scale terrorism – predictable in its timing, trigger-point and duration. The response of the woman is critical in decreasing or increasing the rate at which the violence happens again: crying helplessly is a less useful response than getting out the cast iron skillet. Of course sitting down, negotiating the problem that caused the violence, explaining how violence dissipates loving feelings is the best but most women are totally ill-equipped to deal with the conflict of a man they love who is also violent and therefore appears to hate them. They become demoralized enough to stay in the relationship hoping it won't happen again, or accepting that it will, losing self-esteem every day. Only when the violence exceeded low-level and occasional outbursts do they react strongly enough to stop it happening. The most common pattern coming out of several studies appears to be gradual escalation between a dominant man and traditional woman. By the time the violence got really physically damaging the traditional woman was psychologically defenceless enough not to take any overt action, giving herself excuses for his behaviour, including the one that maybe she 'deserved it'. The less down-trodden women took underhand action, struck some sort of emotional bargain, or if they had alternatives, friends, family and money, just left.

The best strategy for women appears to be direct action, first time, so long as it is successful. But this is not a strategy included in the 'How to make your love last' manuals. It is considered a situation that should never arise in a love relationship. But it does, regularly.

The legal system did not consider itself to have any part to play in the reduction of aggression in domestic relationships until quite recently. However, most women are still reluctant to take this course because it will usually mean the end of the relationship, and unless the violence is life- or limb-threatening it's not worth it.

The recognition that men and women have conflicting motivations, emotions, life plans, communication-styles, micro- and macro-cycles, means that conflict is inevitable. Love is only an aid to communication in that it motivates the couple to find a mutually acceptable resolution. Violence is a means resorted to by those not confident enough to believe they can negotiate a satisfactory bridge over the conflict. The sheer amount of violence argues against it coming only from those who move against people, and since it is mainly men who are the perpetrators, one has to admit much cultural conditioning in the attitude towards women that makes it the easiest means for men to influence their partners. It is quick, efficient and competitive – just what business methods promote for the macho business man.

Of course there are millions of men who never use violence, to women or to other men, but of those who do believe a variant of 'might is right', it is dependent women who are the victims. If a woman earns less than 25 per cent of the household income she is more likely to be violently treated by her income-provider! And the more she pressures him to do housework, whether she is working part- or full-time herself, the more likely that violence will be triggered.

Edward's was a limited sort of domineering. The silent storm to his study and the contrasting loud click of the lock was the only obvious way he tried to control Barbara. He saved this for really desperate situations, like when she brought home several people or when she started talking about having a baby. Mostly he avoided any conflict, and he had been moving away from her as more stress erupted. But he had other subtle means of control. Barbara had grown to hate a cold, withdrawn look on his face, a monosyllabic reply to any attempt to get conversation going, and a body tension that affected her badly.

Ed was using, unknown to him, a wonderful conditioning technique. The stiff face and withdrawn body took Barbara back to childhood days, when disapproval was registered in her mother's pursed lips and stiffened shoulders. She *hated* it, when she saw from Ed's face that she'd invited too many people round or the wrong kind of people, or was going out to too many meetings. So of course the people and the meetings dropped off for a while. But Ed was a paragon in other ways. He called himself a feminist supporter and did an equal share of the housework. 'Well, anyway', said Barbara, 'he kept the house clean and did some of the cooking.' Since she was out every day she did all the shopping and estimated she spent more time on the housework than Ed, but was nevertheless happy – he did enough and she never had to worry about what the house would look like for guests, he was a stickler for neatness, cleanliness and routine.

Barbara influenced the relationship mostly by ignoring the signals and putting up with Ed's 'sulks' if she really had to go to a meeting or particularly wanted to invite students or friends around. She made no active attempt to negotiate a mutual accommodation either, believing she could never change Ed – whose discipline and idealism was based on a stubbornness born from inhibiting desires he knew were never going to be realized in childhood. So she did an internal negotiation, traded off her need for his sulks, and kept the relationship going nearly as well as it probably would have if there had been a real negotiation – which in view of the later happenings, would have been the best idea.

Pauline, on the other hand was quite opposite. She was willing to hand all power and responsibility to Bob, who fortunately for her, did not abuse it. He even attempted, sometimes, not to take it. She agreed with him, even when she knew better, and asked him about everything. She believed Bob was better equipped than her to deal with life, and the more she deferred the more true it became. An accurate assessment of Pauline's happiness depended on Bob's attitude. He was careful not to exploit her, and was sometimes irritated at her willingness to defer to him. Sometimes he wished she had more of a mind of her own. He could be quite sarcastic and hurtful when things were going wrong at the law centre. He would reject her advice or her attempts at care or showing him attention. But they both knew she would keep trying until Bob felt calm enough to accept her solicitations and a balance would be restored. Pauline always knew when he had something on his mind, and would move quickly to conciliate him – he had got to rely on it.

With a less mature man, Pauline's abrogation of control would have been disastrous – she would truly have been a woman who loved too much, trying ever more desperately to please a tyrannical and selfish man. In the issue of control it is mostly women who give in. A girl's childhood is reinforced with non-verbal messages of 'don't compete with men', 'don't make men angry', 'defer to men'. Behind this is the idea that women need men for support for themselves and their children.

Women grow up attuned to disapproval and what others think. They get what they want by sensitivity, and they know that men expect certain things of them, and the extent to which they feel they need a man is the extent to which they will defer and put his consideration before her own. This is called the principle of least interest, and the one who has the least is the one who has the most control in the relationship. They can threaten to end it all unless the other pulls their socks up.

Pauline is the traditional product of a childhood where being a girl meant being good, clean, helpful, gentle, all the qualities that go into femininity, while Simon is her male equivalent, brought up to be competitive, sporting, unemotional, ambitious. Both have a limited awareness of how social and parental attitudes have shaped their thoughts and behaviour, and how that influences what they do in their present relationships. Pauline says:

No I don't think anyone would know if we were quarrelling. Well we don't, we love each other and I want what Bob wants. I would never raise my voice in public. Bob gets irritated but never angry. The worst row we had was after the break-in. He didn't want to move and I persuaded him it would be sensible. But it took months. I cut out all headlines in the local paper about the increase in muggings and burglaries and rapes and stuck them up on a wall chart. I made him drive me to and from the women's self-defence classes one evening a week. I was almost pleased when a maniac started going round sadistically attacking women, police were everywhere and that was what in the end decided him that a security-guarded flat in London would be safer.

Bob said Pauline's best weapon was tears – but he agreed they rarely had any conflict, they were a kiss and cuddle couple, not a kick and conflict one! Bob is in the position a traditional man would like to be in, and he has no real quarrels with it, whereas Jeanne is deeply disillusioned and unhappy with her traditional man. In many ways she is like Pauline, forgiving, trying to persuade by negotiating, emotionally supportive, but was shocked over the housework issue. Pauline would never have expected Bob to do anything, but Jeanne was a liberal spirit believing in personal responsibility and came from a family where equal division of work was expected, as a by-product of the political philosophy they held.

Jeanne had started working full-time when Simon moved in so she could pay half the mortgage on the freehold of the flat which had just been offered. She signed over her sitting-tenant's advantage to Simon, threw in the £6,000 deposit and made him co-owner, and although she didn't think about this, her main preoccupation now was to get him to do his share of the housework. Any attempt by Jeanne to talk about justice and fairness was met by veiled threats and sarcasm, which would escalate to fury and physical threat if she persisted. Yet they still cooperated in the rest of life, companionship, intellectual exchange, sexual relations, and Simon would ask her opinion about other things. So it was easy for Jeanne to say OK, he draws the line at housework and if I can accept that we will have a happy, loving relationship.

Easy to say, but not to do. Over the months the rising tide of anger as she did all the housework got harder to hold back, and every now and then she would try and explain the deleterious effect it was having on their relationship. Until the night of the rape, which was the end for her. She couldn't ignore Simon's lack of respect for her, her feelings, the type of life she wanted to live, and defeated, bitter and humiliated, left to stay at her father's house.

But relationships don't have to be battlefields of winners and losers. They must not be for survival's sake. Excluding violence, the most extreme thing anyone can do when in conflict is simply to withdraw. This is the favoured ploy of the separates, who tend to bring the avoiding-attachment style to their relationship. Even their fights will be mostly in silence. They ignore each other – expressing disapproval by acting as if the other wasn't there. These are the lives lived in parallel, rather than emotionally together. Each will try to get their own way, but in more subtle ways than the other love-styles. Extended discussions with no clear direction or finalization, a part agreement or disagreement with no resolution, avoiding definite plans. All these were Ed's specialities, which frustrated Barbara. When he was in a mood (study door shut, sometimes locked as well), Barbara took the opportunity to go out more, knowing that he wouldn't complain because he would be on the computer day and night:

> After a day or two he'd come down and say something nice, which sort of indicated that the disagreement was over and we could forget. And I'd be wracking my brains to think what it was we'd disagreed over! But even in the middle of it there was something that stopped me saying anything nasty to him, yet at school I can be forthright and assertive, and even angry. I just crumble when it comes to Ed, but I don't give in – just avoid the whole issue until it doesn't matter anymore.

If all the energy put into avoiding conflict had gone into trying to resolve their differences, they would have been able to coordinate active, sustained discussions about their problems and feelings. But they used their feelings to negotiate instead a joint pattern of avoidance rather than a solution.

The submitters are the ones that give in. They will agree to almost anything their partner suggests, and will even seek advice and support when it's not offered. The submitters tend to make traditional relationships and are perfect complements to the immature traditional men who believe they should be in control of their women, and give orders, rather than requests, statements rather than observations, blame instead of taking responsibility, and slowly demoralize the relationship.

The storgics, who make an interdependent, therapeutic relationship, try to achieve a democratic means of influencing each other, jockeying until they reach a position each is happy with. Problems are seen to be the responsibility of both, so they are equally shared as far as possible. As Ann said, she signals well in advance, as she knows her feelings sufficiently well to do so:

> John's in no doubt when I'm angry, he can see it in my face, voice, my
> walk, and the way I bang the kitchen cupboard doors shut, and I can
> see when he's even just a bit steamed up, his breathing is faster and he
> talks a different way. He moves quicker too.

'The difference between an angry Ann,' laughed John, 'and a
contented Ann, is whether the old cat is under the bicycle shed or
in his usual place in the hot water cupboard!' Ann's non-verbal
language is clear enough for even an old moggie to read!

The real message is that they know their good relationship will
cycle around concern to contentment, involvement to indifference
and love to anger. They wait out the negative cycles with tolerance
and enjoy the happy periods, while all the while in the background
is an affectionate, positive expectation. They conceive of it as a
straight line of pleasantness on which circles are imposed. The top
half of the circle are their joyous, close upswings and the bottom
half the downswings of irritation and boredom. They aim to shorten
the duration of the downswings and lengthen the upswings. John's
mechanical analogy is actually a good way to look at all
relationships, in both linear and cyclical terms, and closely parallels
the conception of the macro- and micro-cycles of conflict, intimacy
and withdrawal.

Relationship talk styles

These eight types of messages are used by all couples of course,
but research shows some to be used more by particular relationship
types than others. They are competing, contradictory messages in
the sense that they serve different relationship functions.

The messages are chosen to reflect the continual cycling between
superficial and deeper contact. There is in all relationships a tension
between the ebb and flow of telling the partner all about one's
feeling and the fear of the consequences of doing so. Sometimes
one's feelings may upset, anger or shock the partner. So the types
of message can on the one hand express inner feelings and
thoughts (self-disclosure), and on the other protect the vulnerabilities of the partner (confirmation or an objective edification
message). Messages also serve to organize the relationship
(questions, interpretation), to construct a joint world view
(reflection), and to foster favourable impressions (acknowledge).

Message types most used by the traditionals

Edification: Conveying objective information about how the children are doing at school, mother called about Christmas, the neighbours have bought a puppy, anything that might affect their life together.

Interpretation: Going beyond the information spoken, and feeding that back, questioning the motives ('You're only saying that because . . .').

Message types most used by the separates

Questions: 'Did you pay the telephone bill?' 'Is my dress too short?'

Reflection: Inferring something about the other or the relationship from what was hinted at or understated that might mean you have to change. 'It seems you'd be happier if I gave up working full time.'

Message types most used by the therapeutics/ storgics

Disclosure: Telling the other about one's own feelings, desires, opinions, worries, hopes, fears, ambitions, perceptions and intentions.

Acknowledgement: Some gesture, noise or word to say to the other, 'Yes, I'm listening, keep talking', or 'I'm thinking of a reply', or 'I understand.'

Confirmation: Checking out that the reading of the other's emotions and intentions was accurate.

Advice: Linking past experience to the present for the benefit of the other. 'If you have another glass, you'll get your nasty cough again.'

Interestingly, traditional couples never use reflection (perhaps because of their high use of confirmation and interpretation), and separates never use interpretation (too risky).

Part III
Cooling it: Coping with the Differences

We might compare masculinity and femininity and their psychic components to a definite store of substances of which in the first half of life unequal use is made. A man consumes his large supply of masculine substance and has left over only small amounts of feminine substance, which must now be put to use. Conversely, the woman allows her hitherto unused supply of masculinity to become active. This change is even more noticeable in the psychic realm than the physical. Very often these changes are accompanied by all sorts of catastrophes in marriage for it is hard to discover what will happen when the husband discovers tender feelings and the wife her sharpness of mind.

Carl Jung, 1933 from *Modern Man in Search of a Soul*

In other words, development along the life course is towards mastery, but it's different ways for each sex.

7

Male and female perspectives on intimacy

Love and strife are the two organizing principles of the universe. They correspond to the forces of union and division in realms as diverse as cloud formation and human relationships. This was the belief of Empedocles, a Greek philosopher, but it takes most couples years to find this out.

Sperm-wars

Human nature has been shaped by natural selection, and survival depended on knowing what one's best interests were, and acting on that knowledge. But biologically speaking men's best interests in love and sex are in direct conflict with women's best interests. The relationship between them has been as much shaped by thousands of years of evolution as by the last two centuries of romantic ideology. Women have one precious egg each month, that's approximately 400 in a lifetime, only a fraction of which will be fertilized to become another human being destined to represent her genes in the next generation. These eggs are potential within her from her birth while males can continually remake fresh sperm all their lives. Which amounts to 8 trillion over a lifetime. So she must make sure she gets the best blueprint available and males obligingly demonstrate this for her, by fighting each other over her. Winner takes her off to bed.

It is the winning that is the male optimum strategy, he must win over and over again, and thereby promiscuously spread his megamillions of easily produced sperm (in contrast to her few hundred precious eggs) around on the basis that at least some of them will fertilize an offspring which will be brought up by the female and which will represent his genes. He not only fights with horns, teeth, muscles, roars and claws. The battle for male supremacy is fought in the womb, for the more opportunities the female has to be promiscuous the more sperm the male releases to help in the battle tactics, by killing off foreign sperm. They form themselves into a co-operating team, some sacrificing themselves to further the success of their sperm brothers while the egg-fertilizing committee swim ahead (the best-timed, best-aimed, most lively ones). Absence makes the heart grow fonder and the sperm count go higher! Even in human men the more they are in the company of their wives the lower their sperm production compared to men whose wives were away a good part of the time. So all the appendages males fight with are a back-up to the appendage that has evolved to deliver the sperm to the egg. Natural selection favoured males able to get their sperm high up into the female reproductive tract, thus escaping the foot soldiers of the rival sperm committee.

If only they could go to a genetic marriage bureau and solemnly declare to each contribute 23 chromosomes each to the new being and contract for equal responsibility in contributing to its survival. But then the thrill of the chase would be lost, the hopes and the ecstasies. And so, also, the pain of rejection, the disillusion and the recriminations. Until that rational day we are stuck with men and women engaged in the best trade-off their conflicting sexual campaigns will allow.

Where it all starts

The biological motivations that direct our behaviour are unknown to the individual who has no conscious knowledge of genetic survival or biological fitness and may not even desire children. All they know is that they feel good when they do some things and not others, or that they feel intuitively something is right, or even feel compulsively driven. The things humans enjoy are the ones essential for survival – eating, drinking, finding a mate, establishing a family. The pleasure chemicals are nature's reward for doing what helps survival of the genes. The more complex the behaviour (like bringing up children) the further away from genetic control it is and the less likely it is to be a continuously pleasurable event. But the essential elements are programmed, the desire for sex and the motivation to protect small, helpless humans with round faces and large eyes. Nothing else is needed for the continuation of the species.

The biological negotiation between them is how much time and energy he is going to devote to the family. The female is already fully committed in that it is she that has to give birth and do the breast feeding, the only question is how much bacon he can bring home.

Monogamy is a social institution the purpose of which is to resolve this conflict, at least in an uncertain resource climate. Birds for example must form life long pair-bonds to cope with their fragile existence, their monogamy is biological and necessary, human monogamy is socially prescribed and our social system is based on it. But ideals can't always replace biological motivations which is the reason promiscuity and sexual hang-ups are more frequently observed in men than women. The difference in who does what (called parental investment by biologists) informs the differing psychological traits that men and women admire. She is turned on by competence in a man and in demonstrating his strength he is also showing his potential mate he can be a good provider while she is incapacitated with child bearing and rearing.

The preference of most women for a man of status as well as her upset at the emotional intimacy implied in a husband's affair, parallels his jealousy over the sex his wife's affair involved. She worries about her husband's future commitment and he about whose genes the children have! The mother is always known, but the father could be anyone from the milkman to the gynaecologist!

The psychologies of men and women are fitted around male defence and female child care and human social groups have survived and proliferated because of it. In those pre-pill days women were producing children just about annually. They needed to, to counterbalance the high death rates, and the *sine qua non* of womanhood became all the qualities thought necessary for bringing up baby – gentle, nurturing, affectionate, sympathetic, domesticated and emotional. It followed then that the opposite traits of hardness, logicality, competitiveness, enterprise and head before heart sort of traits should belong to the opposite sex, men.

Instrumental versus expressive

In fact, anthropologists have researched the origin and maintenance of what they call sex-roles and summed up the feminine traits as 'expressive' and the masculine as 'instrumental'.

In almost all societies this division is at least somewhat enforced so that women adorn the hearth place – and further, while they're doing nothing they might as well be getting on with the cooking, the washing, the cleaning and all those trivial little 'nothing' jobs!

These differences hint of sexual excitement, give us glimpses of cave men dragging their women off by the hair to orgiastic frenzies, and a feeling that we will be completed by the other. It was clear from the personality traits of the 3,000 couples I surveyed that the thrill of the chase is still alive in 20th century Britain. The personality scores most associated with femininity (emotionality, empathy) and masculinity (tough mindedness) had a precise relation to happiness. When wives were a little higher on the emotionality scale than their husbands, as well as husbands being slightly higher on the tough-mindedness scale than their wives then they were both very happy with their relationship. It was as if each needed to feel the other was a 'real man' and 'real woman' but emphasizing sex-differences to enhance attraction overrides similarities and leads to strong silent Apollos and desperate Aphrodites, on their dance to disaster.

Men should be heroes and women should admire them

Apollo and Aphrodite were a mythological god and goddess. Apollo is the embodiment of masculine tough-minded attributes, who strives for mastery and control, values order and skims surface experience ignoring the underlying reality. He favours thinking over feeling, objectivity over intuition and is therefore predisposed to emotional shallowness, selfishness and distance in relationships. He dances to no one's tune. He is drawn to his opposite, the personification of feminine qualities. Aphrodite is emotional, irrational, impractical, frivolous, irresponsible – and beautiful. And fascinating to mythological males. In the myths Apollo is true to the mortal male's evolutionary best strategy. He pursues several goddesses, including Daphne, Cassandra and Coronis, all of whom he tries to control. Myths are told down the ages because in the retelling is every human's story. They ring true and illustrate our personal situation, offering us warnings and solutions. The Apollo myth illustrates the differing psychological traits between men and women necessary to pursue their opposing sexual campaigns. The hero she admires is competent while he reserves his attentions for youth and health, the best indications of child-bearing ability.

How the intimacy v. independence cycles can lead to the pursuer–withdrawal cycle

Negotiating sex differences is a delicate balancing act with even happy couples puzzled as to why they frequently seemed not to feel the same thing at the same time. The strong, silent male is the epitome of the instrumental character that most people put under the heading of 'typical male', and a summary would be not dancing to anyone else's tune, like Apollo.

Expressive words that are thought to be representative of a 'typical woman' add up to the empathy necessary to understand the other's reactions – a good recipe for the pursuer-withdrawal cycle when the other partner is resisting keeping in step.

Men have different ideas of expressing love and intimacy to women. Virtually every male/female relationship gets stuck in the pursuer-withdrawal cycle to some degree, and it can take years to work out. It's due to the homoeostatic interaction in a relationship when they work by diffent rules and not the fault of the partners. Close approaches lead to overstimulation and then a compensatory adjustment – in other words the overemotional woman and the unresponsive male. Every couple thought this pattern was unique to them, and the women usually felt it was their fault and that she was letting herself down by staying with a man who was trying to move away from her. Each cycle of withdrawal takes place in slightly different enough circumstances for them to believe that those particular circumstances were the cause, too much pressure at work, worries about money, or the kids, or any number of readily available plausible reasons. So it can take half the relationship to see the underlying pattern and real cause. But most only discovered it after the break up.

If all the people around a boy or a man encourage and expect him to have an Apollian emotional structure, then it's hardly surprising that he does. But he still has a human physiology, and now it is known that men have a greater physiological arousal in response to emotional stress than women, his cry of 'be reasonable' and 'rational' makes sense. Chronic activation of the nervous system is harmful and unpleasant, it makes a man feel tense, irritable and angry. So in the face of relationship stress, emotion is the last thing he needs. It explains why most men fight with their coats – they put them on and leave, withdrawing from the discussion, quarrel and the house.

Talking about the relationship is to him a sign that it's going wrong, if he avoids it the problem might go away – but to her talking about the relationship stops it going wrong. It also explains the different pattern of answers to the relationship satisfaction questionnaire these 3,000 couples completed. Men said they were happy when there were fewer quarrels, while women's happiness was related to how emotionally close they felt, which was indicated to them by kissing, talking things over and showing affection. It is clear from the previous statements by men and much other research that men feel uncomfortable and stressed when discussing emotions they feel. And it was this that caused most of the quarrels. Not money, the colour of the new wallpaper or mother-in-law. She asks for verbal intimacy, talking about subjective feelings of love and he responds with a physical demonstration of intimacy, sex, which is an objective, tangible, instrumental expression of intimacy. Even the dictionary definition of intimacy gives alternative meanings, sexual intimacy or sharing of emotional feelings. It is one thing to have social 'rules' for the regulation of intense feelings. It is quite necessary because we tend to transfer our early family experience to our later love relationships and re-experience all the anxiety, terror and rage of childhood. But it is quite another thing to have rules for each sex, so that men and women ignore and repress important parts of themselves. This often leads to unhappiness, illness, depression and even premature death. At least part of the early death rate in men is caused by the tough, competitive, independent behaviour they are required to don with their macho mask. And at least part of the higher depression rates for women is caused by the passive, helpless role they have to take to be 'feminine'.

Because biological scripts guide us unconsciously, men and women look for different things in each other. Our personalities have been shaped by evolutionary history which guides our thinking on what is 'masculine' and 'feminine'. Although it is these differences that are so attracting, it is the very same differences that make intimacy and communication difficult. The more extreme the masculine or feminine traits, the more likely the couple is to be disillusioned or get divorced. Intimacy and good communication are necessary for health and happiness but each sex has their own definition of it, and doesn't recognize the other's. A usual solution is that she tries harder emotionally and 'manages' his emotions for him, which results in him becoming even more unresponsive, thus leading to the overcontrolled man and the overemotional woman, the most common pattern in marital therapy.

It is the traditional (manic) woman who is the quickest to recognize the pursuer-withdrawal cycle. For her to fulfil her role successfully she needs to have her man's commitment, attention and demonstration of closeness. These are the women whose happiness rose on their husband's retirement, since he then had more time and attention for her. But the more dependent they were the more angry they were, and the more they demanded demonstration of love. The thinking here seemed to be 'If he has power over me then he must be responsible for what's wrong with my life.' Powerless wives are controlling wives, for whom idealization turns to blame and criticism, quicker than most.

Women who put much of their life's energy into making a relationship work are waving an invisible banner which flashes the subliminal message 'you should be doing the same for me'. The response is usually guilt, resentment and withdrawal, certainly when their partners had ludic or pragmatic tendencies. When a woman takes on the job of interpreting and redefining a man's feelings he can become less and less willing and able to understand and cope with them himself. The more she soothes his anger or orchestrates his pleasure the less he feels spontaneously.

She sweeps forward two steps when one will do, wanting 'something more' all the time without knowing that the inner longing for more love masks a need for an identity of her own. The traditional (pragmatic) man puts limits on the dance, the steps are fine, as complex as she likes, so long as he takes the lead. It is the ludic man that takes two steps back to her every one forward and like Barbara and Edward are embarked on a dance to disaster (until like them they get back in step again).

The ludic and pragmatic lovers of Chapter 5 are the Apollos while Aphrodite is the epitome of the manic lover. Of course there are pragmatic and ludic type women and manic type males but the number is very small compared to the other way round – male and female conditioning makes it so. Not to mention the little evolutionary competition of winning in the sexual strategy stakes.

The storgic lovers have managed a balanced two-step that creates its own momentum and harmony. The relationship will end when the woman gives up the orchestration, no matter which relationship style it is that has got out of step. Keeping in step needs good communication and monitoring so as to match the approach/

withdrawal cycles of the other. Having an early warning detector of the other's physiological arousal and acting to de-escalate it is known to be the best predictor of a happy relationship. The tool box of techniques to tinker with the system is the manual of decoding speech styles of convergence and divergence (see Chapters 10 and 11) and the non-verbal and verbal messages of intimacy and independence embedded in the language we use and the assumptions we share.

Sex-linked obsessions: his work, her intimacy

When insecurely attached lovers are asked what degree of masculinity and femininity they feel themselves to be they respond in the extreme, the manic women believing they are highly feminine and the pragmatic male, strongly masculine. The ludic women thought they were masculine and the ludic men, just as masculine as the women!

Ludic love styles (the flight attachment type) and pragmatic love styles (the fight attachment type) belong to the instrumental mode of psychological functioning and speak the language of independence that is described in Chapter 11.

The manic love style (the submit alternative) fits the expressive traits, which go into the language of involvement (Chapter 10). The secure attachers are more androgynous – that is, they have a more equal balance of the feminine expressive traits with the masculine, instrumental ones. These are the traits listed at the beginning of Chapter 8, which couples did as a personality test, rating themselves on a 7 point scale from 'almost always like this' to 'hardly ever like this'. Other items were scattered around the masculine and feminine words so it wasn't too immediately obvious that this was a sex-stereotype questionnaire and not a personality one as claimed. Everyone got a big surprise, they hadn't realized how much social conditioning affected what they thought of as their personality, formed by free will and individual proclivity.

This separation of personality traits which leads to the sex differences in love-styles has tremendous consequences for relationships; at worst, work-obsessed men, and intimacy-obsessed women. Women who were denied power and productivity and so distorted the value of tenderness and intimacy, had developed emotionally expressive networks of friends, family and children.

Men on the other hand were so estranged from emotional expression of love and affection that in a large American survey it was found that most men found it hard to be close to their children. They also experienced much marital disruption and the researchers concluded that most American men therefore have no emotional confidante at all for long periods in their lives. But even at its best the instrumental-expressive separation means a conflict for almost all men and all women who try to get on in a relationship.

Intimacy is a relatively new concept, coming with the idea of a relationship as being something that can validate oneself, and not a concept our grandparents would sympathize with. This growth-promoting, therapeutic view means we are attracted to others who improve our image of ourselves, to someone that treats us more like our 'ideal' self rather than our real, mundane actuality. How girls do this is by talking to each other, sharing confidences, examining fears, supporting hopes, swapping experiences, evaluating others, giving encouragement, asking for help, in other words, a total analysis of each other. Clarifying beliefs, thoughts, emotions and behaviour through another person fosters intimacy. Boys, of course, do talk to each other, but research reveals it to be talk about shared activities more than feelings, and that male friendships therefore are less intimate, or at least that what a man thinks is an intimate relationship is not the same as a woman's definition. Female best friends usually know everything about each other. Male friends know their pal's sporting and drinking preferences but not how he feels about his family's problems or even if they have any!

Because intimacy is seen to be something that women do it is not therefore something that 'real' men should do. The masculine mode of intimacy is activity-generated. He expresses intimacy in what he *does*, round the house, the garden, the garage and in all the things the couple does together. Togetherness for a man is shared activities and interests, togetherness for women is shared feelings, thoughts and observations. Her idea of intimacy is the rapport that comes from the things they talk about they would never tell anyone else. She wants reassurance that he will always be there to talk to. So men and women both feel love but they express it differently, and the potential for misunderstanding and hurt exists in every relationship.

The problem for men

The problem for men is that it is women's version of intimacy that has come to be accepted as 'real' intimacy. This happened after the industrial revolution as places of work were set up specially and everything once done by the family, weaving, spinning, cheese-making, brewing and so on, was now taken out of the cottage-industry sphere by the industrialists and capitalists – who were men. An ideology of efficient work in *public* places evolved while the *domestic*, the women and the children, were relegated to the private sphere, where men returned after work. Home, women and intimacy became associated in opposition to the competitive, male, public workplace.

So the *expressive* versus *instrumental* dichotomy influenced definitions of intimacy. Women can't be convinced that sex without intimacy is love, and men are puzzled at women who say they love them but turn down sex. Although both actions and words must be coherent in expressing intimacy, self-disclosure, the prime-mover of intimate rapport, is necessarily verbal, so women's definition of intimacy wins.

But men's actions do speak louder than words. In a study asking how important parents and family were to husbands and wives, there was a perfect example of this double standard of judgement. 58 per cent of women and only 37 per cent of men said their parents were important to them, *but* when the researchers counted the actual times each visited their parents the proportion was nearly equal (88 per cent and 81 per cent, respectively). There is a big gap between what men say and what women think they mean, especially when it comes to emotional language.

The differing significance of practical help to men and women was demonstrated by a study where couples kept daily recordings of how pleasant and helpful their spouses were. Things like cooking a good meal, repairing a tap, expressing affection and so on were divided into instrumental acts and affectional acts. It won't surprise anyone to know that women were more happy with their husbands' affectionate behaviour. But husbands' happiness was related to their wives' instrumental actions, not their affection. He took his wife's ironing of his shirt as an expression of love but she wouldn't count his washing her car as an equal expression of love!

So, different standards set in childhood create the crisis of compatibility men and women suffer today. Men believe the time put in on their job is sufficient demonstration of love since he is providing the major part of the couple's income. Perhaps this is why most men are uncomfortable when a woman earns more than they do. They have lost their traditional way of showing love. For men with boring jobs the position of 'my work equals my love' can be viewed more sympathetically than men whose jobs provide interest, challenge and status. But in either case this philosophy is based on the traditional mode of relationship, not the newer therapeutic model, and it also reinforces the idea of men as the powerful providers, who have control over women. It allows male power to be visible and accepted and female power to be denied and invisible, because *her* instrumental services are unpaid.

Adding up the hours each husband and wife in my survey spent on work (both paid and unpaid housework) and then dividing those hours into annual income for each, produced a means of two and a half times more money per hour for the men. This was on account both of the men being paid more anyway as well as the smaller amount of time they spent on housework (even if their wives worked full-time) which was unpaid for both. No wonder men insist on work being counted as an expression of love!

But there is another consideration, to be fair. Differences in metabolism (to do with the differing muscle to fat ratio) underlie different time and energy cycles. In contrast to the Victorian idea of fragile women, it is actually women who have more stamina. They are in for the long haul at a lower energy output, therefore needing fewer recuperative periods. Men can exert more powerful energy for a much shorter time. This difference has been capitalized on for thousands of years. Women with their high fat to muscle ratio (and therefore better insulation) did the deep sea pearl diving in Japan where more time swimming underwater got more pearls, and yet the Japanese idea of women surpasses even the Victorian in passivity and fragility. Now that the psychological barrier has been broken, women are breaking previous sports records faster than men, especially in long distance running and swimming, because women have good thigh muscles while men have stronger arm and shoulder muscles.

Bob of Chapter 5 was a typical man in this sense. The day exhausted him and all he could think about was television or light reading. Both pastimes that require little body activity. Pauline's idea of relaxation was going out again, to some cultural event that stimulated her and recharged her energy. Even talking required energy which Bob had to push himself to muster, wearily. It was effortless to Pauline. If she did watch television she would still be trying to talk to Bob, who would respond monosyllabically. Most women are like Pauline, doing several things at once. It is probably due to the double harnessing of their cerebral hemispheres. Men focus deeply on one thing to which they give their whole attention. They can't be deflected while women are holding three different conversations with each of the children at the same time. It is tempting to think that this is the way these brain differences evolved, keeping an eye on *all* the offspring while men developed the silent concentration needed for the hunt.

Men and women have different time and energy cycles but the real question of the century is: does the explanation of energy expended at work so exhaust the male that he is physically incapable of housework? Bob and Pauline's struggle is repeated in millions of households as the woman does 83 per cent of the housework (usually in addition to a job) and resents her husband's inactivity. There has to be some reason for the consistent refusal of educated, fair-minded men who agree that it's not fair that their wives work outside *and* inside the home, to nevertheless, do only a fraction of the housework. Tradition, need for power, fear of being manipulated or emasculated are not the motivations of these men. They wish they could do more (they say), and they often believe, inaccurately that they do, but they are just too tired. Tomorrow will do. As Dianne says:

> Dick always starts with the best intentions, I hear the vacuum cleaner going for 10 minutes and then when it gets to the difficult stairs it stops and I invariably find he's sat down to read some old magazine that he's supposed to be clearing up. And then it's, 'I'll do it later . . .' which never happens. I've realized he's better at jobs that he can throw himself into and get it over with quickly – then back to the couch! You should see him do the lawn. It takes me an hour but he's out there like a demented kangaroo, head down, long strides, as if he's running to catch the mower, flying round the bends. And it's done in 20 minutes. But he doesn't move off the couch for the rest of the day, practically.
>
> My daughter did a leisure and family project at school and worked out that the only chair I had sat on for two months was the dining chair. Even when I watch television I like to be at the table so I can also do sewing or writing letters. The only time I've sat on the new couch (3 years old) was at Xmas the year before last to open presents. Dick spends 2 or 3 hours a night on it!

Until we get a study of sex differences in calorie expenditure and energy depletion in specific tasks men will get the benefit of the doubt.

Loving qualities are not associated with men as any romance leader knows. The tall, dark, handsome stranger is cool and unmoveable, until the last chapter anyway, when he is allowed to fall sheepishly in love, maintaining control, nevertheless. It is this need for control that is so damaging to relationships. Men feel they must keep control, and not give in to something that women have monopolized.

It is this (feminization) of love that has given rise to the myth of marriage being a trap for men and a victory for women. It is only in the last decade that anyone thought to apply scientific binoculars to this well-entrenched myth, and found just the reverse. Married men (or those in long-term stable relationships) have the best physical and mental health while married women have the worst, especially those with young children and little money. The next worst group was the single men!

So, while men protest, they actually benefit most from a loving relationship. But some men believe their own protestations or feel ashamed of their need, thus clamping down on these unmasculine ingredients and becoming an unresponsive man.

The consequence of the polarization of the instrumental/expressiveness dichotomy is that almost all women would like their husbands to be more responsive and most men want their wives to be less emotional. Men felt wives used emotional pressure to get their way, while they tried to avoid conflict. Many women come to an intuitive understanding that no matter what a man says (or, more usually, doesn't say) he is emotionally dependent on her and she may decide to play the game and pretend that it is not so, if she is happy in other respects, while giving him the emotional support he needs. They become unpaid counsellors of husbands and boyfriends and often of his male friends as well.

Other women feel cheated when their hero turns out to be a mass of tightly packed emotions, he might spring a leak and how can she depend on him then? But whatever her response the damage is done. This is what women find so dishonest about male and female relationships; his overt insistence on his emotional strength and independence, while covertly relying on her, as the secret emotional anchor in his life.

This need may be hidden from the man himself as well as others but rarely from her. It brings out a range of responses in women, from welcome protection to contempt. But, when a woman takes on the job of emotional mentor, she is usually dancing to disaster. She makes the emotional running (expresses interest and concern in his day, tells him she loves him, gives in over conflicts of interest, does chores for him, keeps in contact with his friends and family and so on) which he accepts to a certain point. For the ludic lovers it is a smaller point than other men. But he starts withdrawing when he feels her requests for reciprocity to be emotional pressure.

It could start quite early, with a simple request to him to say 'I love you'. One woman in my survey told me that she divorced her husband after 7 years because he had never told her that. Furthermore, although she told him that that was all she needed to hear to stop divorce proceedings, he couldn't say it. Even though she knew he felt more for her than anyone else. But it wasn't enough in the end, just to know that.

The pragmatic men expected all the emotional service, it didn't make them uneasy, like the ludic men, because they saw their return as their work and their instrumental activities (putting the rubbish out, the shelves up, unblocking the sink and so on) as an equal recompense. To them, expecting a reciprocal emotional service was asking too much, that was where they felt the emotional pressure.

The storgic men were a flexible version of the traditional men, they did express affection as well as do the dishes, but they did view their housework as 'helping their wives', thereby seeing her as the legitimate provider. But they extended this to expressing affection and took much more responsibility for this. Emotional expression on the part of their wives was usually appreciated and reciprocated, and they sometimes initiated an emotional sequence themselves, like being the first to kiss and make up or offering unsolicited affection. Consequently their wives were much less likely to recognize the steps in the dance of disaster. Storgic men make storgic wives.

Of course, it is not inevitably the man who is the retractor in this oscillating pattern of pursuer/withdrawer, but the differing patterns of socialization of boys and girls make it more likely. It certainly appeared to be the case with men I interviewed. Whether they were ludic, pragmatic or storgic lovers, much of the responsibility for the emotional health of the relationship was viewed as the woman's province. But the more he left the expression of love to her the more he felt he was living up to her expectations and the more she talked about the emotional aspect the more he felt like he was going to fail an exam she had set on some unknown subject.

The problem for women

Ever since Jessie Bernard, an American sociologist, looked at the decade of wives' complaints that husbands don't talk enough in the way that women want, share their worries or listen to their wives enough there has been an understanding of two different relationships going on in the same household, a 'his' and a 'hers'. Most women yearn for more responsiveness from their man, and relationships break up for the lack of it. It implies being cared for, understood and being taken seriously.

For the last decade voluminous research has uncovered the detrimental effects of male sex-typed communication on intimate relationships. A man can't be seen to be strong, independent and competent if he is *also* emotionally expressive and vulnerable enough for self-disclosure that creates intimacy. Dr Chester, in his survey of 10,000 women for example for the BBC programme *Horizon*, found one third complained about their husbands being ineffectual confidantes.

Maureen Green, a social historian researching into contemporary relationship patterns in the United Kingdom, illustrates the struggle of the two sexes to understand each other. Husbands judge their wives to be dependent and clinging and wives feel husbands to be appallingly incapable of intimacy. Emotional demands were resented by men who felt inadequate to meet them, whereas wives resented decisions made without reference to their wishes or needs.

Jack Dominian, a widely respected marriage counsellor and researcher and head of the department of psychological medicine at the Central Middlesex Hospital in London, confirms the emotional withdrawal pattern in men and the consequent feelings of being misunderstood by women. Emotional honesty and openness are sacrifices most men are forced to make to keep control. The result in relationship is hurt, misunderstanding and anger. A pattern of mistrust, blame, demand and withdrawal is established. Instead of each stating their feelings and responding to the other, they state their demands and then condemn each other, all the way to the end of the dance to disaster.

Men do discuss and reveal more positive emotions than a decade ago. The stiff upper lip is now known to be the precursor of heart attacks and stress-related disease, including cancer. But there is still a barrier to revealing innermost worries, fears and fragile hopes and fantasies, even to that one special woman. Men feel this is the slippery slope to emotional dependency. In any relationship telling another information that is not for public broadcast (prejudices, discreditable tendencies, disgraceful histories, innermost anxieties) gives the recipient a leverage. This is why we hesitate to volunteer information unless it is reciprocated. If I know that you know about my innermost secret sexual desires I'm not likely to tell anyone about your worrying, murderous feelings towards your teenager! Reciprocity is a safeguard as well as an intimacy generator. But reciprocity is also an equalizer – and sometimes not a welcome one. To a man who feels he should be in control, there is always that last resistance to opening up. He is frightened of the vulnerability it may entail. To tell a woman all about his feelings gives her the power he feels should be his. She can reject, respect, accept, laugh at, or broadcast his revelations.

There is also the feeling that it is an unmanly thing to do – since it is what women do. So the issue of responsiveness often comes down to one of power – implicitly understood and struggled over by thousands of couples. In any group the powerful one knows more, bosses know all their workers' personal details, they are on file to start with, but workers know only what is gleaned from gossip and may be inaccurate. The powerful group cannot allow themselves to be vulnerable and true intimacy involves vulnerability.

It's as if a man felt that once he'd shown his soft side to his partner he wouldn't be able to act out his hard masculine persona to other men and might lose his place in the masculine world. Talking about our feelings is so important to happiness and intimacy that some couples fooled themselves and exaggerated the other's contribution. Women in particular were continually making excuses for their men's lack of responsiveness. Others divorced, or weathered it out until the next stage of the relationship life cycle when men grow into their 'intimacy-phase' – after the realization that career and competence are not life's real rewards (see Chapter 8).

Sex differences in ability to communicate and match intimacy cycles are responsible for the frustration of the hopes members of a couple once had, and the slow decline into indifference, bickering and selfishness. They get used to a lower level of satisfaction, finding other sources of contentment and fulfillment, and chug on, on half cylinder. But it is possible to be on full sparks all the way, by re-establishing the rhythm of intimacy that first made them want to share their life together.

A man needs that supercharge of love to talk about love, but once that fuel is spent he is stuck. Partly he feels that now he has won fair lady that's the end of that part of the fairy tale. After all, all the prince had to do was get the princess, there are no precedents in our fairy tales for how to keep her happy. It was just presumed to happen. Instrumental activity is his sphere, emotional house-keeping her responsibility.

She was his reward and, additionally, the emotions that create intimacy, the monitoring, the positive feedback, the exchange of loving sentiments, the empathetic listening, all these he sees as 'women's skills', like cooking, ironing and typing. Like anything that women join en masse, it becomes easy if *they* can do it. So trying to establish relationships of loving intimacy becomes disparaged by men, who can then keep their own need for intimacy hidden while still satisfying the need.

A love relationship between the sexes can only go according to the romantic, happy ever after story if biologically programmed sex differences are accommodated. It is these differences in the first place that arouse sexual passion, the strong competent man and the soft emotional woman. Each sex wants a slightly exaggerated stereotype in order to fall in love – very few women go for soft, rounded emotional men, or men for hard, independent and clever women who want control.

But it is these same sex differences that cause problems in the relationship – from minor frustrations to disastrous, torn asunder families. The average man has been socialized to ignore emotions, even though he does feel them. But he feels uncomfortable talking about love and intimacy once the passion has faded. His view of intimacy is guided by his childhood relationships which involve doing things together.

The average woman has been socialized to display emotion, thoughts, and feelings and feels responsible for anything that needs emotional work, like relationships, just as he feels responsible for the instrumental work of tyre changing and rubbish disposal. Her idea of intimacy is talking and sharing with another innermost feelings, desires, fears and so on, and they don't recognize each other's definitions. Men don't wholly trust women because they are not *like them*. Further, they are usually exhorted to protect them, and women's helplessness places an unwelcome responsibility on many men. But then they find women helpful and emotionally supportive (as *they* have been taught) – this must seem too good to be true and as it reminds them of mother (or teacher) they will accept it as a recompense.

The trade-off between his emotional dependency and her physical dependency is underwritten by biology, and sold by socialization but the struggle now is the higher valuation of her strengths for the benefit of both. Each sex strives to attain from the other sex the type of power that they are most discouraged from attaining themselves. His power is the overt, public contracted for influence, hers the subjective, hidden one, which she wants written into the contract, and recognized.

Oscar Wilde once observed that nature had given women so much power that very wisely the law had given her none. But it wasn't so wise, it ignores the human desire for a just world and the inevitability of strife until this desire is satisfied. We have passed through the 'hard man' stage where the threat of violence is always lurking behind his competitive behaviour. And also the 'new lad' stage – these do their own washing but still judge a person's personality from the car they drive. The 'new man' is like a storgic man-in-waiting.

Then there are the Wildmen of America – professors, computer operators, plumbers, salesmen, teachers . . . who all disappear into the American woods to reinstate the maleness they feel feminism has splintered irrevocably. Their brotherly and uninhibited cavorting and chanting is not a retreat to regroup and emerge reunited and strengthened, to vanquish the new woman in her high-powered career. It is to develop the 'inner warrior' and it could be a very significant step in male evolution. As women have reassessed their role in the light of contraceptive technology and new economic opportunities, masculinity has seemed increasingly redundant. Feminists poured testosterone down the drain with the wild warrior, and maleness polarized into defensive Rambos or apologetic wimps.

The inner warrior is engaged on a struggle within to find new ways of using his energy productively instead of in obsessive competition with others. This develops an intimacy and recognition of emotional vulnerability which enables him to generalize to family and community. It sounds like little girls' groups – the sharing of confidences, the playing of cooperative games, the touching – and it may herald the future of a 'feminine culture' replacing the masculine values of patriarchy.

Every couple is affected in at least some degree by these sex-differences in emotional communication, more in their first years, when their relationships tended towards the ludic, pragmatic or manic. The best message is that the older you get the more storgic you get.

An emotional quotient re-education programme

Species that have more sophisticated communication systems fight less, and the same applies to human relationships. The more a man can talk, the more he can defuse his arousal when it gets to unpleasant levels. Whether the inability to talk about emotions comes from his fewer hemispheric connections or his social programming matters less than the practical. Many volumes have been written about the relative contribution of biology and social-political-economic forces that account for the difference between men and women. Very valid points about what can and can't be changed, but these discussions are lengthy, academic, philosophical and in the long run of no practical use to men and women trying to operate a *modus vivandi* with one another.

Since this was a universal problem for women it seems that it is women that have to embark on a long-term re-education programme, called

'Improving his Emotional Quotient!'

It simply means showing by example the range of emotional shadings that go with our limited words. It means discussing people and events in terms of the emotions they evoke, how emotions can be conflicting, co-existing, repressed or magnified, sometimes inexpressible and hard to identify. Of course it means knowing how to match a physiological state with an emotional state yourself. One of the problems with teaching is evaluation, how do you know when the student has learnt the lesson? Even if there is an exam there may be other benefits from the teaching that are not examined. And how can you examine emotions anyway? Good teachers don't get discouraged in the face of lack of motivation of their students. They find a way to make the lesson interesting, of relevance and one that the student will remember. The best teaching practice is the one that involves the students. If they set their own goals instead of passively copying the teacher's example they understand at a deeper level and change their conceptual thinking.

So, since the emotions men find hardest to talk about are fears, worries, imagined inadequacies, needs for closeness and intimacy, these are the ones that must be taught. All learning needs a reward whether it's a mule or a man who is the learner. And the best reward is one that allows a learner to learn for its own sake. Such intrinsic motivation develops creative learners who may one day surpass their teachers. The intrinsic reward which will keep your man motivated to learn more about emotional expression is, the reduction of unpleasantly high arousal. It's like the relief of the endorphins kicking in after prolonged stress. But recognize that for some men it's as hard work as chopping wood. Unused emotional muscles have to be built up just like physical muscles. Look on it as a challenge. After all, the best teachers get bored with willing students, and devise ways of getting complex information to a confused mind they know would not pick it up by themselves.

A simple linking of emotional concepts in a non-threatening way, as a daily lesson, is the start. Talk about other people's emotions first, fictional characters, the neighbours . . . discuss how they solve emotional dilemmas, ask about other solutions they might have adopted more profitably, get him to imagine what other men might have felt in current newspaper accounts of death, divorce, accident, bankruptcy and so on. And don't do it at a predictable time so that he comes to recognize 'Emotional re-education lesson; day 10'! It's a life-long continuing process that needs patience, tact and all the womanly skills you are capable of.

Start with simple feelings:

> Something happened to x, that made them feel happy,
> sad, frustrated, confident, despairing;

add consequences:

> Something happened to me a long time ago that made me
> feel x, now I think it influenced me to do y;

then work up to mixed feelings:

> Something happened that made me, x or anyone furious
> and yet I understood . . . or . . . I was glad for them and
> envious at the same time . . . my admiration was mixed
> with a tinge of irritation that they had done it this way.

Distinguish between actions and motivations (did they mean to do it, do they have a different framework, can I judge them from my reaction). Spell out the benefits of talking about emotions (reduced stress, shared understanding, feeling needed, lack of ambiguity, more likely to get their needs met). Underline that we all run the gamut from saintly altruism to murderous revenge; feelings are all legitimate, they tell you something, even if you can't act on all of them.

The corollary of course is an instrumental re-education programme for women. The sense of achievement at unjamming the vacuum cleaner roller yourself after the repair shop told you 'it's going to be a big job lady', is incomparable – except perhaps for figuring out the circuit wiring diagram and tracing the blown fuse minutes before the guests arrive for the important dinner party. This feeling of competence is one many women never experience – and it's only a matter of paying attention to what the plumber, electrician and mechanic does. Of course you won't reach the proficiency standard of these professionals but you can grasp the ground principles of piping and drainage, power and mechanical action so that you can follow a reasoned explanation of what has gone wrong and even attempt simple repairs – just as he can for the relationship:

> I never thought I could be so proud of myself, said Thelma, as when I fixed the washing machine when my husband was away on business. It had emptied all over the floor before he'd left and he'd fixed it saying you won't have anymore trouble with that! So the day after he left and it flooded the kitchen floor again I felt helpless, cross and abandoned. I phoned my sister who is more practical than me and after a pep talk replaced the outlet pipe which my husband had jammed into the inflow pipe, blocking it because he was in a hurry. He was more impressed with me fixing that than the winning recipe I sent into *Women* magazine, which won a free meal in a classy London restaurant!

You could even swap lessons in emotional intimacy for lessons in logic of machinery. Or change your view of each other through studying your characteristic communication styles.

8

Coping strategies

The best evolved organism is the one most independent of its environment. An animal that can fend for itself, in the face of heat, cold and all attackers is more highly evolved than a plant which can be trodden on, flooded out or scorched by the sun. Similarly in humans, the establishment of independence is the goal of growth and development of a child to a fully functioning and psychologically mature adult. Because men and women grow up with different experiences they become proficient at particular and differing tasks. These are loosely labelled Instrumental and Expressive.

The strong, silent male is the epitome of the instrumental character, and other words that most people put under the heading of 'typical male' are: competitive, analytical, aggressive, ambitious, assertive, athletic, defends own beliefs, dominant, forceful, independent, individualistic, having leadership abilities, making decisions easily, self-reliant, self-sufficient, willing to take a stand, willing to take risks, living according to one's own beliefs, feelings, values and morals, i.e. not dancing to anyone else's tune.

Expressive words that are thought to be representative of a 'typical woman' are: yielding, understanding, gentle, loyal, soft-spoken, warm, eager to soothe hurt feelings, shy, sympathetic, sensitive to the needs of others, affectionate, compassionate, not a user of harsh language, flatterable, cheerful, tender, loves children, i.e. having enough empathy to understand others' reactions.

These are sexual stereotypes, to which every man and every

woman is exposed in our culture (some more than others of course, but no one escapes). Even the most adamant non-sexist parents have to let their children go to school, where sex-typing is strongly maintained by the children themselves, if not their teachers.

Thus in many senses Jung's rather mystical explanation of unconscious animus buried in a woman and the anima in a man can be reworded in terms of childhood conditioning of girls and boys. Women suppress 'male' traits of aggressiveness, assertiveness, tough-mindedness, logicality, independence, emotional control, leadership and so on.

And men take care not to seem emotional, passive, gentle, disorganized, too sympathetic, too polite, hysterical, incompetent or yielding. The more masculine or feminine one believes oneself to be, the more the 'wrong' traits are shunned with horror. This was evident in questionnaires couples completed about personality traits they thought would belong to a man or a woman respectively. When completing questionnaires on other subjects the women who had accepted all the feminine traits as part of their personality rated themselves as *not* toughminded, assertive, or non-conforming. And the men who had enthusiastically claimed the male traits as their own, said NO, NO, NO, to any questions about behaviour that implied emotionality, indecisiveness or irrationality. And yet in an average crop of situations in life that must be dealt with we need assertiveness as much as empathy.

How sex roles are created

Psychologists don't agree on very much but most will accept that the criteria for psychological maturity involves four elements. These are:

1. Self-esteem – the feeling that one can cope with life events, a confidence that generalizes into the future.
2. Autonomy – the ability to act independently according to one's own beliefs, feelings, values and morals.
3. Accurate perception of self and others – the empathy necessary to understand other's reactions and to be able to reflect on and identify one's own feelings.
4. A capacity for intimacy – this is implied by the former condition, but adds ability to give and take, not being too selfish to fit in with others, to be able to talk to them and exchange hopes, fears, desires and problems, and get them to want to talk reciprocally.

The sad fact for opposite-sex relationships is that boys and girls are biased towards only half of this ideal personality. Little boys learn that rough and tumble play is OK, especially if he gets the better of the namby-pamby next door. Even getting filthy in football is OK, particularly if he is on the winning side. Exploring away from home is OK, and even better if he comes back regaling exciting adventures and stories about how he got the others out of some fraught situation. In short, boys learn mastery.

Girls learn almost the opposite; she learns that enjoying active games gets her a masculine label – a tomboy. She learns that adults smile approvingly at her when she is clean and pretty and pressed. She learns that danger lurks outside the home for her so that she is encouraged to bring her friends home instead and that others will look after her. In short, passivity and helplessness are the lessons in life for girls.

Dolls and guns are old-hat stereotypes now, but the essence is still valid. Girls are encouraged to develop social skills (dolls stand for people) while boys are encouraged to master objects. In later life women can work out problems to do with weights and measures only if it is put into the context of cooking, while men will attempt the same problem if it's to do with mechanics. This is how women come to be the emotional 'experts' and why the job of keeping the relationship together falls on them. Men's role is still a variant of the old defence role – he is still seen as the provider, and a complex network of social and economic forces supports this function – even though only 15 per cent of households have a full time wife and mother, who is financially dependant on her husband.

How society does the job of biology

Men and women have been shaped up for their roles over a lifetime. Looking back at the elements of the mature or optimum personality, it becomes clear that the first two – self-esteem and autonomy – are heavily reinforced in men. Winning, of course, enhances self-esteem, but even for the also-rans, exploring life's opportunities (away from home) gives a perspective on life that helps the boy gain confidence in his ability to cope in the future. It also encourages independence and autonomy. But boys do not have the same pressure as girls to develop intimacy skills. In fact, constant activity pretty well precludes it, as well as self-reflection. You can't wonder about the meaning of vague sensations inside you or whether mother's silence meant anxiety or disapproval while you're pelting down a 1 in 10 grade in your go-kart at 50 miles an hour!

The kind of people that men want to be differs from the kind of people that women want to be, and this research was done over several cultures. Men thought it would be great to be practical, shrewd, assertive, dominant, competitive, critical and self-controlled. Women described their state of perfection as loving, affectionate, impulsive, sympathetic and generous. Women wanted interesting experiences from life and to be of service to society; men wanted power, prestige, profit, freedom and independence.

During development and under stress the 'masculine' mode of maturity that is, confidence and autonomy can breakdown into bravado and rebellion. The 'feminine' style of maturity degenerates into an excessive need for social approval and hypocrisy, and these low-level attributes of maturity are the emotional basis of the coping strategies.

So each sex grows up to be the complement of the other. If one man and one woman were rolled up together – as some of the ancient Greeks thought they were originally, and we all went round searching for our lost half – then one man and one woman would make one mature fully-functioning individual.

But ideal people only exist in ideal worlds, and the interdependence of the marital roles which were designed by evolution and emphasized by society have got out-of-sync with changes in our way of living. Men and women are separate beings and neither can live life's tasks or solve life's problems through the other. The consequence of this biased development of maturity is a deficiency peculiar to each sex. Women shrink from achievement and men find it hard to talk about loving emotions. It takes an equal amount of courage for a woman to say 'No' to anything as it does for a man to say 'I need you'. And the harder it is the more likely it is that this couple will end up as the most common problem in marital therapy, the overcontrolled man and the overexpressive woman.

Not being able to consider multiple alternatives and come to rational decisions according to the demands of the situation handicaps growth to emotional and social maturity. To adapt to social conditioning without questioning whether all men should be competitive and all women emotional prevents each individual realizing their real limitations, abilities and potentials and using this knowledge in trying to transcend the constraints of society. There are people who can accept and overcome with good humour many of the misconceptions and imperfections which they experience in everyday life. They are also the people who can fight vigorously against social injustice, child labour, political torture, cruelty to animals, corruption and hypocrisy, things often beyond the normal conception of legal morality. But these are our exceptional figureheads of humanity.

There are several kinds of maturity each individual must go through from the egocentric to the prosocial. Most of us get past the midway level – the conformists with an eye-for-an-eye mentality, to the stage where we can perceive, understand and tolerate ambiguities, in ourselves and in others. A test often quoted in the psychological world is that of the football supporter who is not unduly upset if his team plays well, but is beaten by a better team.

But very few of us reach the fully social and emotional maturity of both a deep understanding of others as well as an empathy and sensitivity for them, not permanently anyway. A prerequisite is the understanding and empathy towards a significant life partner. Responding to another in this intimate way unleashes new areas of brain functioning – which enlarges social consciousness still more.

Any stress will close down this enhanced functioning and the individual will regress to earlier stages of maturity which matched that level of emotional upset. Maturity isn't a permanent frame of mind, except perhaps for meditators on Tibetan mountains. Remember in Chapter 3, the evidence was that life partners are attracted most powerfully to each other when they have similar levels of maturity, self-esteem and happiness. Packaged with each level of maturity is a healthy version of the defence mechanisms of the last chapters, the defences against anxiety. But now they are coping strategies, and still used to cope with anxiety – but in a less self-repressing way. They range from avoidance to confrontation and cooperation. The higher the level of maturity the more likely the coping strategy is to be cooperative, and the lower it was the more likely each was attracted to what was missing in them that they feel the other could supply. We all to some extent try to compensate for our faults by choosing someone who exhibits strengths in that area. That is what we admire and notice first.

Maturity solves the 'do birds of a feather flock together or do opposite attract?' question. When a person is at the higher levels of maturity he or she is attracted to a similar other. Couples where one or both is at a lower level of maturity will often choose others who have complementary or opposite traits. And because we are consistently shaped towards masculine and feminine behaviour and the inhibition of the customary opposite sex behaviour there is an almost magnetic attraction to these opposite traits, perhaps more important to compatibility than physical attraction. It is more lasting and provides the launching pad to maturity.

There are myriads of cues to whether a person takes a masculine stance to the world or a feminine one, and we can all read these cues, although we probably do so fast enough not to be aware of it. Years ago research showed cues like body posture and gesture, eye and facial movements, speech and meta-speech, all differ, according to whether it is a man or a woman. And there are women who exhibit masculine body language and men who use feminine. More recently a fascinating study got people to rate themselves on masculinity and femininity and then videotaped them in various activities. Then they got experienced judges and asked them to watch the videos and judge the level of masculinity and femininity or androgyny (an even mixture of male and female). Although the judges used different cues – some made their judgement on voice, others on body-language for example – they were nevertheless amazingly accurate. Somehow what we think of ourselves, whether dominant, passive, gentle, logical, assertive, compassionate, emotional, reserved, sensitive and so on, is expressed in our body language and verbal language. And of course the implication is that all aspects of our personality can be conveyed the same way, most certainly through the emotions. This is the subject of a later chapter – interpreting emotion that a partner finds hard to express verbally.

The fundamental attraction between couples is the repressed opposite sex traits each intuit in the other and all sorts of mixes are possible. The right mix of complementary qualities is essential to long-term happiness and balanced coping strategies. When couples are asked what mixture of male and femaleness they feel themselves and their partners to be, the happier ones will place themselves in the same relationship on their own scale as they put their partners on the opposite scale. In other words, wives who thought they were about 75 per cent feminine thought their husbands were about 75 per cent masculine, and those who decided they were 15 per cent feminine thought their husbands were also 15 per cent masculine. Opposite sex relationships thrive when male and female elements stimulate and nourish each other. Problems occur when both husband and wife are somewhere on the masculine dimension so that there's not enough femininity between them, and vice-versa.

When divorced people did the same exercise the results were quite unbalanced and anomalous. Women believed they were more masculine than their ex-husbands and some men thought they were more feminine than their ex-wives. It seems as if the gap between masculine and feminine was so insuperable that there was no bridge to equilibrium. Each felt the other was usurping their roles. It does suggest the marriage broke down because it felt out-of-balance, and the compelling coping strategies of masculinity and femininity were unable to be harnessed.

The perception of masculinity and femininity is really a judgement of future coping strategies in the face of conflict, insecurity, anxiety and crisis. After all we choose a helpmate to face life's problems with, and one of those problems is becoming a well-rounded personality. Somewhere inside us lie buried the opposite sex traits that have been held down since babyhood and yet are such an integral part of our personality. These traits are continually making themselves felt, in cycles of conspicuousness and regression. Men want to be more expressive and women to be more assertive but just can't bring themselves to do it. It goes against a lifetime's reinforcement, so the next best thing is to have a close ally that will do it for us.

Many other traits go along with assertiveness and emotionality and each individual has a particular hold or emphasis on a whole constellation of masculine or feminine traits according to their particular experience. Each person recognizes unconsciously the particular blend of opposite traits they have undeveloped in themselves and which they need for psychological growth, but which they can't develop in themselves for fear of seeming too feminine (if a man) or too masculine (if a woman). When people with these opposite sex linked traits live together in secure attachment and open communication what they learn from each other helps them to become something they couldn't have done by themselves.

Division of labour in coping strategies

Women tend to the feminine constellation of coping strategies, which can be roughly summed up under the heading of 'sensitizing'. These are the confronters. Men mostly used the masculine typed strategies which can be summed up as 'repressing', these are the avoiders. The two words give you an idea of the strategies and in happy relationships a sensitizer balances a repressor. There are very few powers on earth that can match the combined forces of a repressor and a sensitizer standing together to cope with some adversity. They literally have the situation covered.

This is how it works: the sensitizer copes with anxiety by excessive activity – talking about it, phoning others, going out to see others who have faced this problem, imagining a whole scenario of 'what ifs'; an imaginative rehearsal to cope with the reality, when it occurs. Every conceivable response will have been considered, pored over and tucked away for future reference. Because of their emotional responsiveness they are seen as enthusiastic, dynamic leaders. Everything is done quickly and urgently. Any other solution seems lazy, passive and lethargic. The high energy and activity level helps to keep the anxiety at bay while the situation is being resolved. *Immediate* action is the password and they will rush in where repressors fear to tread.

For every sensitizer in a happy relationship there is a repressor who provides the contrary and stabilizing balance. His immediate response to anxiety is to block it from conscious thought by intellectual processes. Piece by piece, detailed information about emotional events is stored in the memory and slowly dissected for logical analysis. As each fragment is emotionally defused and rendered harmless, additional details are sought for further examination and organization. These facts serve as an aid to erecting an emotional barrier. Repressors offer these minutiae of emotional events as an explanation, it is a description of their feelings, divorced from the anxiety that precipitated it. Repressors are attracted to sensitizers with the excitement and spirit they bring. The sensitizers on the other hand, feel the repressors will keep them on an even keel, stop them flying over the moon and letting anxiety disintegrate them.

Repressors have difficulty mastering emotionally-charged issues, and, because of their fears of emotional arousal, are seldom able to integrate emotions and intellect and reach the heights of emotional maturity. Under stress, they tend to withdraw, become detached and demotivated in situations requiring an immediate emotional response. Self-deceptive logic and intellectualization is the danger and being caught by surprise leaves a gap that only the spontaneity of the sensitizer can jump into and cover.

Interestingly, there is a difference in endorphin levels between sensitizers and repressors which suggests that differences in social contact and intimacy affect coping strategies.

The machinery of repression
and sensitization

It was discovered after people had strokes, epilepsy or injury to one or other of the hemispheres of the brain that there were two ways of knowing. In fact, the basis of different types of knowledge has been debated by philosophers for hundreds of years:

ying	–	yang
unconscious	–	conscious
intuition	–	reason
emotion	–	intellect
wholistic	–	sequential
faith	–	logic

These and many other opposites have become embedded in our culture and language, illustrating that even the ancients suspected there were two ways to process information. These two different modes of perception have been accepted for years, and now new evidence shows that parts of the two hemispheres play different roles in our emotions and moods. This emotional division of labour means that the frontal lobe of the left hemisphere handles the positive emotions, while the frontal lobe of the right hemisphere underlies depressive, even aggressive feelings and behaviour. There is a reciprocal interchange between the two, and disturbances in that switchover give rise to disturbances in mood.

For example, injury in the left hemisphere leaves patients moody, pessimistic and depressed because the left hemisphere can't then maintain the control it once had over the right hemisphere functioning, and, conversely, injury to the right leaves the left hemisphere free to put the person into a manic euphoric state. There have been cases of right hemisphere damaged people having tried to walk on air from the fourth storey hospital window!

But there is more to it. The main division of the brain may be more than just a right-left one. There is a frontal lobe and a back one, each specializing in different functions and a top-bottom division between the hemispheres and the older part of the brain below the cortical hemispheres. When all these links are hooked up, the left hemisphere is the guardian of emotional states tinged with alert expectation, the vigilance of the sensitizer scanning the horizon for danger. The right links are more involved in reflective emotional states, both relaxed awareness and negative states such as depression. This is the withdrawal of the repressor to mull over emotional experience. A very tricky question now arises. Does the emotional restraint and avoidance of the average male come from the right hemisphere link-ups or from his social conditioning? And the emotional impulsiveness and confrontation of many women from the left hemisphere or the prescription for female behaviour?

There is one more piece to this jig-saw. Women tend to be left-hemisphere dominant more often than men, which is why girls are earlier and better speakers than the average boy. Men have the edge on right hemisphere skills, which is how most of them come to be better at mechanics, engineering, architecture or anything that needs seeing where shapes fit (this is called spatial perception, and it refers to the relationship things have to each other). The right hemisphere controls non-verbal activity, which fits with the chewing over of emotional data and fitting it piece by piece together method of the avoider, while the instant talking of the sensitizer is allied to the left hemisphere.

The further finding that women have larger bundles of connections between the two hemispheres means that women can match emotions with words more easily, while things of emotional significance that enter the right brain in men (this was done in an experiment) just stay there fermenting!

But, strong though the physiological case looks for brain suppression of a man's emotions, it's worth considering what we know about culture and the way it can influence brain development. Some research suggests that stress and the hormones it releases in pregnancy slow down the development of the left hemisphere of the foetus. Testosterone, a male hormone which the male foetus itself releases, inhibits the growth of the left even more. Activities like sports and active play develop spatial and right hemisphere attributes, as reading and speaking promote the left.

People whose faces respond expressively have lower levels of physiological arousal when measured than people who have non-expressive faces. This signifies suppressed emotion in the people who have the non-expressive faces. This corresponds to the repressing or internalizing of emotion by men, and the sensitizing or externalizing of emotion by women – who have lower physiological arousal, lower rates of heart disease and stress-related medical conditions. Socializing a boy to ignore emotions is thought by some to contribute to their higher rate of stress.

There is much evidence that points to more men being right-hemisphere dominant than women and that the higher rate of disorders that boys suffer in any left hemisphere task – stuttering, dyslexia, learning difficulties, autism, verbal fluency – and the inability, when he grows up, to say 'I love you'!

The bottom line is that for whatever reason, nature or nurture, brain differences between the sexes alter their responses to stress. How we cope with stress is an important part of compatibility, and we are attracted in a complementary fashion. Male rationality and female sensitizing are both valid enough responses in the face of incomplete knowledge about the situation, but when you can't react in the opposite way – even when it's appropriate – you are handicapped. And it is our upbringing as a boy or a girl that decides the power of this handicap. And worse, there are destructive components; when the stress level is raised so the behaviour is extreme, and when conflict from the previous cycles leaves unresolved residues of resentment, the coping strategies of the couple are turned against each other instead of being used jointly, to cope with stress from outside.

The confrontational strategies are the style of the emotionally expressive. The anxiety of the situation precipitates them into cycles of energy, restlessness and activity. This makes the avoiders look lethargic, lazy, boring and detached to the confronters. To the avoiders, however, the conspicuous activity and ceaseless talk of the confronter, which once seemed to signify a person who would never run out of steam, now looks like panic, childish impulsivity and uncontrolled emotion. This is the cue for the automatic withdrawal of the avoider to underneath the ramparts, putting up fingers to the wind to test for emotional blowover before he emerges. Increasingly frustrated by the avoider's restraint and non-availability, the confronter escalates.

Under the general headings of avoidance and confrontational strategies are related styles (see Table 8.1, p.204), which all tend to hang together, but not inevitably so. The confronter will tend to be impulsive, undercontrolled, idealistic, active, disorganized and externalizing under stress. But due to particular family and upbringing circumstances might be less idealistic and more organized than the table suggests. It is possible to have a sensitizer who is highly controlled or aware enough of the limitations of reality to be careful and factual, even controlled in their coping strategies.

Or the avoider might tend towards stability, internalization, restraint and overcontrol but still be disorganized under stress – their usual preciseness and organization falling apart, sleeping late, eating unpredictably, staying undressed, going out unkempt or unshaven. In whatever balance these seven coping strategies are matched, they each cycle within an individual from extreme to normal, according to whatever else is going on in their lives at the time. At the normal point of the cycle the individual matches their partner's normality point to create a couple cycle of adaptive and harmonious coping mechanisms with which to face everyday life. At this point they would each like to be more like the other's normality point. For example, the realistic person would like to be more spontaneous, or the disorganized one more disciplined. As they use each other to achieve this, they can become more like their ideal, but, under stress, these opposite qualities become irritating as they move out of the harmonious couple cycle and into the extremes of behaviour, emotions and reactions.

They each believe the other is being deliberately antagonizing, but the truth is that each is compelled to play out their scene once the 'programme' has been activated by the stressor. Coping strategies learnt under stress have the same compulsive quality as any other addiction – they act blindly, half-aware that they will feel better when the programme has been run through and 'filed for storage' and the intense feelings dissipated.

When the vigilance scanner of the brain goes into its 'stop, look and listen, something I didn't expect is happening' mode, the rest of the brain is wholly taken over by the primitive self-preservation programme that has kept individuals surviving from tree-clambering days. It's a total focusing on self, what this new information means for emotional and physical survival. This can lead to abnormal selfishness. The person in 'stop, look and listen' mode is literally paralysed with fear and unable to see anyone else's point of view at all. The automatic response is 'what about me', as they fall back on their coping strategies, grimly sorting every paper clip into graded lengths (the avoiders' coping strategy) or bicycling down the middle of the motorway at night, with no lights, while the cause of the stress is left unattended (the confronter). Whatever the conflict started over, the telephone bill, the unexplained dent in the car, the disappearance of the last bottle of wine, now turns into a personal attack. *You* talk too much, drive too carelessly, drink too much and so on. Whether your relationship is going to be a loving one or a fighting one depends on the response the one on the receiving end of the criticism makes. Conflict, once into the self-defence mode, must be de-escalated and the response to the personalizing of the conflict must deactivate the rising tension. This means conciliating, negotiating, talking (not shouting), explaining, justifying, withdrawing temporarily, using humour – anything that

Table 8.1   Coping Strategies

extreme (under stress)	*Avoidance norm*	*Confrontational norm*	*extreme* (under stress)
HATE			FEAR
1. emotional withdrawal	emotional restraint, meticulousness, orderliness	impulsive spontaneity, creativity	hysteria recklessness irrationality
2. obsession paranoia	overcontrol of self, needs to control others to feel they matter, but avoids being controlled by others; associated with curtailment of freedom;	undercontrol of self, ambivalent about controlling others, associated with care and responsibility;	disorientated
	needs to lose a bit of control	needs to develop more control	
3. compulsive, righteous indignation	realistic, objective	Idealistic, subjective	fantasy, illusions, denial of reality, escapism, dreamer, wild grandiose plans
4. obstinate	stable		
5. resistant	watches and waits, the 'audience'	active, get up and go, the 'show'	manipulates, inconsistent, exhibitionist
6. defensive, rigid, more organized, pettiness, machinelike	organized	disorganized	disorientated, unable to cope with daily routine
7. introspective, shut off, feels guilty, withdrawn	internalizes emotion, quiet, complies with rules of social convention, self-conscious, wants someone to provide emotional support without having to ask	externalizes emotion, self-confident	blaming others, psychosomatic symptoms, tends towards aggression, uninhibited, audacious, needs someone to admire their performance

avoids more anger and potential explosion. There are many good books on techniques for reducing conflict, but more important than leafing through them on the brink of cataclysmic upheaval, is the motivation to implement these techniques. We all lose our carefully worked out assertive and rational responses under stress and conflict. The single most important thing you can do for your relationship is to control your angry non-verbal behaviour. A quick warm hug of concern and sympathy or a diverting bit of humour, even if you have to grit your teeth to do it, is the immediate first step to wind down enough to use your assertive conflict-reducing techniques. A recent sensible guide is *What to do when he won't change* by Dan Kiley.

A body posture and gesture that communicates understanding and a willingness to negotiate and talk through the problem are *de rigeur*. All important is voice, the tone of which can communicate anything between love and hate. Relaxation techniques based on deep slow breathing relax muscles and vocal chords and help damp down the arousal of both.

Nodding your head positively and attentively while leaning forward and looking your partner directly in the eyes as you explain gently that the dent must have been done in the supermarket car park, helps your credibility and the arousal deactivation of both of you. Refraining from crossing your arms or legs or pacing round agitatedly also helps, as does listening to the full complaint, without interruption. Then, in replying, try to lower your voice, not raise it, as is the normal reaction. The idea is to break the normal links between your emotional state and the outward signs of anger that set the other off before you've even opened your mouth. These are all unconsciously signalled directly to the other's nervous system, which goes on automatic red alert.

This plan of action only works, of course, when both of you have goodwill to each other and want to improve your relationship, or at least stop it deteriorating. When one is determined to get their way in every conflict a book is not going to help, it's either separation, therapy, or giving in, to your eventual detriment.

The brain is monitoring our daily lives all the time, predicting from past experience what should be happening in the future. When there is a mismatch there is a sudden halt to ongoing, creative, new behaviour, geared to the current situation. To scan the horizon for possible happenings over which you have no control releases stress hormones which shut down future options. Whether we magnify or ignore the disturbance there is an arousal of anxiety which has its effects on the body eventually. It is considered that 25 per cent of visits to the doctor are a direct result of relationship conflict. The constant overarousal of the nervous system is a consequence of a biological programme used to looking for explanations when the expected and the actual are not the same.

When one of the past macrostage conflicts – for example, the commitment or the closeness macrocycle – has not been resolved, a state of anxiety, vigilance and expectancy will continue off and on until resolution. Two people living together so intimately are bound to interrupt each other's ongoing plans and predicted regularities anyway – but adapting to minor, daily changes is only a matter of good communication. But when the interruption of important life plans and relationship stages is seen as uncontrollable, resentment, frustration, hostility and depression are the by-product. Anxiety and uncertainty simmer away underground, ready to come to boiling point and overspill at the slightest rise of temperature.

The questions being silently asked relate to the unresolved conflict from the previous long-term cycles, even if the spoken questions are about daily short-term explanations – like making love, talking about a particular subject, or anything that needs the other for completion. The long-term plans that need the other for completion are universally conflictual, just because of the differing biological and socialized natures of men and women. But we mostly address long-term cycle conflict at short-term cycle level, which is why our major malcontents are neither understood nor resolved.

When long-term cycles are resolved satisfactorily, short-term interaction goes smoothly. There is what is known as 'behavioural meshing'. Each knows what to expect and how to reciprocate it, how to fit in with the other's expectations and communicate their own. Interaction goes so easily they don't feel it's an effort – as many social encounters are. It is impossible to live with someone without some interruption of plans and behaviour, so the value of similar expectations in both long- and short-term cycles is the nervous energy saved in prolonged conflict resolution.

When things aren't going well there is a physiological reflection, or linking of one nervous system to the other. Fear and anxiety are communicated at a subliminal level. The unpleasant high arousal of the nervous system of the partner whose plans are interrupted sets off the same unpleasant arousal in the other. Usually neither is aware of this. They experience only a vague tension and upset but they can't locate the cause. As the cycles of painful activation escalate and swamp the natural return to baseline deactivation cycles, they set off the learnt coping strategies which get played and replayed, whether they are appropriate or not. And, unlike tapes, they *never* wear out.

Margaret, a mature student, explained:

> Everytime I came back from the library with all my books and papers and plastic bags I would dump them down in the hall and go into the kitchen for a cup of tea, intending to put them away later. Then as I sat drinking tea and musing over how to start my essay, Dan would come in. Grim-lipped, he'd start putting things away in cupboards, sweeping up, washing non-existent gunge off bottles. It drove me crazy, when I wanted to relax, so I'd turn up the radio trying not to hear the crockery and saucepans being washed, rewashed and categorized. And Dan muttering the same words about the pig-sty we lived in.

On the short-term level the conflict was about organization, with Marg's lack of it setting off Dan's excess of it. There were also long-term conflicts. How strong was Marg's commitment? Dan worried that once Marg got her degree, a car-part specialist like himself might not be good enough any more. He didn't really understand why she was studying anyway. His stand over the kitchen was a reaction to what was dumped in the hall. Marg described the high point of their struggle which fortunately they can both laugh about now:

> I had put off and put off my third year assignment write-up which accounts for 25 per cent of the marks. So this weekend I had to do it, the deadline was 2pm Monday. I did and hardly stopped to eat. On Monday evening I arrived home to find a lock on the kitchen door and Dan announcing he was taking over and I was only to be allowed in to make a cup of tea so long as I cleaned up straight away afterwards. The menus were all set for the week's meals with the ingredients out in little piles!

Dan was concerned with the long-term cycle of commitment falling apart, so he set about making sure all the small cycle stayed together. 'That moment was critical. If I hadn't laughed and had reacted in anger I think Dan would have attacked me,' Margaret recalled. 'But I could still just see the funny side of it, as if we were one of those sit-com television programmes. So I said, "Well you've made your point, so don't let's go on being silly," and he agreed ruefully. I know now when something is worrying him because he goes around tidying up. When I see all the flour, sugar, tea and coffee tins in a perfect row I go straight to him and ask him what's up. He thinks I have some magic intuition, I've never told him how I know!'

So Marg and Dan manage now to help each other deactivate their high arousal levels sufficiently to stop using their coping strategies against each other, destructively. There are personality differences in the trigger point for automatic coping strategies. Those who suffer more anxiety in normal circumstances are, a surprising recent finding, men. Men's happiness in relationships can be predicted by a much more simple equation than women's. It's the old one of rate of sex minus rate of quarrelling!

This is a tongue-in-cheek way of describing male nervous system patterns and of course there are beliefs, talents, thoughts, goals and meaning in a man's life that alter his emotional responsiveness. But underneath these complexities lie a greater responsiveness to both sexual activity and quarrelling. A higher emotional arousal does not mean the same thing as closer emotional bonding. In fact, it may preclude it. The closer and more intimate a couple are the greater the emotional effect on each other. So for those, and it appears to be more men, who have a tendency to quicker and higher unpleasant emotional arousal, intimate bonds are an ever-present destabilizer of the nervous system. Put that with the cultural prescription for male control and cool emotion, and you put a man into quite a double bind. Be close, be cool and ignore your consequent arousal!

So he is repressing, defending, trying not to show emotion while she is magnifying hers. This makes her seem like the overemotional one, swamping the reasonable cool of the rational male. So her demands are easy to dismiss as female hysteria. The answer to the automatic shoot-out of coping strategies is to each develop in themselves what attracted them to each other in the first place.

Rather than each becoming an emotional specialist and an instrument specialist it makes for a more balanced relationship to each be able to choose the best quality as the situation dictates. It is these traits that feed into the confrontational (emotional/feminine) and the avoiding (instrumental/masculine) coping strategies. If each by watching the other can move towards the centre, at the same rate, the major male/female conflict can be avoided. Instead of turning against each other they can harness up together and face life's problems in tandem and with extra strength.

This means thinking of each other's coping strategies as valuable tools to borrow. Instead of pushing restraint into withdrawal, control into obsession, impulsivity into hysteria, activity into manipulation, and so on, draw up a new table of coping strategies and recognize the value of each. Try swapping coping strategies one by one, for a week or so at a time, just to practise them. Then give them back with an embellishment from the opposite strategy!

Table 8.2

Repressors need sensitizers to:	Sensitizers need repressors to:
• generate new possibilities, solutions, ideas	• keep track of the essential facts and details
• foresee any coming problems	• read the fine print and bottom line
• show enthusiasm and initiative	• supply patience and stand firm
• go beyond the information given	• consider the actual evidence
• imagine, conciliate, persuade, and empathize with others in the situation	• analyse, organize, observe
• advertise, sell, perform, display	• produce, fix, reform, save
• look to the future	• pay attention to the here and now
• appreciate and inspire	• concentrate, find faults
• create ingenious adaptations	• maintain stability and routine
• take risks	• calculate risks, keep feet on the ground

As a summary-label, the sensitizer could be called radical and all for cathartic change as a solution to any problem, while the repressor favours conservative stability and security. They both have their advantages in any situation.

9

Life paths

It is not often that a scientific observer breaks down into tears over their fieldwork, but Sarah Hardy does so when she describes the horrifying moment she realized that females can threaten, starve, and abuse each other. She was watching an infant monkey being literally pulled to death by a struggle between an invading dominant male and two females.

A common picture in biology books is the males slogging it out in a competition to get the female. No one notices that the girls aren't sitting round a cosy campfire, swapping recipes and knitting up yoghurt pots. They're in there, mixing it up, making sure they get a better deal than the next woman – and the result is total confusion among all parties.

Female primates who are in heat, advertise that their fertility is up for grabs to the best males of the species. But other females can also read this message, and if several are in heat at the same time there is a competition for the genetically superior male. This is the one that can beat off all the other males and provide protection and food for the females. If the food and shelter necessary for bringing up baby are limited, the dominant female will take exception to other females giving birth at the same time as her, since her own babies' chances of survival might be limited. So, she will harass females on heat, which stops them ovulating. Ethologists have often noticed how a new male, on overpowering the dominant male, will take over his harem and kill the infants too. Whereupon the bereaved mother will quickly come into heat again and conceive a new pregnancy with the new dominant male. Where is the female solidarity? The girls' club could combine their wiles and overpower the infanticidal male – but they don't. Not only that, some females invite the bachelor male bands around to coffee.

Human females also have to compete. Women marry to avoid problems; it provides protection from other forms of exploitation. But it is *not* biology, it's a social and political situation justified by dubious recourse to biological principles. Resources in our society are plentiful, none of us wants a huge brood of children, but our social system still ensures competition among women by paying and promoting men more.

The usual answer to the question 'Why aren't there more women presidents/tycoons/airline pilots/directors?' is male discrimination. And that is certainly part of it. But the whole answer has to include female discrimination against other females too. While men have no option but to choose a job and stick at it, trying to advance if they can, women are still brought up with the idea that their real life's work will be their family. Except today they are expected to have a nice little career on the side as well! But, because women are still trained to admire and depend on men who exercise power, they believe themselves unable to control their own or other's destinies. The admiration of power has many unfortunate consequences – some authorities even use it to explain the high frequency of incest from father to daughter, the inability of many women to leave violent marriages, and the many other negative things that women allow men to do to them.

The high flyers

There are women who put everything into their jobs. The oldest of these will be members of the post-war baby bulge who, after working twenty five years, will be in middle management, while men of their age and experience will tend to be in top management. These women are now wondering if the dedication to the job was worth it. The high flyers are also jealously guarding their position from younger, better qualified women coming up through the ranks. Unlike the men who have put twenty-five years into a job, they will usually not be senior enough *not* to have to worry about competition. When work identity is shaky, it's easy for a career woman to blame herself for not finding her self-worth through traditional female avenues.

The low flyers

Then there is the woman for whom the idea of a family being a woman's mainstay and major fulfilment still operates in the background. Of course she will train for a job, but it is seen as expendable when family commitments arise. So she will take the mundane path, never trying for the higher levels. After all, it's just for now, and just for money. But the low flyers are threatened by the high flyers, who are rising too far above them. They prefer strong, male leaders in control of their companies, and will sometimes do a bit of sly wing-clipping.

The battle for attention

All this is spelt out in grisly detail in *The Uncivil War* which details the way that women with differing lifeplans lower the credibility of women in general. When you have career-women, full-time working mothers, part-time working mothers, and women who work unambitiously with the plan of marrying and not working at all, it makes the general category of women-as-workers inconsistent, and therefore risky for promotion and training material. The usual pattern in the 1980s and 1990s has been a full-time working man with a part-time working woman, which will either be genuinely part-time (20 hours per week), or part-time in the sense that she will work a few years, have a few years off to bear and rear children and then go back to work.

Competition between women for money and husbands separates them, and this results in a division of attitudes, between women who are dependent on men and those who are not. Men's lives centre on their jobs and most women's on their families. The dependent, unambitious woman who doesn't want to fend for herself must devote much of her attention to her man, while the independent career women hasn't the time to do so. In consequence, the career-woman may suffer a backlash, an ultimatum to cut down on work, or else divorce.

In the middle of the attention battleground are those women who balance their lives between total dependence on a man and independence of the career women. These women often give inconsistent attention to their men, and expect more help with the housework and children, which may be given willingly to start with, but goes into reverse when the children start to need attention as well.

Other partners in the dance of attention

There is another player in this game, one who, though off-stage and unnoticed, actually has the greatest influence. This is the one who has different stakes in evolution's game – mother.

It is not only men and women who have different stakes in evolution's game of biological pay-off – the amount of genes an individual can get into the next generation. Mothers are prime movers in this sequence; a son is the answer to her biological prayer. A man has an almost unlimited potential to father offspring. Nature doesn't go in for quality-versus-quantity arguments, and neither do we all want to fulfil our biological capacity; nevertheless, the possibilities generate subtle distinctions in parental treatment of sons and daughters. Sisters are the losers in this competition.

In the race to become male from the Y chromosome to the mature man, much can go wrong; from conception on, males are more likely to die than females. This means that neither their own nor their parents' genes will make it to the next generation. Too many male eggs in one basket means mothers have to place their bets, biologically speaking, both ways. It helps to enlist aid. Survey after survey reveals that girls are required to look after their brothers, and sometimes sacrifice their own education, so the family resources can go into the brothers' education and later career. The recipe for maternal satisfaction appears to be successful sons and married daughters with children, a perfect fit to the genetic survival blueprint.

If girls are trained to manage the domestic and emotional labour of the relationship they will, reasons mother, be able to attract successful men, who will be better able to provide for the grandchildren. Successful men and early-marrying women have the best chance of progeny, goes mother's script. So, in our society, it is mothers who unwittingly contribute to the battle for attention.

Mothers have been shown in many studies to pay more attention to their sons. Part of this may be that male babies are more active to start with (although research is equivocal on this), and therefore unavoidably attract more attention, but it seems that mothers look at and talk more to sons than daughters. Girls are touched more. Sons who have had more of mother's attention grow up believing that other women will pay them more attention too. Dale Spender shows how, in every type of interaction between men and women, the two-thirds rule of attention operates. Whatever the circumstances, boys and men get the two-thirds. It is so pervasive

that if a teacher gives more than one third of her attention to the
girls, everyone, girls and boys, feels it is unfair! If women speak for
more than one third of the conversation, the man will feel he can't
get a word in edgeways.

In the animal world the dominant one is the one that the others
must watch, in order to keep out of his way. The symbols of
dominance in the human world are the amount of space you can
take up, the amount of time you are *not* kept waiting, and many
other freedoms which Nancy Henley convincingly makes a case for
as the prerogatives of men. It seems plausible that the male babies
who get the most attention should monopolize the status symbols
when they grow into men, but many complexities about social,
racial and religious class would tend to obscure any conclusions.

What is not obscure is the reaction wives and girlfriends get when
their partner perceives that her job or hobby or other interest is
taking her attention away from him. Many of my interviewees
mentioned male resentments about lack of attention when children
arrived. Not getting a woman's attention apparently makes a man
feel deficient. According to Herb Goldberg, women have been
coerced into appearing passive and dependent to attract and
manipulate men. The reward for men is affirmation, but when
women are successful they feel more self-confident and competent,
and are less likely to play this game. Some career girls, like Brooke
Shields, have publicly stated that boyfriends require more attention
than they are prepared to give at this stage in their career.

Bebe Campbell describes the reactions of husbands whose
careers took the attention of their wives; they ranged from ignoring
major successes to outright sabotage. Sadder still is her description
of the men who used criticism, anger, rage and violence to
communicate. These men wanted more attention without having
to ask for it, surely a sign of its link to primate behaviour and a
guarantee to the men of their wife's fidelity. Bebe links attention to
male control, and feels that men's fears are connected to a
subconscious belief in the old tale that women are either dependent
and pure or independent and wicked. And that powerful women will
use their strength to a man's detriment. Folklore provides numerous
examples of success and 'come-uppance' for women. In most tales
women are punished if they forge ahead and glory in their
achievements.

Bebe feels that the 'backlash' she observes from husbands is the
result of men having agreed to participate in relationships on an
equal basis in the heady consciousness-raising days of women's

liberation, but now finding they don't like equal nappy-changing and dish-washing, after all. She thinks the backlash phenomenon is a widespread attempt to re-establish male dominance and undermine equality in the home.

In a sense this is true, but the underlying reason must be biological: the old male dilemma of keeping an eye on the woman to make sure it is his offspring she is nurturing while he is away hunting. Women have also been punished more for adultery than men, and the double standard for sex still applies to 98 per cent of men says Shere Hite. Women working away from home for hours and meeting other men raise primitive reactions in even the most civilized of men. He needs her attention to reassure him that he is still the dominant male, and that he has 'seen-off' the competition. When women don't show interest, or try to make a man jealous before he's committed to her, the result is likely to be a rapid cooling off. The possessiveness and jealousy come *after* the uncertainty-to-hope dilemma (see Chapter 1) has been solved.

When women interpret the backlash as a struggle simply over who's doing the washing up, they are likely to leave even more dishes in the sink, literally and metaphorically, putting more energy into their jobs. This increases the tension at home, which increases the amount of time she will spend away to avoid the constant conflict.

Another phenomenon related to the biology of sex-differences is the cautionary tale told in *Jennifer Fever* by Barbara Gordon, an analysis of the 'bimbo' culture. In 25 per cent of marriages, the man is more than 10 years older than the bride, and it is usually his second marriage, not hers; he is then invariably a man of wealth and status greater than his bride. The overriding causative factor is attention; biology would predict that women want love and men admiration, and all the interviews Barbara Gordon reports reveal the worshipping attention that the younger woman gave her senior-status man. Women, Gordon says, are raised to please and men to perform. But life's experience teaches the first wife that pleasing her man means losing control of her life. No matter how perfect a wife and mother she is, her husband can become alcoholic, win a political seat, or the pools, or become an invalid or get promoted or divorced or any number of a thousand things over which she has no control. Nothing much that she does has an effect on the circumstances that control her life – her husband's income and support.

This is the recipe for depression, and by mid-life she has

discovered that feeling better means being more assertive and less attentive, and is on the road to becoming a 'Janet' (a deserted wife). When children leave home, the reaction of some women can be to rush off and sign up for a course on space technology or an expedition to outer Mongolia. The other pole of this reaction is 'What shall I do now', and in the absence of a child to mother, this sort of woman may pay more attention to her husband. One reaction challenges the myth of incompetency, the other reinforces it.

It is not children who put women in a weak position in society – it is the dependent relationship she must make with a man. Of course, this increases as she is bringing up children, but it is not the children that devalue her opportunities. Symbols for motherhood have always been strong, creative and powerful. There is nothing powerless or passive about maternal emotions. On the contrary, these emotions are actually quite frightening to a man, and women that are strong as mothers are made weak as wives in consequence.

There is a real financial dependency, but more inhibiting is the psychological. If, in childhood, you take one set of people and train them up to become passive and uncompetitive, and another set of people to be active and competitive, then it seems pretty inevitable that one set will come to dominate the other set and define them according to the dominant set's needs. Put plainly, this is male domination – the tendency to assign the highest value to roles and skills executed by men, and proclaim that it is the prestigious things that only men can do.

Emotional expression becomes not the quality needed for mothering, but a quality associated with dependency and sexiness. Expressiveness and nurturing characteristics are then downgraded and redefined as sex-related and sexy.

Virgin or whore

The role of mother is given less respect and encouragement than the role of sex-symbol. Compare the attention given to mother of the year versus any week's page 3 girl. How to have a family (which has an emotional value) without losing value and status in the work-world is a real dilemma.

Biology is feeding back the consequences of overpopulation to us, and social organization has superseded the use that large families once were. Before technological society arrived, nobody would amass huge wealth or property, and advantage between people was measured by the amount of kin they had to back them up in disputes or help them when ill. Social institutions, like the legal system, hospitals, and welfare plans perform those functions now, so family isn't of so much value any more particularly in the west.

The experience-seekers versus the empty-nesters

By midlife, a woman's story takes on new complexities, and brings two new realizations. Barbara exemplies one:

> I loved my children and was involved with their lives as much as I could be, but I could see other women do things I didn't have the chance to – things I'd have loved to have tried. I was editor for our newsrag at school, and it galled me when one of my school chums who never had anything ready on time for publication got to be an editor on a Fleet Street paper. Our local paper had it all over the front page and here was I driving the kids to and from school – the only way for me to get on the front page would have been to drive the car through the newspaper office front window!

Barbara has taken a creative writing course at a local college, and intends to finish the novel she has been working on in spare moments over the past twenty years, she hopes to have more time when her last child finally leaves home.

Leonora reacts differently:

> The day there was no one to go home for was the worst in my life. At work, one of the girls was leaving to have a baby, so everyone suggested going to the pub for a farewell drink. I was on the point of saying no, I've got to be back for the kids, when I realized my oldest had left home and my youngest was going out to the icerink with friends and wouldn't be back until 11pm. My husband is never home till 7pm anyway, so I could if I wanted to . . . so I did. But it was a farewell to a life that was so suddenly over. Everything I'd planned for and spent all my energy on was over. The children are fine, no longer need me or want me, and I just can't understand where all those years went; and what now. The best time was when we were close. Even my 16 year old has a girlfriend, and the last thing he wants is a hug from Mum. So it's a long time since I've been putting off the day when I had to sit down and think about getting rid of the children's things. My husband wants to buy a smaller house. I never even thought about life after our happy cosy family grew up, I sort of imagined they would stay like that for years and years with

me at the centre for the rest of my life.

But babies don't stay babies for forty years, and forty years is the average life expectancy between the last child achieving independence and the death of the mother. A lot of time to fill up if you've no plans. Barbara and Leonora illustrate the differing confidence levels in women's lives. While men's self-esteem and confidence stays roughly the same, women's starts lower in the first place, and trails off after 40, further widening the gap between male and female self-esteem.

However, within that depressing trajectory there are the Leonora and Barbara sub-groups. The self-esteem of Leonora's group goes down, while dependency on the marriage goes up. She turns to her husband, who is now usually realizing the futility of unachievable ambition. Barbara is the opposite, as her self-esteem increases with her explorations of the outside world after the children have ceased to take all her energy, her happiness with the marriage depends entirely on her husband's reactions to her new enterprises.

The Leonoras were the happiest in the middle years. They were fulfilling a socially sanctioned ambition – the creation of a harmonious family, from which the individual who would replace them and create a new, perhaps better society would be nurtured and sprung. The Barbaras also put their energies into the family, but kept their fingers in a dozen other pies, keeping their options open for their eventual long-term goals. The pressure of these two decades filled with children, extended family, career start-ups and career-breaks can be enriching and stretching, or it can take its toll in sheer fatigue, failure to meet goals, feelings of impossible pressure and sometimes alcohol or eating problems or escapes. In either case, mid-life brings relaxation, more time to concentrate on fewer goals, and liberation from deadlines. Both types have had a frustrating lack of control over their lives, which is perpetuated in Leonora's case and overcome in Barbara's case. Consequently, the future looks very different to each.

Battle of the sexes

The myth of incompetent women is slowly being pulled apart by women, baby in one hand, screwdriver in the other. But the myth of inexpressive and independent men is still working against men's health and intimacy. Women have three life options:

- To be taken care of by a man and remain dependent, do all the housework, defer to major decisions and be dozens of times more likely to be on the punching end of any dispute;
- To depend on a man for the main support but provide the frills;
- To be independent, have a career and no children unless there was someone at home for them.

Men have one option: to work. A man's life satisfactions depend on his career. If it is an interesting one, or his ability to provide is adequate, he will be happy. Even boring jobs have camaraderie between workmates, the pub after work and football at weekends. (Or the lifelong invention going on in the garage.) But, whatever it is, it is unlikely to depend on his wife's job. Work is so important to a man's sense of worth that when he defines a woman as *not* working (which means anything that is not paid) some generalize that view of worthlessness to women.

By midlife there are two groups of men, differentiated by the degree of attention they can dispense with. There are those who continue on with the macho mask, remarrying women much younger than themselves – anything to paste over the emptiness. And there are those who do a slow change into the 'new man', helped by their wives.

The possibilities, then, are *macho man,* who stays married to a Leonora who doesn't turn into a Janet. And the *new man*, who stays married to a Barbara. (Any Barbara married to a macho man would have divorced long ago – the majority of divorces are initiated by extroverted women who work.) Defensive, hypermasculine men need a safe area of their own, peopled with dependent and obedient children, workers or wives to confirm the myth of their machismo. These are the men who don't make the androgynous switch over. Any expansion in this type of man's wife towards a wider range of interests is a catastrophe – or symbolically, a castration. He wants the respect and attention that he fears are going to go into something else. The myth of invulnerability, of being in charge of everything that affects their lives, is undermined, and revealed as a consoling lie.

The usual goal of dedicated parents is to launch healthy, happy children into the world, but for the Leonoras, this spells the end of their life's meaning. The family story of nurturing, closeness and dependence is blown apart by the children's independence. Leonora-type mothers need the presence of grateful children to justify their belief of maternal good. She may have died for them –

but more than likely she will die without them. One thing these couples will share between them is the level of self-esteem: Leonora's and macho man's will both be much lower than Barbara and her new man.

The androgny switch

The divisions of masculinity and femininity are so fundamental to the way we organize our lives that we can't afford to recognize that even this apparently unchangeable difference has a particular life-course, and that once the biological purpose of the two sexes is finished we are left to make of ourselves what we will – transformation or depression.

The biological reason for having two sexes who are at certain times in their life attracted to each other is to produce children who will live long enough to produce their own children, and so on. Both the heterosexual couple and the whole of society, which need future workers, warriors and wives, have an interest in this.

You would think that an enterprise so closely tied to the good of the species has a built-in programme to make sure it all goes according to original design. The ethologists say you would be right. In the primate world, the mothers trade-off sexual favours to the dominant male, who will protect and provide for her while she devotes herself to the care of the young. But after they've brought up baby, these mothers can come to the defence of any others in the troop just as quickly and threateningly as a male. So, to her own offspring she provides early emotional security, but when that's done she takes up the role of helping to provide physical security for all the group. By this time, the dominant old male is usually over the horizon, *still* trying to fulfil his biological fitness formula! If he can't join another troop, he will be reduced to loping around holding out the begging bowl, frequently dying alone.

Psychoanalytic studies find a gradual peeling away of the illusions about life, strength and mortality as a person assumes parental roles, and a more realistic evaluation of their capabilities, motivating them to be less reckless, and therefore help the child's survival. Throughout the primate (including human) world, social organization has a similar pattern. The young female is submissive, allows herself to be pushed around by others, and is attracted to a male who will best be able to look after her and her children. At menopause she becomes the matriach, avenging all, especially in the service of her grandchildren. She shifts to the active end of the mastery continuum. She passes her previous partner in the enterprise, who is headed the opposite way to the passive end, and the power balance between them changes. This crossover is helped by hormonal change. Just as Jung thought, the male hormone (testosterone) falls in men to its lowest point at age 50, while the female substance (oestrogen) rises. And in ageing women the male hormone rises, while the female declines.

Boys have always had achievement, self-reliance and exploration encouraged – in most societies there are painful initiation rites to manhood at puberty. He is frightened, sacrificed and humiliated to test his courage and endurance. And girls have had the expression of aggression most severely sanctioned – of all the things girls are warned against, aggression in a little girl is the most horrifying to a parent. But she becomes a gentle mother, no matter what the provocation of the children.

In some sense then, parenthood is limiting. The evident joy of post-parental women, who can suddenly please themselves – be late, outrageous, stay in bed, get drunk or whatever they please, with not a single person to be harmed from such irresponsible behaviour, is revealing: 'No examples to set,' gloated Marni, 'I'm off on a trip round Australia for six months, in spite of the fact that I pressured James to go to university instead of bumming round Europe for a year.' Often, such women find their children now play the parent role towards them. Their children become the serious responsible ones warning their errant mothers not to persist in their eccentricities – which are really long-repressed 'masculine' traits – exploring, assertive, independent 'perimeter' qualities.

In a study conducted on female flight attendants, the first finding was that they had to be nicer in exercising authority over drunken or otherwise misbehaving male passengers than the male flight attendants. The consequence of daily holding down of anger at disrespect was a compensatory flight from feminine qualities in private life; or sometimes an estrangement from self so severe that these women were plagued with feelings of phoniness. Even those who could distinguish 'real self' from 'self in uniform, on the job' felt their feelings to be bought and commercialized by the airline. When girls are brought up to be mothers, this hidden agenda silently attaches itself to job descriptions. As outlined in the chapter on coping strategies, suppression of sex-inappropriate traits leads individuals to be attracted to a member of the opposite sex in whom they sense a completion. That will be the individual who best depicts the potentials they have surrendered for themselves.

Men too can change, and they do. In my study, personality traits changed at mid-life, and this had strong effects on the happiness of the couple. Men became much less tough-minded and outgoing, and more empathetic and affiliative. Hormones, primate behaviour, personality scores and socio-anthropological research all tell the same story: in the androgyny switchover, the sexes become more equal in power and intimacy expression, due to the hormonal dip which allows them to reclaim their long lost 'anima' and 'animus'.

The happiness curve

Although different cultures allow mildly diverging behaviour before parenthood (compare California with China), once a family is established, you could hardly tell whether you were in Afghanistan, Australia or Timbuctoo. Parents universally feel a sense of meaning or purpose on the birth of the first child. Unbidden, unexpected feelings of pride, protection and purposefulness arise. It might be elaborated into joy in India or downplayed into just one of life's satisfactions in New York – but a change does occur, for both. Men who have children have different perceptual habits, memories, tolerance for intimacy and cooperative/conflict strategies than those who don't.

The motivational pushes behind the periods of fertility create a sexual architecture of the family, with different staircases for men and women. These different life-directions expected of men and women, cause common crises that have predictable effects on relationships. At a man's active peak of mastery (during the parental years), his ambitions are lofty, ideals and artistic expression are assertive, even grandiose. His concerns are to provide for the family. And in cross-cultural studies in both traditional and modern societies, the major source of satisfaction in the life of a father is how productive or rewarding his work is. Conversely, what makes him unhappy is anything that interferes with his ability to provide – crop failure, unemployment, illness, war.

In later life, the competitive drive is diminished and older men become more passive – and happier. In some societies they become the acknowledged spiritual leaders, in modern societies the conciliators. A study of American divorce lawyers for example, found that the younger ones were concerned to get the best deal for their client, while the older ones acted more like marriage counsellors – the only way men over 50 can compete with the younger, aggressive men who have both muscle and information technology at their disposal. This is the older man's route to social contribution as he inevitably loses touch with his children. His new found tranquillity and reflectiveness are welcomed by his wife.

The happiness phases of a woman's life are opposite. As she moves towards more power and competence, she keeps her connection with parenting more than her husband, although in a modern society it is the powerful matriach who is most displaced and who will seek other sources of competence on which to use her psychological muscle. Biology relaxes its developmental push, and from mid-life on, relationships can become more like the religious ideal of marriage, the two as one. The differences become less.

Many sociologists have researched and given names to the changes in perception and energy that mark life-cycle transitions. Most agree on a seven-stage developmental cycle, each unfolding different aspects of the potentials within. How these life stages fit into relationship stages is most powerfully obvious in the U-shaped curve of relationship happiness. The slippery slope down to the trough starts with the birth of the first baby, and doesn't climb up to the other arm of the U until the children start leaving home.

But within this U-shaped relationship cycle there are predictable macro-cycles – each with their own concerns and conflicts. First, the concerns of individuality, expanding boundaries and increasing interdependence, followed by the struggle over sexual power, and all the while the parenting macro-cycle with its different satisfactions for each sex. Finally comes the post-parental rapprochement, with its androgynous switch.

Every stage involves a particular type of vulnerability, characterized by a set of assumptions and protective illusions. The death, divorce, delinquency, illness or financial hardship a couple sees around them start to impinge as possibilities – something that could happen to them. Often, complicity and collusion in defending against them deplete the energy to cope with the next cycle's conflicts.

Knowing that there are specific tasks and objectives unique to each stage allows a couple to develop their own macro-cycle checklist, recognize that their dissatisfaction is not global – the whole relationship is not in trouble only specific stages have gone wrong, due to the particular stress inherent in that cycle.

With these relationship perceptions, which tend to be age-related, since childbearing and rearing are concentrated round 25-35 years, there unfolds a sub-plot divided into pre-parent, parent and post-parent stages. And even within that uneven family story, there are two different narratives – his and hers; they diverge most sharply in mid-life, when his happiness and confidence remains stable, or increases, while hers goes down.

The macro-cycles of conflict

Coupling

On meeting, their romance was established as the most important ingredient in a couple's relationship. Talking about their eternal feelings, making love, constructing idealizations of the other and so on. This headlong approach is all the while held in check by fear of rejection. Sexual energy is harnessed to please the other at nearly any cost, and they are cooperative and energetic. The first year or two brings the highest levels of happiness they will experience.

Commitment . . . pre-child

On commitment, which is the next stage, submerged fears of intimacy from childhood experience and social conditioning anchor the approach, and steps of avoidance counterbalance it.

The idealization described in Chapter 1 is a façade that must be drawn aside gently at exactly the right point for it to be continued both realistically and idealistically. But few manage this denouement gracefully, since happiness levels fall rapidly at stage 2, after approximately 2 years of marriage. Chapter 2 was about greater depths of truth being revealed on commitment and living together (which is also a delicate point of discovery), and how a balance has to be struck between accepting the other sufficiently to provide understanding so home is associated with security, protection and acceptance – the basis of emotional healing that we need after the daily stress of job and social interaction.

Both are involved in a presentation of self that they are both happy with. Happy couples appear to collude in a version of each other's personality that is self-esteem enhancing to both, while unhappy couples refuse to recognize each other's 'act'.

Since 3 years is the first divorce peak, the assumption has to be that it is those for whom idealization turns to illusion who never get the relationship going and decide to abandon it. The ones who stay are happier with their negotiated selves, but the added stress of the birth of the first child coincides with the downturn in happiness. It stays at this lower point for several years, and doesn't rise again until the children are starting to become independent and leaving home. These years are characterized by varying regrets over opportunities missed, lack of time and money, dreams dashed, unresolved conflicts from childhood imported into the relationship; all interspersed with moments of harmony, family warmths and satisfactions. Attention is directed towards working out possible solutions to the problems, and realizing the complexities involved.

Children

The couple begin to appreciate and use their new understanding of the way the world works, and structure their relationship into subjective stages: 'years until we start a family'.

When children impose an extra burden on energy they are disrupting the synchrony of the couple, and their established energy/attachment cycles. This makes it harder to deal assertively and productively with inevitable clashes of interest that will arise. Children give great reward and joy, but also great fatigue and disruption. To fit in, an adult's characteristic rhythms of daily life must change, and daily work demands be fitted around the children's cycles. Sometimes this is impossible, and mothers who have more than one young child at home often complain of fatigue, disturbed sleep and depression – especially if their relationship with their husband is inadequate. This seems a good description of the jet-lagged passengers who did not interact with the locals and the reason could be the same – inadequate synchronization of their oscillating rhythms. The women who were happy with their husbands were not depressed – so were possibly able to use them as a 'resynchronizer' of their circadian rhythms.

Whether interdependence is established satisfactorily or not (it took Barbara and Edward 11 years, while Simon and Jeanne never made it), children will be usually conceived. The physical and psychological can be wildly out of synchrony; babies will be born whether the couple feel loving or murderous. And once that happens life's different paths are set. Pregnancy itself has different meanings; women must necessarily focus on it, men can feel excluded, neither can take the other's place.

School
Then the differing nurturing responsibilities of each – as just described in this chapter. This is the most intense period of power

struggle. She would like more help in the house and he a bit more financial contribution (but not to the point of equality). In the middle of exhausting laundry and endless chauffeuring through traffic jams, they each think about forgone alternatives and frustration and blame surfaces between emotional comfort. Time is now counted in 'years until the children leave home'.

Adolescence/teenager

The conflict now is over control, sometimes fought in the sexual relationship, sometimes over the upbringing of children. This is the lowest point of happiness for them both. And it is when the clock of life is ticking at its most audible. By 35/40 the questioning of self, purpose and meaning in life goes on, with the added question: Have I done the right thing? The finiteness of time energizes priorities with some dreams being jettisoned to make others more likely to be realized. The contribution of work and children to the meaningfulness of life is reviewed, and it is here that the happiness of men and women differs.

The sources of competence are less easily found than the sources of intimacy, and it is the Leonoras that miss out, and mourn in their empty nests, particularly if their husbands don't do the intimacy shift of the new man.

Choice and change, the trade-off: the post-parental stage

If mastery and competence were developed in men they are now revised, and the delights of intimacy substituted. Conversely, for women, the mastery drive increases. But much conflict attaches to the cross-over. He is afraid of being seen as a wimp, and she fears being rebuffed as wanton and unfeminine if they act out their fantasies. Usually neither realizes the universality of this stage, its hormonal back up and its potentials for transformation. Often they feel eccentric and ashamed at this apparent loss of 'the right stuff', and struggle harder to repress it, or sabotage it in each other – ridiculing and deriding the hesitant steps out of the sex-role strait jacket. By excluding each other, they block the growth of their sexual equality.

But good communication, non-verbal monitoring and intuition can overcome the fears and stop the couple locking themselves into sexual segregation. This third stage, after about 15/18 years of marriage, sees satisfaction rise to nearly first flush of love levels, as new interests and activities are taken up and substituted for the coming losses of the life-cycle, menopause, parental illness and death, the family at home ending, and failing strength. This of course is the time when the couple are likely to have the most money – children independent, mortgage paid or rent having secured a tenancy. Depleting hormones can be buffeted by the exercise of new expectations, and middle-aged couples now have a real choice in life, unlike their prior lives, when the sex hormones compelled them towards each other, into courtship and children and their care. Some physiological decline is more than matched by the psychological enhancement in their lives.

Sex may cease, or increase. Communication can be for or against more self-revelation. Whole lives can be arranged to please themselves. Selling up to buy a gypsy caravan and roving the world, or starting a refuge for some disadvantaged group or taking up the forsaken novel put aside in child-rearing years. Perceptions of their own lives change as they see themselves between their own parents, ageing fast, and their grown-up children, with all the vigour and unrealistic convictions they once had themselves. Some may react defensively and resist any change in their lives. But the choice is theirs. Society, their parents and their children have no prior interest in their arrangements. The only important thing for the couple is that whatever degree of change mid-life brings, they do it together – or least accept and tolerate varying change rates in each other.

Compensation and convergence . . . retirement

By 60, most other relationship opportunities have receded into the background. Some ludic attachment types can stay in a relationship for this long still vaguely hoping to find a better partner, but by now, even these Peter Pans will realize they had better make the best of what's left. After all, there's still more than a decade left for those who succumb to death at three score and ten, and maybe 3 decades for those with more genetic luck. Reviewing their life together, watching the lives of their children unfold, clearing up misunderstandings from the previous cycles, bring a satisfying subjectivity. In comparison with single people of this age, the gap in psychological and physical health is the most it has ever been, with the alcoholism, disease and depression of the single contrasting with the comfort, contentment and consumption of the married. The subjective experience of time boundaries is now 'years left to work'. As the couple slide into the fourth stage, of retirement, reworking life's experience into a meaningful whole, it becomes 'years left to live'.

Unless couples realize that each cycle has an inherent conflict for the different sexes, the different personalities and different psychologies, they are likely to blame each other for the tensions that arise. Understanding the inevitability of such problems permits them to acknowledge them in advance and head them off. Instead of turning away from each other disapprovingly, they are able to appreciate what each has had to overcome to get to this stage, to appreciate the amount of active loving involved – the giving in, the listening, the kindness and turning the other cheek, the support, the stifling of criticism. Thus they are more motivated to relax and overcome the next conflict resolutely.

The natural history of conflict

Cooperation, satisfaction, contentment and happiness fluctuate with coolness, conflict, bitterness, disappointment and anger. These recurring ingredients repeat themselves at every cycle – for some the ambivalence can be tipped in the favour of cooperativeness, love and understanding strengthening the threshold at which conflict will spill into the next cycle. The first law of relationships is that nothing can go right *all* the time. The repeated negative cycles are woven into the pleasant ones, so we can make a global judgement about the relationship. But the strands are different for every relationship. Some will be satisfied with their sexual relations while at the same time unhappy about the way the children are treated. You can be a great companion *and* a lousy housekeeper.

Happiness waxes and wanes, but demoralization under the strain of continuous conflict is stable. The accumulation of dissonance eventually forces the whole relationship over the edge into negativity. The conflict becomes out of normal control and balance. The couple feel an emotional 'stuckness' which leaves them no energy or motivation to cope with the conflicts of the next cycle. So they ignore it, constructing defences and illusions to protect themselves from recognizing painful reality – and fail to move on to cope with the next cycle.

Plans to overcome the conflict of the macrocycles

Plans clarify goals. Use different goals for every relationship stage. Put yourself on a training course for promotion to become best partner of the year! Work out what such a training course would have to teach you. Your partner is just that, an equal partner, with equal rights and responsibilities. How you want to allocate housework, decisions, money is up to you and you two alone. Go through the 6 macrocycles, discuss the conflicts each one will dredge up for you both, your fears, the experience of others.

Contract stage charter

1. Each stage should have a visible, specific, foreseeable timing. Not 'until we get tired of each other' (you surely will) but, 'until one of us leaves college, the job, until we have children' or even 'this time next year'. 'Till death do us part' is a bit like the top of the escalator, you can't visualize it, so setting such a goal doesn't have the same psychophysiological consequences that precipitate new attitudes and new behaviour. This doesn't mean that such a long-term goal shouldn't be part of your life plan, but that there should also be change and renewal at the various relationship stages. Marriage for life but with 5-year contract stages, where each side sets out new requirements or relinquishes old duties, for example. Since the developmental theorists tell us that we all develop a life structure that feels comfortable and meets our needs, but which changes every 5-7 years, this seems a good base on which to dismantle and reorder life and relationship phases.

2. Import some of the quality management concepts that big business uses to establish the expectations each of you have, how they diverge, how they can be improved. Think of the feelings you want to encourage between you, love, affection, mutual emotional support . . . use these as emotional vaccines that are daily prescriptions. Keep negative comments and criticism for a specific 'review' time, after hearing each other out, have a drink, listen to music – or whatever reward you choose.

3. Think of yourselves as producers of emotional services for which there is a supply and demand market – each has the right to complain of shoddy and unreliable goods, not delivered on time. And the responsibility to match the other's output. Establish a profit

and loss account for the times when quality control has a lapse. This doesn't turn emotions into machines, but it does make the couple exercise more freewill and choice in their reactions to the other and take more responsibility for their emotional behaviour. Unlike animals who respond to a good or bad event, we have a choice – we can ignore negative remarks, or reply with understanding.

4. Review each stage at the end, plan how different the next one will be, how different you will be, i.e. last stage wife and mother, next stage self-employed business woman, or mad artist in garage growing old disgracefully. Keep a life-structure 'maintenance' notebook. Enter your service records as if you must submit them for a relationship M.O.T. at every phase.

The more definite and more finite you can make the plan, the more the psychological commitment to it. The adaptation, boredom and tolerance cycle must be matched with new challenges to keep the relationship interesting, alive and vital to both.

Part IV

Communicating Compatibility

Concordia discors: 'Harmony in discord'.

Horace 65 BC

10

The language of the brain

There are millions of fibres joining the two hemispheres of the brain, and you could see the sex-differences in these hemispheric connections as a metaphor for female connection and male detachment. It seems that the two halves of the body, including the brain hemispheres, grow at different rates in boys and girls even before birth, and these asymmetries have far-reaching repercussions for communication between the sexes. Brain organization for various problem-solving abilities is related to hand-preference (the 'lefties' make good architects, musicians and engineers) and to gender. It looks like we have several different types of cognitive abilities, based on several levels of brain organization. At various periods in life they undergo more or less rapid growth, according to the hormonal state of the body, which itself undergoes lifelong fluctuations.

There are brain differences in processing information that lead women to a multi-level verbally expressive style of communication, (the auditories of the next chapter) and men to the visually biased way of seeing the world. These differences are strengthened by the prohibition of the expression of anger in women from babyhood on, and conversely the taboo on emotional expression in boys and men (see Chapter 7).

So far, the hormonal and neural biological sex-differences that have brought communication problems to the couples surveyed have been:

- The differences in sexual arousal and fade-out point, which alter the pacing to commitment and which persist throughout their life; men being quicker to arousal and orgasm than women – on the whole.

- The differences in brain organization which mean men have discrete areas of brain functioning for some cognitive tasks involved in spatial and verbal reasoning and also, have fewer nerve fibres connecting these 'work centres'. The large bunch of fibres connecting the two hemispheres, the *corpus callosum,* is much larger in women (and, interestingly, in left-handers too, and abnormally thickened in schizophrenia), so they are able to match emotional processing to the 'work centres' more easily than men. This means women are more sensitive to the emotional attunement of the other, and tend to speak the language of involvement.

From these spring the fundamental incompatibilities of men and women, the differences that swamp the similarities.

Women are also able to process more sensory information, making them more sensitive to sound, smell, touch and stress. Women are more likely to let stress activate their whole brain and men more likely to damp it down, which has bad effects on male health. Some cognitive functions operate in different parts of the brain in males and females, and even when they are the same and each person is doing the same thing, different amounts of blood are taken up, meaning that the brain's activity fuel is used differently between the sexes.

In one study investigating brain sex differences, it was found that female rats had thick left cerebral cortices, while males had the thickness on the right side. This suggests that the brain differences are related to sex hormones, and are generalized to other species. Some theorists believe that our brains are structured to think of others in two major ways . . . affiliation or control. In many experiments describing people all the adjectives used are found to correlate with one or other of those two dimensions. Words like cold, quarrelsome, warm, agreeable, dominant, ambitious, lazy, submissive, gregarious, aloof, and so on line up pretty well to one or other of these superordinate categories.

Inevitably, the similarities on which attraction was based are overwhelmed by differences, the differences that gender brings. With the best will in the world, men and women mystify each other, unless they understand that brain differences and sex-role conditioning mean they approach the same situation in opposite ways.

The importance of the connecting fibres in the brain was understood when a man was discovered without a *corpus callosum* – but with an otherwise intact brain. He was never able to communicate his true feelings to others, or to comprehend the emotional motivation of those around him. Actually, there is a word for people who are unemotional, present-orientated, and interpret words totally literally – alexithymia. It's a condition seen in psychosomatic patients (often men) who, in spite of many stressful events, react quite impassively. Like Woody Allen once said: 'Me? Worry! Never, I just grow a tumour!' In these alexithymics emotional life remains out of awareness. This sometimes happens to epileptics who have had the connecting fibres severed to reduce their fits. They reported that they had stopped day-dreaming, and their thinking style became concrete and rigid. The brain differences between men and women suggest that alexithymics are a highly exaggerated version of men's fewer connecting fibres. The consequence of their relative inability to verbalize feelings is their higher stress and earlier death rate.

But what has control got to do with emotional disconnection? You can't be affiliative and unemotional at the same time, so the male of the species is trained in an incapacity to share. Chapter 7 suggests that male control of female sexuality is biologically based, and it's a short step from that to control of the social systems that regulate our lives. Naturally then, women avoid conflict because it is a threat to affiliation, but to men conflict is a means by which status is negotiated and control affected. So women propose, cajole, suggest – or, (in men's language), pussy-foot around – pressuring men. He will prefer a direct fight, which he sees as a form of involvement. After all, you only fight intimately with someone you're involved with. Some men habitually make contact this way – with other men, through physical fighting, play-wrestling, back-slapping and so on. With women, it is the underground intrusiveness of the endless hints, and strained discussions that makes him seem at a disadvantage from which they withdraw. Sometimes rage is a substitute feeling for the pain of not being able to connect emotionally. When men lead emotionally attenuated lives, all their feelings can become 'sexualized' – and they go back to base, biologically speaking.

Connectors and detachors

There are also two information processing systems which conflict and cooperate with each other – a sort of trade-off between short-term, flexible memory and long-term, durable or 'habit' memory. According to animal research, the flexible is constantly being updated due to experience that is emotionally tinged and has links to the emotional memories. The other is simply a matter of external attention and habit-formation. You could say the qualitative versus the quantitative. There is also evidence that the flexible one is affected by information out of consciousness, and this 'implicit' memory is the basis of what is seen as intuition.

The abnormal often throws light on the normal, and some types of brain damage, which has left patients with one or other of these types of memory impairment, give clues to their differences. The 'hows' of the information processing types build up associations and can learn by rote. They are good at mental arithmetic, financial reckoning, chemistry, history. The Trivial Pursuits players . . . or explicit memorizers. The 'whys' want to know what relevance this information has before they can assimilate it. They integrate present learning and experience with wider events, past, present and future, and ignore facts that they don't want to clutter their memory network with, until someone proves the necessity and gives them a frame of reference to fit the details into. Their best quiz game would be the old B.B.C. quiz game that asks what the connections are between several different people or objects. These connections were always very esoteric and lateral. These differences are consistent with the sequential, attention-to-detail thinking of many men, and the asequential, holistic thinking of most women.

Barbara recalled the time she was talking to Ed about his job. He felt his career wasn't going well, his clients were incompatible, unreliable and he was just a dogsbody, providing greedy companies with a more efficient means for ripping others off. He had these feelings regularly, and would then look round for more creative, worthwhile work. Barbara responded by telling him she felt exactly the same about teaching. Going over the same old material she sometimes wondered if she should have done a degree in English literature and been something that allowed her to go beyond 'Shakespeare made simple'. 'There you go again,' he had suddenly yelled. 'You encourage me to talk about my feelings and then start interrupting with yours!' Barbara was amazed. She thought she was showing understanding and solidarity by swapping a similar experience. But Ed took it as her taking control of the conversation and changing the subject.

Barbara's multi-channelled conversation, talking about her, him, maybe something else in between, and back to him, was confusing to Ed. He couldn't cope with her lightning shifts of subject, let alone the meta-messages of involvement she was trying to convey! He felt Barbara had just grabbed the conversational ball and kept running; every time she tossed it to him, he missed it. He didn't want what he perceived as parallel conversations, he expected it to stay on one subject, elaborated, certainly, and even skewed, but not dropped. *Then*, he would have been happy to have talked about Barbara's career. But of course by then Barbara had been hurt and withdrawn her involvement in the conversation.

Jeanne remembers when she sent Christmas cards from her and Simon the first year they were together. She liked writing both their names, it made her feel intimately involved and as if she was creating something. She was surprised when Simon said angrily she should have asked him first, he might have wanted to send his own separately. Barbara said the same about Ed. She knew he was actively against animal suffering – he was a vegetarian for that reason – but when she signed them both up (she had to because it was a joint cheque book) for an anti-vivisection society after an emotional appeal at school one day, he amazed and upset her by shouting at her that she was trying to take control of him. Men are constantly on the lookout for being told what to do because as boys status and respect was achieved by resisting being pushed around in a male group. They tune into status fluctuations the way women monitor the affiliative messages from others.

The irony for women is that they usually feel it's natural to consult their partners first before any such joint decisions, and when they do men believe they're indecisive. But if they don't, they are transgressing men's freedom. He certainly feels he should make his own decisions without reference to her, or he would lose respect. Respect is as important to men as approval is to women.

The couples I surveyed, and millions more over the world judging from other studies, have different rules for good communication. Establishing the rhythm necessary for rapport is difficult when each has different brain-based communication patterns. (Although not impossible, because there are cultural and national differences in these communication patterns, which means they can't be immutably sex hard-wired.) The expressive, verbally fluent style of affiliation-seekers seems exaggerated to control-seekers, who are usually men. And the affiliation-seekers, who are usually women, interpret the male style as coolness, aloofness, indifference and insensitivity.

These ways of saying words mean that each sex makes inaccurate assumptions about the motivation of the other, and can change the whole meaning of what is said. Each interprets the other's experience according to their own reality, and it ends up with men questioning women's competence and women questioning men's emotional capacity. To be misinterpreted tells each they are not understood, and this further distances them.

A further consequence of the freedom-seeker's style is a penchant for playing by the rules, sticking to logic and external rationality. Much-quoted American research shows that boys were more likely to think in terms of rights and principles which reflect their assumptions about independence and autonomy. Women will tend to think in terms of human interdependence and make compassionate rules that take in responsibility to others.

Boys and men feel at ease with each other by fitting into prescribed rules of masculinity. Playing the game properly is very important in male playgrounds and clubrooms, down to the undeviating dark suit and tie. Imagine the same uniformity in women! Girls and women dispense with rules when necessary (to them). Their asequential neural processing makes them more flexible and inclined to waive the rules for the one-off unique case or person who can't fit in.

Change is not something men welcome, as anyone who has moved the furniture round while the man of the house was away has discovered. One lady told me her husband sulked for a month after she moved the dining room table and chairs out of the sound reach of the television while he was away.

After, that she couldn't stand it and moved them back. He was even more irate then, because he was just getting used to it he said! This mechanism explains men's rapid return to base when a relationship breaks up. Women tend to allow themselves to be changed by the time they had together, and keep using his way of mixing the daiquiris, or keep up the jogging. They incorporate the best aspects of the past into their present. But men seem to breathe a sigh of relief, kick off the uncomfortable façade and go right back to their old bar stool in the pub, metaphorically speaking.

He calls foul when she wants to change the relationship in some way, the rules are the rules, he will feel implicitly, and resist. Men think it's good teamwork when the job gets done without much talking. This is a reflection of their separate, fairly independent brain functions. Transferred to opposite sex relationships this means that women appear chaotic and disorganized to men. Women do high-powered jobs, negotiate contracts, and *still* talk about the baby and where they bought that stunning outfit, in between signing a contract. Men worry that the contract is as trivial to the women as the other details are to them. They can't trust women to be competent and create rapport at the same time. Men like organization and procedure – things in the proper place at the expected time means that he doesn't have to activate so many brain areas at once. Keeping track of things in time is really harder cognitive work for most men.

Social-rhythm experts demonstrate that cultural differences in timing can wreck communication between people, and getting the rhythm of a language is as important as learning the words, to be able to speak it understandably. Within these cultural rhythms there are male patterns and female ones. Time is an integral part of a relationship, from microseconds to a lifetime. The informal culture of shared understanding about the world and the way it works is different for girls and boys. In many cultures, there are women's words and men's words, and neither is expected to speak the other's language, or use the other's non-verbal gestures. Time and space are perceived differently enough for there to be serious problems of misunderstanding when intimate communication is necessary – as in a close relationship. Male rhythms are geared to the long-term, time is seen as linear, not to be wasted, everything has a logical beginning, middle and end. Adherence to preset schedules means activities must be task-orientated to be taken seriously. Communication then is for exchange of information and so interruptions, disputations, challenges, opinions, direct declaration of facts, are all legitimate. Most men appreciate practical communication and this adds up to a language of power. And power means controlling others and is a sort of extension of involvement.

Woman-time is more informal. It is viewed as relative, and transactions are lengthy, as everyone has to be taken into account. Time is a process of discovery, jobs are isolated activities which can be left if colleagues or circumstances are not congenial. This is a foreign idea to a man, who will put up with effort and enemies knowing that these are temporary obstacles to the long haul of career. Women keep communication lines open with small talk, questions, encouraging responses, acknowledgement of each other's points and a whole range of non-verbal involvement.

Women tend to use the language of involvement and *solidarity*, which is resisting being controlled and is an extension of independence.

Wendy, writing her first assignment for her new job (having finally been promoted from sub to journalist proper) asked Bill to read the first draft critically for her. He glanced at it and then put it away for when he had time to concentrate on it. Wendy remembers:

> I was amazed when he gave it back days later with neat red crosses in the margin every few lines. They all denoted when he thought it should have been a colon instead of semi-colon, or a grammatical fault or spelling mistake. 'But what did you *think* of it?' I asked him. It turned out he'd not read it for the meaning – only the mistakes. I had wanted to know if he thought it was an interesting piece, would it have caught his attention if he hadn't have known it was written by me – ironically, though, it didn't get his attention though when he *knew* it was written by me. I really wanted to know what he thought and I must admit I expected a bit of praise, I thought it made some good points about our economy, but he took it as an exercise in proof-reading, something I've been doing for a living for years!

Wendy took this as a *statement of power*. She thought Bill was suggesting:

- He couldn't learn anything from what *she'd* written;
- She was asking for correction about things she didn't know about, notwithstanding the fact that she must have been good enough at grammar and spelling to have been paid for it for the last eight years.

She wanted constructive criticism as an equal, she got destructive criticism in the form of a lecture in grammar. In fact, she knew about the typing errors (which he had taken of evidence of her not being able to spell) she just hadn't bothered to do the corrections until she was ready to do the final version.

What Wendy had wanted was a *statement of involvement;* interest in her, her work, her ambitions, and some encouragement, even a little praise! She felt Bill was condescending to her and she was frustrated and hurt, particularly as he had taken so long to read it. If it had been her, she would have read Bill's article immediately. Now she realized why Bill had put it away, he was going to go through it in a detailed way when he could concentrate alone. Ironically, she could see incorrect spelling and punctuation at glance – Bill did it painstakingly, step by step. (This is a fairly common sex difference.) What Bill wanted was to *help* her, he had spent a couple of hours going over her article and was surprised and upset at her reaction. Silly little incident to make a fuss over? No, these are life's daily trivia, around which we build our relationships and which are ultimately responsible for the happiness of our lives and the compatibility we achieve.

When women ask for involvement from men they are usually misinterpreted as asking for help, and get advice, which they resent, because that's not what they meant. Offering solutions takes the power out of their hands. For men's part, women appear not to follow the advice offered and yet keep on complaining. Bill was concerned with the 'Hows' – the facts, the instrumental. Wendy was concerned with the 'Whys' – the significance of the article to the reader, how good was it.

We must have a long talk, dear

Transferred to relationships this difference in perception creates one of the most serious divisions between men and women. Women's superior verbal reasoning means that they think with words, and they do it aloud when they're with friends, as a problem-solving exercise. With other women this furthers an understanding of the problem – together they empathetically pursue all the nuances and possible directions and then jointly decide on a solution. This, they call emotional support.

So, when she turns to the man in her life and starts talking in the same way she expects the same, a joint emotional exchange session. To him, though, it means things are getting out of control. He assumes that, like him, she has worked the problem out with spatial reasoning, non-verbally and is now going to put her conclusion into words. But then, she starts to ask him what he thinks. This is her statement of involvement – to include him. But he is alarmed now and assumes she is asking for help, not emotional ball-kicking, so he gives her advice! This appears to her, as it did to Wendy, a statement of non-involvement, condecension and arrogance. And it appears to him yet more proof of duplicity – why ask him if she is not interested in his advice.

So she withdraws – he is confused and crushed because male conversions *are* about giving and receiving practical advice; he feels rejected and also withdraws. The emotional expression she sees as support he sees as warning signals. If he refuses to talk (his usual suppressor approach to stress) this imagined problem might go away – he hopes.

Men take the role of advice giver, and, as every counsellor knows – all advice is implied cricitism. When women discuss their problems with their men expecting understanding and acknowledgement that their feelings are valid, they are upset when they perceive disinterested academic advice that could have been got from a stranger. Her feelings seem embarrassingly out-of-proportion. A woman friend would sympathize, offer similar feelings and reactions and reassure her that these feelings are quite normal. Women's conversation are explorations in matching feelings to words, images to constructs, and making metaphors out of emotional lives. Because of it, they have a richer emotional framework with which to interpret the rest of life's experiences. When women try to use that framework on their men, something awful happens. Whenever she tries to empathize with him, tell him she understands his feelings – he is piqued! The language of control interprets affiliation as denying his autonomy – the uniqueness of his experience.

'You don't own my feelings as well' Ed shouted to Barbara, leaving her wondering what else he resented her owning – his loyalty, living space, his name? This had been one of their 'red herring' arguments. Whenever Ed drew away and gazed into the future distance, refusing to make plans, Barbara would try to relate his fears to his relationship with his mother. His fierce independence might have been a sensible reaction once to an ambivalent family, but it was only damaging his relationship now. This was Ed's cue to snap on his guard. He reacted as if Barbara was belittling him. When she thought she was communicating 'you're not alone' he picked up 'you're not special'. Suggesting today's feelings were any sort of hangover for yesterday's childhood meant at least one day of sulkiness and back-to-back sleep at night. She felt hurt that he wouldn't trust her enough to talk about his fears and past crushed hopes. Ed took the view that talking about emotional problems only made them worse, left him feeling out-of-control and couldn't change anything anyway, so what was the point? And this is the way men who speak the language of control and independence feel. A problem shared is one to be dissected, solved and dismissed. They feel women go on and on and wallow in feelings. Their sympathy feels like condescension – as if women know better. The consequence of women's better linking facility of the emotional and speech processing areas of the brain is misunderstanding. Men fear that in things emotional they will be found wanting. It's better to stick to being the expert on the factual, mechanical things of life.

So, according to their attachment history, they will either attack first, by ridiculing, withdraw altogether, sulking in silence, or, less often, submit and negotiate a compromise.

There is then the further complication of saying straight out what you mean or want, (the efficient strategy of the sequential instrumental-type thinker). Or fencing around working out what the other wants before assuming too much and trying to harmonize with that. This is the strategy of synchrony and tact. Except in emotional expression, men are usually direct and women indirect, the usual result being that they each do what they *think* the other wants – and the further consequence is conversations about 'You said so' and 'No, I didn't'.

'I was beginning to think one of us was going a bit doolally,' said a frustrated hint-dropper. 'I would swear I heard Leo said such and such and he was just as adamant that he hadn't. Even over little things you wouldn't normally be bothered denying.' But the worst was when after a small windfall they had enough money to put down a decent deposit on a house or buy a charming little houseboat on the canal near the university they were both studying at. The houseboat was a delightful, impractical fantasy, but they ended up buying it instead of the house. It was inconvenient, it leaked, too small, they both hated it once installed on it but they had each thought they were doing it for the other. When in one of their later rows this came out they were both amazed: 'I agreed,' said Leo 'because I thought *you* wanted the romantic life, and I was intrigued with it although I knew we'd be sorry.' At this Tina had exploded and accused him of putting them into this position – the only capital they were ever likely to have lost in an unsaleable boat. 'I didn't want it at all,' she yelled 'it was you.' He yelled back 'No, it was *you*.'

The direct communicator asks 'Would you like . . .?' as a real question. But the indirect one will think that's a hint, because if *they* said it like that it would mean they *did* want it themselves. And so Ms Indirect says if that's what you want, O.K.; and Mr Direct thinks she never knows her own mind.

It's not the words said that are at issue, it's the implications drawn from them. We act on the implication we draw, which was not the implication the speaker meant. Then the speaker quite legitimately denies that he ever said anything of the sort – but by now the hearer is convinced that he did. Even a transcript or recording wouldn't settle the issue because each would be saying 'But I thought you meant such and such.' Differences in directness means that the vague hinter will drop hints that aren't picked up, and act on hints that are actually *not* dropped. The indirect communicator will want to be told 'I love you', without having to ask, and the direct one will be mystified by the apparent irrationality, veiled meanings and total incomprehensibility of the conversation.

Striking the balance between affiliation and involvement versus keeping one's distance and independence is helped by the strategy of indirectness/directness. We all have to judge whether being nice, polite and human calls for showing involvement or not imposing. Do you, for example, bring up the subject of the son's suicide in order to commiserate, or is it better not to upset them by mentioning it?

Misjudging this means being thought inconsiderate or pushy, or else unkind and cold. The benefits of being indirect are protective – if the other takes umbrage at assumptions of involvement then the indirect one can back off with 'I didn't *say* that' etc. It's tactful, to say 'No, I'm too busy' rather than 'No, I think you're a nerd', which is another reason women tend to be indirect, while men believe efficient communication is fostered by directness! In relationships, the biggest issue in conversational strategies is dropping hints. The right mix of hint-dropping and hint-catching creates the balance between rapport and defensiveness. An indirect strategist will drop them all over the place, hoping they are picked up and understood – the direct strategist will miss them altogether and also state his wishes in a way that seems rude, presumptuous or aggressive. When hinters share the same strategy a rapport evolves. To be understood without words and by giving only minimal signposts means similarity on the meta-message level, and being on the same wavelength.

Even single words have multiple different assumptions behind them. Girls define friends differently to boys for example. To her, a friend is someone to tell things to; for him someone to do things with. Of course boys talk when they're doing things together, but these subtle differences alter the way each sex perceives the interaction, and each other.

Similarly for the word 'freedom'. Divorcing men thought freedom meant less responsibility and claustrophobia in their lives, but divorcing women felt freedom meant less fitting in with family needs and more autonomy for themselves. The rules of social interaction are learnt from schoolfriends, and this is when the two sexes have least to do with each other and therefore have less opportunity for finding out that conversational rules are different between the sexes. It follows that brothers and sisters who interacted closely would make better communicators in their own later relationships.

Women tend to be more attuned to the meta-messages of involvement and affiliation, because that is how relationships are maintained, while the freedoom-fighters will often refuse to admit that words have meta-messages, and any attempt to interpret his meta-messages infuriates him because she is denying his ability to know himself and have control over his own communication. Men who are literal about words have common sense to appeal to – after all, he didn't *say* it, this can eventually make his partner doubt her own senses. Some men may miss the meta-messages of involvement, others deliberately ignore them to concentrate on the messages of independence. In reporting an event, men tend to give brief summaries, but women will include the tone of voice, their exact wording and timing and impression of all the participants in the event; in other words their accounts will recreate the meta-messages.

When you have different 'languages' of control and affiliation, you interpret situations differently. A person who stresses their own independence and control of life believes people are individually responsible for their actions. No one made them do it, so whatever they do, it must be what they themselves wanted.

Those who speak the language of control cannot understand how those who speak the language of affiliation do things *for* others, to please them, to support them, and to be involved with them. So the independence-seeker interprets the affiliator's actions as something she wanted to do, therefore not something they need to feel gratitude for – or to reciprocate in any way. If she tells him her true motives he will only feel pressured and believe she's insecure, indecisive, and a typical nagging woman. Her agreement or her listening, intended to demonstrate connection, closeness and involvement, are to him a reflection of his status, power and ability to control his woman.

When Wendy wanted Bill to listen, read her words and appreciate her, Bill misunderstood – because this was not his role. It is women who listen, agree and applaud. Since he saw himself in the role of information-giver he did the only practical, instrumental thing he could have done with Wendy's article. He checked it for accuracy. Those who speak the language of control are information-givers who need listeners, especially if they agree and the affiliative ones are the listeners and supporters. Each believes they are doing it for reasons, reasons that the other misinterprets. Some men feel obliged to trot out interesting stories of their exploits when women ask them about their job, holiday, interests and so on. The 'Getting on with your Man' guides tell you that. But some men actually would rather not, they feel forced into the heroic situation by the attention of the woman. So each can be playing a role they find boring. Once a man has launched into his story women won't interrupt, so he is forced into a monologue he believes is interesting because she is giving those non-verbal signals. He must then also believe that she has no opinions of her own, when she is actually only waiting politely, not interrupting, challenging, or sidetracking as his male friends would. When a man uses the competitive style of speech to a woman, she is hurt and usually tries to be nicer, encouraging him to reciprocate, but he perceives it as having won her over – more mistrust.

Women who give information, opinions or try to tell stories are not listened to by men, it's too uncodeable according to their language of control. If a woman has an official role as an information giver, policy-maker, lecturer, manager, her words are given less weight and credibility than a man in her position. Newspaper headlines will pronounce 'Professor gives warning about end of World' for a man but 'Professor *claims* world about to end' for a woman. So women often feel invisible or ignored when they do try to tell their partners new information or interesting stories. Research shows that girls find their stories of derring-do ignored by the grown-ups, while the same story told by boys is a source of interest and encouragement. Deborah Tannen wonders if this is because the lessons of damage, risk, sustaining injury and displaying technical expertise are not lessons deemed relevant for girls. So the family listens to the boy's stories, so teachinig him how to hold the centre stage and the girl how to listen appreciatively.

Girls grow up to listen and boys to say something worth listening to! Women then feel men aren't listening because they don't give her appreciative support. And men feel all that encouraging interest and attention, the fillers, the 'reallys?', the 'how interestings', mean that she's doing as much talking as listening to him! When a man does try to listen he may be judged as dependent and subordinate, just as a woman who tries to tell a good story sounds unfeminine.

Table 10.1   The Double Standard of Conversation: Affiliation or Control

Because we ostensibly use the same language, it's hard to interpret male and female differences in usage. But a decoding manual would read like this:

Questions:

> **For men:** a request for information.
> **For women:** what you ask to keep the conversation going.

Which is one reason men believe that women are uninformed and unsure – they keep asking questions! But she thinks she's showing involvement and interest! Men rarely ask questions (think of the last time you drove around for hours hopelessly lost because he was reluctant to ask someone the way), especially of women because it puts them in a one-down position and therefore undermines his language of control and independence.

Linking your utterance to the last one:

> **For men:** you don't bother, launch into your own opinion, they'll be interested.
> **For women:** you must make a connection to it to change the subject, otherwise it will seem as if you're taking control of the conversation or interrupting . . . or trying to attract attention.

Maintaining the conversation:

> **For men:** adhere to the topic till exhausted and then go onto something else.
> **For women:** keep adding, embellishing, share experience, reassurance, explore it jointly, tangentially.

Women tend to work harder at conversation, using longer sentences, a more expressive tone of voice, more 'listening' signals – which seems over the top and beside the point to most men. Men's conversation strives for unemotional rationality (unless they're trying to entice a woman to bed).

Conversational fillers:

> **For men:** Nods, smiles, 'uums' mean agreement with the speaker. But only when you DO agree.
> **For women:** Nods, smiles, 'uums' mean 'I'm listening', so do it a lot.

This meta-language confusion is responsible for the two most common complaints in relationships: women who say men never listen and men who say women are always changing their minds. If she thinks she's conveyed listening and he thinks he's communicated agreement it's a sure conflict. Combined with the fewer fillers men use it means that women think he's not listening while he thinks he's indicating that he doesn't really agree!

Directness:

> **For men:** honest and desirable (fits the information-exchange model of conversation).

For women: impolite, untactful (violates the small-talk model of conversation which establishes conversational rhythm and rapport).

Indirectness:

For men: dishonest, incomprehensible.

For women: basic to rapport, avoids confrontation, useful for being understood without saying exactly what is meant. Being indirect probes the other's preferences and likely reactions before you put your cards on the table.

Syntax (tags, hedges, qualifiers):

For men: not necessary, everyone will listen to you.

For women: necessary to state an opinion, you may be wrong.

Linguists have an index of tentativeness, on which women of most cultures score higher than the men of that culture. On this index are phrases such as I wonder, perhaps, do you think, maybe, shall we, sort of, don't you?, which are all used to avoid conflict by not speaking assertively and authoritatively. This, however, is seen as uncertainty and lack of independence by men.

Silences:

For men: must use to keep control of the conversation.

For women: must fill in to cover the awkward gap and keep conversation going smoothly.

The male tendency to control conversations is called 'minimal response'. Waiting for him to respond from anything to 3 to 5 seconds after you've finished speaking kills the conversation. You don't know whether he's quietly forming a considered response or just not bothering to reply to something too inconsequential/upsetting/boring/gossipy/emotional etc. To him though it means controlling all that conversational expressivity she is putting in – silence can regulate both when and how the conversation will proceed.

Inflection:

For men: falling intonations mean a command – especially when shortened. i.e. 'Sugar?' (Sounds like you WILL have sugar with your tea, or else!)

For women: rising intonations sound like uncertainty, asking for approval, 'Is it alright if I have sugar with my tea?'

Interruptions:

For men: necessary to keep the conversation going in logical direction.

For women: just try!

When women do interrupt they tend to leave it until the end of the other's sentence so it doesn't change the subject too abruptly, whereas men tend to interrupt earlier, thus leaving the speaker's train-of-thought unacknowledged.

11

The language of the body

The true story of Clever Hans, the horse that could do maths is one worth retelling. Much research went into how his equine mind worked – how and what sort of problem he could solve – and he was carted around Europe in the early part of this century to be put on show, tested and retested. Hans was a very clever horse – but his cleverness was not at mathematics, it was at reading non-verbal cues. To a level that could put clever human males to shame. When his beloved master was put behind a screen to read out the problems to Hans, the poor old horse was at a loss – he couldn't read the subtle head nods, eyebrow raising, facial muscle tightening or arm gestures that told him he had arrived at the right answer and could stop tapping with his hoof. He tapped uncertainly and nervously, unable to seek the approval he wanted from his owner. I've never been able to discover whether he had a nervous breakdown after this – he had every right to!

Hans would have made a wonderful mate, responsive and an accurate decoder of the unintentional messages of his partner. But his partner didn't understand him, and furthermore dominated him. Another oft-repeated story in male and female relationships!

Non-verbal behaviour can reinforce the verbal message, negate it, or compensate for the inadequacy of the verbal. Dr Robyn Skynner tells a lovely story in his Radio Four *How families Survive* series. In one of the sessions his patient had brought a floppy rabbit which kept falling over. In the frustrating session the psychiatrist felt he was getting nowhere, and for some reason felt compelled to keep propping up the rabbit, thinking how ridiculous the whole thing was. In his frustration at not being able to be more helpful verbally, Dr Skynner offered support non-verbally to the floppy rabbit – which was interpreted by the patient correctly, as a non-verbal offer of support to himself.

This is the key to relationship survival. When disagreement prohibits a verbal synchrony, a non-verbal reassurance can still be going on underneath, 'I disagree with you but I still love you' and the positive expression of intimacy goes on. The other way round is harmful, to say the right thing but then to negate it non-verbally. At the sublimal level it makes the couple uneasy and pushes them into the negative withdrawal cycle.

The evolution of language

Long before the development of language, individuals conveyed messages without words through sounds, posture and gesture. In time there was a pictorial representation of signs and symbols. With language came the written word, and very precise messages as well as more abstract and imaginative creations. As the human mind evolved, it developed the capacity for automatic disguise, and hidden messages became part of our communication, understood at an unaware level. A separate system of preconscious coding is probably the human brain's greatest achievement. It is automatic and takes place without the awareness of the encoder. Sometimes this can be recalled under special circumstances, like hypnosis, or great emotional intensity. But even stored away subliminally, these messages affect our feelings.

His language and her language

In the last chapter it was suggested that the objective v. subjective perceptual categories of the brain meant that reality is different, depending on which way you look. There are even different parts of the brain for processing concrete words as opposed to abstract words and there appear to be sex-differences even in those small parts of the brain, or at least, men and women make differential use of them.

Male-speak is an instrumental language, purposeful, factual, rational, and designed for the competitive world of the workplace, sportsfield and bar. In the male-speak dictionary, the well thumbed words are challenge, takeover, duel, match, thrust, tackle and synonyms for these. Woman-speak is an expressive, but indirect language, replete with cooperative words. And it must be spoken a particular way. Women are trained in babyhood to speak with a higher pitch and softer tone – adults speak this way to girl babies and in louder, lower tones to a newborn boy! The lessons are well learnt, so that by womanhood their voices sound totally different to men, much more so than the slight physiological differences in the vocal chords can explain. Luckily for men, soft, high-pitched voices are eminently interruptable.

'Male-interact' is hierarchical; that is, someone will be dominant, holding forth until another man successfully interrupts by speaking and getting more attention than the first dominant, and so on. Men compete for the floor, while women rotate democratically. In mixed sex interaction, the competitors win over the cooperatives. They speak more, and they speak about subjects other than human relations, which women's talk generally goes back to. So males talk more, talk longer and louder but not about the one thing women want them to talk about – feelings. And women would like men to listen more. Women together talk and listen to each other equally – this is why they don't need to interrupt each other as much as men.

When men and women talk together, doing what comes naturally leads to him talking instrumentally, in emotionally flat monotones, without intensity or elaboration but with competitiveness. Points are scored with gestures of dominance, and the goal is to establish one's own point of view. Simple emotional ventilation is seen as indulgent by many men. They feel that talking should be *about* something, and will invent it rather than admit that all they really wanted was companionship. So, women's supportive communication is interrupted and controlled. To them the delicate probing of the state of their feelings, the manoeuvring to fit in, all seem as if she doesn't know her own mind, so they feel irritated. He feels a foreigner in the land of uncodeable meta-speak, not understanding that cooperation, the maintenance of empathy and the offering of support is what he is turning down. The real man is a doer, and he is as economical with words as with emotions – never using two when one will do! And those few words will be about a fact, an activity, preferably sports or E-type Jaguars – it comes from little boys' play groups and later big boys' pubs and clubs. In these competitive groups the way to maintain status is to talk about the fastest, the biggest, the best – or keep the attention with the risqué joke. Talking is rarely about feelings like groups of women or secrets like little girls' 'heart to heart' groups.

Non-verbal warmth or reserve triggers vicious or benign cycles

When couples start to misread each other, feelings run high and start on a predictable cycle. A rigid reciprocity of the negative messages is invoked, because each is supersensitive to negativity and any cricitism launches cross-criticism. Matching an eye for an eye leaves no space to be creative. They start to punish each other instead of rewarding each other, and this negative spiral gives them the trapped feeling unhappy couples describe.

The manifestation of non-verbal behaviour during fluctuations in degree of closeness is felt by the partners, and what counts in maintenance is how much couples will keep up the touching and kissing when they don't feel like it. The sequence is important. Unhappy couples look at their partner during negative messages, especially when they are speaking rather than listening. This suggests a competitive non-verbal monitoring of the partner's behaviour. There are lengthy pauses between speaking, which are not filled with the usual verbal reinforcers, and it is as if the couple have taken a mute stand, and decided they can't speak or move towards each other more. The whole effect is arhythmic.

Happy couples do the opposite, lean towards each other, place body and head so as to be facing forward rather than away from each other, they talk more and talk more positively, look at each other more, especially during listening, smile and nod their heads more and use more arm and hand movements. This animated conversation says involvement, pauses are short and matched, speech is intense and also matched in duration.

The silent messages

Some men are sensitive to others' feelings – it is after all only a matter of training and experience – but these are not the average men. Growing up in English-speaking cultures means the majority of men are less able to decode the emotional meaning of speech than the average woman. Most of what we talk about isn't earth-shattering and full of pithy wisdoms, but if talk is trivial, the meta-language is not.

Movements, posture, gesture and vocal pitch, tone, tempo, loudness and articulation have great emotional meaning; over 50 per cent of the message comes from the non-verbal aspects. Much of the unexplained attraction and eyes meeting across a crowded room syndrome is due to the non-verbal signals we give off and receive, and the continuing compatibility of the couple is entirely down to the non-verbal signals of reassurance and approval we exchange daily. This is the currency of compatibility – the attitude underlying words and actions. Thoughtless words and rash actions can be overlooked when basic attitudes towards each other are positive, loving and trusting. Conversely, following to the letter the best communication guide published won't improve compatibility when the covert attitude is clearly ambivalent.

Because men are less practised at identifying their emotions and putting them into words, their unintentional message is expressed non-verbally and sometimes at total variance to the words. Dozens of women told me they had got used to ignoring what their men said and watching for the foot shuffling, the tell-tale eye blinks, the tempo of pacing, arm waving, forehead creasing, set of jaw, or any of twenty characteristic movements they knew meant a particular feeling. Some had embarked on a sociological enterprise, asking their husbands what they felt, and mentally cataloguing it for future prediction!

Because of the male taboo against knowing himself, a man's self-concept is often a semi-disconnected construction. We are all piecing together pictures of ourselves from the reactions of others around us, and our personal identity can only be understood through these interpersonal relationships – the closer the more self-clarification. We develop unique body styles, matching the pictures others feed back to us. Men's styles are less complex and more readable to women, because they can't integrate the emotional strands of their personality so well.

The more accurate she is, the more powerful a position she is in. In fact, predicting others behaviour and reactions is the goal of psychologists, politicians, economists and bookmakers and a huge amount of time, money and science goes into it. Since most women grow up communicating with others and therefore reassessing themselves daily, they are in the powerful position of the professional predictor, although the stakes are different. Unlike the professional, they don't want knowledge for control and profit, but for communality and relationship.

In a study of communication in marriage, couples were asked to participate in problem-solving tasks and discussions that were bound to be at least stimulating and perhaps distressing. This took several hours, and they were videotaped, their non-verbal body language coded. The couples were given several weeks' marital communication training (these were well-paid volunteers) and did the problem solving exercise again. When the husband was irritable, critical or put his wife down in some way she would react back negatively. When he smiled, showed empathy, defused tenseness with soothing gestures and so on, she also reciprocated positively.

But the same reciprocation did not happen for the husband. Whatever his wife had said or done, his behaviour matched not hers, but his own original feelings about her, scored the very first day of the experiment. In other words, his underlying attitude towards his wife was echoed in his non-verbal communication (as well as some verbal) and the communication training had not changed his sensitivity to the present emotional situation. He was still interpreting today's events through yesterday's feelings, almost as if once the relationship is crystallized, that's it, he never has to think about it again!

The inability of some men to interpret and put their own emotions into words leads to their inability to decode non-verbal expressions of meaning. This leaves them vulnerable to the person who can decode non-verbal messages, sometimes better than he can himself. This can lead to a fear of being controlled, and many men did make this statement about women. The study quoted in the first chapter illustrated this; men feared emotional entrapment by women, expressed as being 'swallowed up' or 'engulfed'; while a woman's enduring fears are of physical danger to her person. The motto for men appears to be control or be controlled, and for some men who cannot control their emotions, the alternative is to control the behaviour of the people that affect him, notably his partner.

Joe Tannenbaum says he has noticed in his men's workshops that when the men know he is in charge they relax, so it's only that men feel *someone* ought to be keeping an eye on the rules. He presumes that if a woman knew the male rules of control, took charge, and appeared competent, then she is likely to be given the referee's whistle. But if she resorts to feminine group behaviour, like trying to get everyone to participate democratically and cooperatively, then the men will feel she is not to be trusted and will take back control.

The language of what matters

We all attend to what has most significance for us, and in relationships it's the degree of involvement for most women; and the degree of independence for most men. The language of control rivals the language of intimacy not only in every verbal exchange but also in the *way* the words are spoken and through which non-verbal medium they are expressed.

Watching for the visual clues

Because men don't volunteer emotional information, women are reduced to asking questions, which are often brushed off. Or else they will judge his emotional attachment by his facial expression. Lower-status people with quieter voices will have trouble in getting attention in conversation, and must watch and wait, ready to jump in when the others are ready to stop speaking – this is a ploy of the traditional wife. She gets her way by using subtle, manipulative but skilful non-verbal messages, while unsuspecting, insensitive husbands believe they themselves are the final arbiters.

The woman in the therapeutic couple is just as good a decoder of non-verbal clues, but instead of putting up such an elaborate defence will negotiate just as subtly for equality. The poorer decoding skills of the 'separate' wife perpetuate whatever disadvantage she started out with. When the relationship is unhappy, women give up watching the face and switch to what now has more relevance for them – the voice.

Listening to the vocal clues

The vocal channel carries the non-verbal message of command, confidence and charisma. Deeper pitch and louder projection are associated with dominance and authority. Both sexes can acquire this, but men start out with a natural advantage from puberty, even men who are not trying to control those around them. But when they are it is the voice that directs the campaign for control. Pitch, loudness, articulation, rhythm, fluency, silences, intonation pattern, stress contours, dialect and accent all affect the messages we abstract from words.

The charismatic can alter people's emotions with their voices. Think of the oratory of moving political speeches, the deep, striking and varied voices of singers. Of course singers and speakers practise voice and breath control to enhance their performance, but confidence and authority, or lack of it are clearly conveyed in everyone's voice. It is the hardest non-verbal cue to control under emotional stress.

These are the messages that men attend to when their women talk, and it is the message they send back. 'Who's in charge round here' is conveyed by raising the voice, lowering the pitch, talking in a flat monotone, leaving longer silences between sentences and not replying back as quickly as the other, they are all control mechanisms. Conveying intimacy by vocal channel means deliberately softening the tone, increasing the rate of speech, speaking with a greater pitch variation, leaving fewer pauses between sentences and shorter silences before replying; but it is still done with louder, lower voices than women.

Crossed channels

Unhappy men, like unhappy women, abandon their usual non-verbal means of monitoring the relationship, and switch channels. Men who assessed their wife's non-verbal meaning through her voice, now look at her face – and women who watched their husbands' faces listen to his voice instead.

Another influence is the fact that men send more negative messages anyway – less smiling, nodding, emotional support, sympathy. The sequence leading to the channel switch is not clear, but the research referred to earlier suggests that the woman looking for facial cues of involvement becomes disappointed with the inexpressive face of the man. When she has learnt that the real carrier of his feelings is his voice, she starts to hear 'close enough, no further' messages.

Because of the greater numbers of negative messages sent by men to accompany their verbal communication, the effect of a higher rate of distancing non-verbal language is a controlling, authoritative tone. This would demotivate women to search for intimacy cues, and become more concerned with their power: who makes the decisions, what does he intend for the relationship in the future and so on. But by then men, puzzled at the decline, start to search for intimacy cues by looking at her face!

Frozen faces and harsh voices

This was repeated over and over again:

> As soon as I see her frozen face I know we're in for an evening of nit-picking and what's wrong with me.

or:

I try to have everything nice for when he gets home and then I hear him speaking curtly to the children and my heart sinks, I know the weekend is going to be all short, sharp monosyllabic conversation.

The messages of dissatisfaction for the unhappy man are from the frozen face of his wife, and her messages of dissatisfaction are in his harsh voice. They are, unfortunately for them, accurate messages, because the unhappy attend to the right channel, the one which they were sent.

An untested possibility is the increasing deepening of the voice in women, with their social experience and age (remember the androgyny switch). Over time this says, 'I want less intimacy and more control' to the men, who are then on the defensive. Some women had cottoned onto the simple equation of:

lowered voice = I get what I want easier.

The sensory language of rapport

There are other physiological differences in the coding of incoming information that affect rapport. To get on well with someone you must share their sensory reality and they yours. Unfortunately, for the majority of men and women there are subtle differences in this reality, which mean they are very rarely able to share each other's experience exactly.

We experience and interpret the world through our senses. The universe is full of rhythms of energy, light and sound which provide important information for the organisms that can detect and analyse it. There have to be changes in our patterns of neural activity that correspond to the physical events in the environment. As the philosophers say, we can never perceive reality directly. We have sensory receptors to turn the environmental energy into the electrochemical energy of the nervous system, this patterns a neural code which lays down memory and allows us to compare the incoming information with previous experience.

We can all recite the five senses but the two that are specialized for women and men are hearing and vision respectively. Some 60 per cent of the population are thought to use primarily visual means for getting their information about the world, and more of them are men. Perhaps because of men's better spatial processing, referred to earlier. But the proportion of people using their auditory sense as a major means of processing the world is quite high too. Those with the most sensitive hearing can actually hear up to ten times better than the average person – and they tend to be women.

Women's reality

Women want to *hear* things – their better hearing sets off the endorphins located behind the auditory system; even new-born baby girls are more responsive to another baby's cries than a new-born boy.

Caroline waves her husband, a scriptwriter, off to America regularly, where he can stay for weeks at a time. She doesn't mind she says – as long as they talk over the phone most evenings. 'Just to hear his voice makes me feel content and safe', she says, 'even though I know he's 5,000 miles away and could never practically help me'. The cost of love and endorphin release can be counted – in telephone bills!

A person who receives their impressions of the world and the people in it through the auditory channel is a good verbal communicator who enjoys dialogue. They are distracted by all sounds, disharmonic and pleasant. These are the people who tell you what they hear on their holidays, describing the tinkling of the cowbells on the Alps, or the Immans' call to prayer from the mosque, the strange music of other lands, and can discriminate the sound of every bird in their garden. They talk to their pets, their flowers and their ancient cars. They are eager to listen to others' stories and tell their own, and are good at putting their thoughts and emotions into words. Familiar? They are more graceful and rhythmic, and are drawn to people who speak eloquently. You don't find the flat, monosyllabic talkers in this group. Because their breathing style is regular and rhythmic, and uses all of the diaphragm, they have well modulated voices with varied pitch, tone, timbre and cadence. An expressive voice.

Men's reality

But if women want to be *talked* to, men want to be *looked* at by their nearest and dearest. Men tend to be visual processors, solving problems by 'seeing them'. They have an ability to see things in relation to one another, the sort of ability that makes good engineers, jigsaw puzzle assemblers, algebraic formula decoders, architects, and avid *Playboy* readers, or perhaps more accurately, lookers. If you relate to the world through images, then how people look is quite important to you, just as those who relate to sounds focus on what people say.

Some never forget a face, others always remember voices

If vision is a guide to your mate's world of experience, then it means going to plays and art galleries, sports fixtures and exhibitions, not concerts and debates. It means having holidays in spectacular, exotic places rather than postcard tranquility, and making love with the light on. Because a visually dominant person *sees* the answer to questions, they see themselves in these images when they evaluate their feelings. Their mate is an integral part of this picture show, which is why those who people it must look good too. So, he counts attention in terms of how much she looks at him, and she, in how much he talks to her. Based on mother's shaping, it was something he became addicted to, his visual mode of processing lapping up the eyes of love. Glen told me of his unease when his wife started working.

We'd agreed beforehand she should continue her career once Jamie was at school. And I've always done a fair share of the housework anyway – but there was this feeling hanging around. I wasn't happy. Every time she was late I would wonder why, with all sorts of disaster scenarios, including the one about running off with the boss. Then when we went on holiday I realized that it was the amount of time she was away, and even when she was home she was always preoccupied with someone else. The first morning on holiday over the breakfast table she looked at me and laughed about something and I knew what it was I'd missed. I'd not had her full attention in the whole 8 months she'd been working. Not more than a fleeting glance in all our conversations.

Glen firmly believes in the old proverb, 'out of sight, out of mind'.

Matching each other's reality

A popular theory gives advice for remedying the reality gap. Auditories should start talking to their visual partners in terms of picturing this, seeing that, bright ideas, colourful views, illuminating opinions, foggy perspectives, the point dawning on them, looking for a solution and so forth, and looking, with eyes wide open, pupils enlarged if possible. (The ancient Egyptians used to do it with

Belladona eye drops.) Use any visual metaphor that helps them discuss their experience closer to how they see it.

Meanwhile, visuals should be tuning in, sounding off, resonating, vibrating, hearing this, having crescendos and talking. Talking about things as clear as a bell, sounds a good idea, the tone of the conversation, and talking more. Because of their hearing sensitivity, auditories shouldn't be subjected to harsh noises, and are reputed to be emotionally sensitive in general, questing for harmony. Visuals, on the other hand, are claimed to have enthusiastic, extroverted rather insensitive personalities.

The hardened psychological reader immediately sees sex-linked stereotypes embedded in these descriptions; but whether because of socially conditioned stereotypes or specialization of brain hemispheres, the two sexes do have different verbal and non-verbal ways of experiencing reality, which causes much misunderstanding when they are not recognized.

As poor Clever Hans the horse discovered, it is not enough to read the unintentional message, you have to share your partner's reality to establish an equitable rapport.

Two skills to acquire

1. Learn to decode body language, and to defuse tension. It takes considerable emotional discipline to change attitude while emotionally aroused, but this is the secret of a successful relationship – to stop the negative cycle before too much damage is done. Non-verbal means are more important in altering the negative cycle than verbal communication.

2. Examine your conversational styles, the timing of speech that illustrates to each the degree of your involvement, and the compromise you want to reach between involvement and independence.

The language of involvement

Music of the spheres

Music is an echo of the rhythmic quality in all things – and no society, however poor, is without music and dance of some form. Mystics and composers have made much of the universal harmonics of the world they believe are etched within all of us.

The information we get from the world around us comes in rhythmic waves which our sensory receptors translate into rates of vibration that can be understood by the brain. There are many neuropsychologists who believe that the division of labour between the right and the left hemispheres has evolved to couple the linguistic capacity of the left with the para-linguistic/kinesic (that's the emotional memory of the words, as conveyed by voice and body-language) capacity of the right hemisphere of the speaker and listener – respectively.

An auditory-motor reflex in the brain synchronizes the listener's movements with the speaker's voice faster than conscious reaction time. So, when one person speaks, the thoughts are translated to muscle movements and then into airways that hit the other's eardrum, which starts to oscillate in synchrony with the voice; a few milliseconds for the sound to register in the brain stem, then the left hemisphere. The left brain-right ear system is particularly sensitive to the rhythm of spoken syllables.

Left hemisphere damage, like tumours or haemorrhages, which impair speech, will usually also impair gesture and correlate with the ability to recognize word meanings. This means that gesture and speech are processed in the same part of the brain – right-handed people will use right-handed gestures, whereas left-handed people will use both because left-handed people usually have speech processing areas in both the left and the right hemispheres.

Basic rhythms are a fundamental feature of our brain programmes, and are controlled by biological 'clocks' linked to external rhythms like daylight, and internal ones like heart or pulse rate. These millions of rhythms are all interrelated, and resonate with other humans. Synchrony is a hidden force that, like gravity, holds groups together. Exemplified at its best in good jazz groups, team games, professional groups like firefighters, and at its worst in lynch mobs and mass hysteria. An emotional response develops when the signals transmitted through the nervous system stimulate a limited number of brain areas. Emotional responses are structurally timed within the brain, giving rise to an electrical signal that can be picked up by electrodes and read on a computer screen. Emotions such as anger, fear, excitement, panic, anticipation, anxiety all have their characteristic waves and spike pattern as the emotion sweeps through the inner areas of the brain. Matching positive emotional rhythm in a couple is rapport-building, but too much negative matching can drive both people further.

Uncoupling of the rhythm happens when each becomes more aware of self, and starts to check the equitable contribution of the other. Of course this 'who's doing all the work around here' attitude invites hostility, and the relationship becomes distant. The couple lose the ability to synchronize with each other, as they move from rhythmic, implicit routine and stability to a life laboured by rules, shoulds and oughts.

The evolution of relating in rhythm

Animal communication has implications for humans, with its calls based on rhythmic movement. Evolution would have preserved early humans learning to speak in time with others. In the heat of the hunt, synchronizing with each other would have been a matter of life or death. The creation of life is a rhythmic process, and sex rhythms are the ultimate matching, creating harmony between the couple. Animals have rituals to express aggression and dominance too, but humans can appease with words as well as rituals – they reassure each other by what they say and the way they say it.

The way we speak to each other choreographs an intricate dance to time. Voices raise and retreat, mouths open widely or narrowly, lips curl and stretch, eyelids are lowered or raised, blinked anxiously or invitingly, eyebrows lift, foreheads crease, heads are tilted every which way, shoulders shrug and arms wave, pupils constrict and dilate, fingers flex and wrists are turned, legs are crossed and feet shuffle and jiggle, trunks lean towards and away to each other – and all to mother's original beat.

Rhythms of sunrises, saxophones, clocks and conversations

Staying in synchrony is staying together. Communication is like a dance – each taking their part in the intricate steps to understanding. Microsounds go with micromovements and all are embedded in a macrocontext of whole words with whole movements. All the movements, micro and macro, follow the same beat, a beat that organizes the speech, links the syllables, words and phrases. But we only keep in perfect synchronization while remaining attentive and involved.

The overall function of synchrony is identification with each other behaviourally, non-verbally and verbally. The matching of rhythms gives us the feeling that 'this person is sympathetic to me'. Emotional intensity has a vibration rate that is similar to the rate of people in a state of anticipation, expectancy and attention. Each level of speech is accompanied by a contrasting pattern of body motion, so that one paragraph will be marked by gesticulations of the right arm, and the next paragraph with the left arm, right down to the smallest movements – kines (like twitches) – and all picked up by the nervous system at a subliminal level.

Just as there are millions of sounds humans can make, but only some of which we regard as meaningful, there are many different movements the body can make – but we attach meaning to only a finite set. There are about 60 meaningful movements for the whole body and 30 for the face, head and eyebrows.

The way speech and body movements go together has been dissected by microanalysis, slowing a film sequence down to the speed that each mini-movement goes with a phoneme (the smallest part of speech). Pronouns such as I, me, we, us are accompanied by a handmarker – a movement towards the speaker's body – and when it's in the plural the movement ends with a little sideways sweep. Future and past verbs are emphasized by a movement forward or backwards, respectively, and there are many other body movements that enact the grammatical structure.

There are two attention-processing systems, one conscious, the other a monitor which only comes into consciousness when something in the background leaps into significance. But the impression the background generates is still stored away with the conscious memory, even if there is no change to remark upon. When something is repeated over and over, the movements that go with the speech for instance, the attention filter lets it through. So if the movements are acting as a back up for the meaning of speech, communication will be clear, the relation with speech and movement synchronous, and the speaker well understood. Even watching people on video can reveal previously undetected rhythms of speech and emotional pitch that can be described in mathematical rhythmic equations.

Relationships can be described in the same fluctuating pattern as stockmarkets and weather cycles. The repetitive cyclic and unseen patterns we generate resonate with one another in an interactional synchrony. When two or more living things oscillate in the same field at a similar pulsation rate, they lock into each other, which is why we feel so alive when we develop a rapport with another person.

Conducting your conversation

Conversational rhythms are stable, repeated and characteristic of the individual. Most people have an old uncle who is known as a garrulous old so and so, never letting anyone get a word in edgeways, or a friend who can never seem to string more than a couple of words together and seems to have gone to sleep while you're waiting for an answer. Everyone has a summation of their physiological and emotional states, which is their unique identifiable rhythm. So, attraction can be conceived of as synchronization of brain waves – and that depends on how you entrained with your mother's speech, how she mirrored the babies' cycles, and how we 'tuned into' the waves of sound and light which travelled in particular frequencies to the time and place of birth. We feel 'comfortable' with those who have a similar pulsation rate, and the possibilities are endless. Research on people being interviewed shows they have the same pattern of listening and speaking, time after time. We have different speech rhythms for different people though, perhaps habituating to a characteristic rhythm with one person and using a sub-rhythm which is a mathematical multiple of the internal beat for other people. Some people are flexible, and have many sub-rhythms – and friends – while others don't. One study showed that psychiatrists and their patients synchronize their heart beats, a true 'heart to heart'!

The whole body participates in voice and speech production. Underlying this dance of understanding is the brainwave we produce in synchrony. The saying 'on the same wavelength' probably comes from the way volume and pitch of voice interrelate with the timbre or tone quality, which is a generalization of the vibratory energy of the voice. The closer people are emotionally, the more they are in synchrony (measured in millisecs) and it has long been known that disturbed families are movement disordered. Couples not in synchronous communication have a vague feeling something is wrong, something is missing that they can't put their finger on.

Life is a series of breaths

Comfortable conversations are when a smooth rhythmic flow of interaction keeps the couple involved from moment to moment – like a piano duet, each harmonizing to the other's movements. It starts with breathing, an accurate mirror of our emotions. The rate of exchange of oxygen with carbon dioxide which powers muscle, heart and lung is altered by emotional states, which affect breathing patterns of inhalation and exhalation rate. Rapidity or shallowness has an affect on oxygenation, heart, digestive tract and liver, which are all massaged by the diaphragm as we breathe. Most of us in western culture breathe at 15 to 20 cycles per minute, when the natural rhythm is 5 to 8 cycles. Correct breathing is relaxing, calming and actually releases energy. Slow, deep breathing activates the endorphin receptors in the lungs. Hyperventilation happens when people under stress catch their breath and breathe in a laboured way, causing changes in blood chemistry, allowing toxic substances to build up and it causes giddiness, numbness, fatigue, headaches, palpitations, nausea. These symptoms will disappear within six months of being taught correct breathing.

Healing by breathing therapy has been known in China for centuries; the quality of breathing can gradually heal emotional wounds and negative attitudes. As breathing patterns change they affect the pitch, tone and tempo of the voice, and when those cues are combined with slight changes in facial muscles, emotional meaning is detectable. The tiny changes in facial muscle patterns are registered below conscious threshold, but nevertheless affect the feeling we have about the person. Breathing patterns are as idiosyncratic as fingerprints and voice prints.

The language of involvement

To have a rhythm you must keep a beat. Beat sets the turn taking, tells the other when to pay attention, and is done by the body movements accompanying the speech. Remember the last time you tried to have a conversation with someone from a different culture (even if it's the same language); it's a strain, as you wait to see if that drop in pitch means he's going to stop talking, and just as you launch into your account of the car accident in which you nearly died, you find out that the drop in pitch was merely for dramatic emphasis – his punch line is to come and you've just ruined it. The beat of language stresses the meaning of what is said, and it's vital to communication because the same sentence can be understood in different ways, depending on where the stress is. Beat is a source of predictability used to prevent cognitive overload and focus on the bits that carry the message, that need special attention. Exchanging key information and changing subject are done on the beat our hands, arm and facial gestures score. We slow down or speed up the words in between the major points of stress to keep the beat. Then the conversation flows easily and feels effortless.

To achieve rapport a couple has to adjust swiftly and without thought to each other's levels of loudness, duration of speech and response to it, length of pauses between sentences, rate at which the words are spoken, preciseness with which the words are spoken – and also match the language type and adjust to the accent. The orderly exchange of speaking turns is signalled by one and monitored by the other, several non-verbal cues exist to manage it smoothly, and adaptation must take place within the first three minutes to make each feel that this person is worth getting to know. As the speaker comes to the end of a grammatical clause, he or she will drop in pitch and loudness, inhale audibly, drawl on the last word, leaving a pause while glancing down and gesticulating appropriately. Movement goes with emotion, and when two people are in such temporal congruence, both interpersonally responsive, the conversation is described as 'warm' by observers. The pick-up rate (the time between turn-taking), is quicker than when they are with people they are not attracted to, and the length of pause between words will be less. One long sentence will invite another long one in return and similarly, short sentences are reciprocated. The whole conversation goes smoother, quicker, the subject is changed effortlessly – no hesitations, false starts, uums and aahs, and time seems to fly. Parts of speech and associated movements which are in time with brainwaves lock into a single unified sequence. Each yields the 'floor' to the other easily, so there are no energy-consuming pauses while the other is waiting to jump in. Neither are there any simultaneous speaking, or interruptions – even accents become more similar, as well as the style of language, in terms of its formality or informality.

Synchrony is an automatic response of each individual to the impact of the other. We all have a characteristic level of activation, that responds in kind to the varying impact of another person, a compatibility of the nervous system.

Relationship rhythms

Matching 'wavelengths' modulates arousal. Relating in rhythm is a natural outgrowth of a world in which just about everything moves with a beat, from atoms to humans, and it is the way we send up the antennae of our neurochemical state.

Love is never having to explain what you mean

Microseconds in timing can make the difference between being thought pleasant, pushy, warm, sympathetic, domineering or conceited or any number of other traits.

Pauses

The length of time one waits before replying after the first speaker has stopped can be different from region to region, north to south, country to country. City-dwellers will feel there is an awkward silence and jump in to fill the gap, while the country-dweller is thinking 'How rude, these city slickers are so aggressive'. Meanwhile the city-dweller is thinking these country people aren't interested in anything. If it's a job interview, the slower turn-taker will be judged as incompetent.

Pauses in conversations are repeated thousands of times, even in a day, so the cumulative effect of repeated judgements takes on a durable quality. A lengthy pauser will never know why the shorter pauser dropped him off her invitation list. Neither will she, she just feels he's boring and perhaps not too bright.

As we come to the end of what we're saying, we drop our voice, slow down and pause. If communication styles aren't shared, the second speaker may fail to take the turn when the first speaker expects it. Or they may try to interrupt *before* the speaker is finished, i.e., misunderstand a gap between words as a turn-switching pause.

This is a classic transatlantic difference. The British expect longer pauses and the Americans shorter, so they clash enough in communication style for the British to be thought reserved and unfriendly and the Americans enthusiastic to the point of being overbearing. Finns have about the longest pauses, and their are numerous jokes about the stereotypical lack of Finnish sociability, like the Finn who raised his glass and said 'Skol' whereupon his companion grumbled 'I thought we came here to drink, not talk!'

Loudness

Increasing the volume at the end of the sentence means 'Wait, I'm not finished yet.' Getting louder can stress important points or links in the story, while softer means, 'by the way', additional information, an aside that's not crucial. Women complain that they are literally not heard by men, they find it almost impossible to break into a conversation and are continually interrupted by men once they are speaking.

Pitch and intonation

Intonation comes from the combination of pacing, pausing, loudness and changes in pitch. Changing the pitch on a word can change the whole meaning. A woman might use a rising intonation to be agreeable, and it often sounds like she doesn't know her own mind to a man, who uses a falling intonation. Extreme shifts in pitch convey sincerity, earnestness, emotional involvement; to someone with a varied pitch, the lack of variety in someone else's conveys blandness, emotional disengagement or repression. To the level pitcher, the varied one sounds overemotional – a frequently voiced male opinion about women.

Instead of asking our partners why they don't say what they mean, or telling them they're not listening or that they don't understand; we should be asking them why they paused, their pitch rose or fell, their volume increased or decreased, and so on. We make adjustments in volume pacing, pitch, speeding up or slowing down, leaving longer pauses or shorter ones in an attempt to get closer to a shared rhythm. The pacing, pitch, pauses and intonation make up speech styles of converging or diverging. In relationships these two different speech styles fit into larger patterns of sub-missive, domineering, avoiding or democratic communication styles.

Speech styles and attachment styles

The three attachment styles manifest themselves in these speech styles too, with the manic attacher at the involved end and the pragmatic and ludic lovers at the independent. Put on a scale it looks like this:

		most	most		
INVOLVED	[manic	women	men	pragmatic . . . ludic]	INDEPENDENT
STYLE					STYLE

Conversation regulates arousal, and each relationship style has its own level. The way couples talk to each other embodies assumptions about their relationship – who has the most control, who cares the most, who will do what. They signal a whole range of meanings by verbal and non-verbal means, which continually alter to elicit more intimacy, avoid confrontation, and renegotiate their couple identity over the years.

For example, Simon would often say to Jeanne, in loud com-plaining tones, 'Why don't you do more ironing, I can never find any clean shirts.' Jeanne would usually answer along the lines of, 'You're just as responsible and should do an equal share of the housework.' This would be interrupted or ignored by Simon. Pauline, by contrast, would have apologized profusely, speaking quickly, and rushed to rectify 'her' mistake. Edward would simply have got the iron out and done one, not expecting his partner to do his shirts. John might have said 'What can *we* do about getting the ironing done, so I don't have to be late because I can't find a clean shirt.'

To identify the mode of the message is to ask is it *domineering*, in that the other is expecting something unreasonable, or blaming. Or is it *submissive*, like Pauline, who often said, 'I don't know what to do Bob, tell me what to do about such-and-such'? Or is *democratic*, 'I think we should do such and such, what about you?'

Therapeutic relationships are characterized by complementary democracy. To transform domineering, submissive or avoiding communication to democratic, Pauline should start to preface her remarks with, 'I think such and such', before asking Bob's advice. This would encourage her to think and plan for herself various alternatives, so she could offer Bob more interesting conversations and give herself more credibility.

Simon should find a public laundry! Male selfishness is women's worst problem in relationships, because traditionally domesticity is equated with women. Simon, like most men, had seen his mother iron his father's shirts and just assumed that when he set up home he would also have a woman to do the same. Jeanne could only refuse to do his laundry at the expense of unpleasantness. She tried in democratic fashion – we must do equal shares, or, I do all the cooking, you are responsible for your shirts, darling – but with Simon it was unsuccessful. There are rational men, however, who see that as the economic situation has changed for women so must their traditional roles.

Edward's self-sufficiency encourages Barbara to lead an equally self-sufficient life. It is democratic in the sense that neither impinges on the other, but then the corrollary is they don't make an impact on each other either. Their communication used to be 'I am going to do such and such', *fait accompli*. The other was left to remonstrate or accept; there was little friction, but it was a language of simplicity, a sort of yes/no communication, which allowed them to drift apart.

A democratic communication style is an equally participating one – both contribute ideas, feelings and thoughts, and rework them until the final product is different to the initial input of each. Each had added more and transformed it to the mutual benefit of both. Matching a domineering, submissive or avoiding statement with a democratic response is the most important element of long-term compatibility.

The separates (both) start out with the language of independence and diverging speech styles, and in their own way are quite happy with this, fearing the joys of full involvement. They are at least matched in speech and communication style, and if no outside stresses put too much strain on the relationship, may stay together in stability and harmony.

The therapeutics both monitor and match and use the converging speech style, with the language of involvement and democratic communication. Undoubtedly the highest levels of happiness are here, but so are high expectations – so deterioration can result in a split up, but they have the best weapons with which to combat it.

Many traditional couples appeared to lie between the convergent and divergent speech styles, certainly if they had been together some years. They had a shorthand, habituated communication style, probably a result of the clash of the male's diverging speech style with the woman's converging one, but its goal is to prevent change and maintain stability. An agreement to differ, quietly. Happiness varied quite a lot here. Unlike other couples, one could be happy and the other not, so the suspicion is that they were eventually on their way to communication breakdown, even though neither felt this or expressed it at the time.

Table 12.1   Tips for altering typical male and female speech styles towards incorporating the other's style.

FOR WOMEN

- Don't leave pauses which men will fill – if you do you'll feel resentful and domineer and he will think you emotional and unassertive.

- Reinforce that with non-verbal signals of 'I'm not finished yet' – holding up your hand with eyes fixed on his, increasing your loudness and letting intonation rise slightly but firmly.

- Drop your pitch, don't go up at the end of sentences, he will think you more decisive than women who do let intonation rise.

- If you're only asking questions to keep the conversation going and he's answering in monosyllabics or not at all, stop, and either volunteer new information, or let there be silence. He will take you more seriously.

- If you're being interrupted too much for non-verbal signals and conversational devices to work, try saying 'Hold on, I want to add to that point.' Then have your say, speaking louder and slightly slower than usual, dropping pitch register with unwavering direct eye contact.

- Overthrow a lifetime's conditioning and talk simultaneously with him, joining in, echoing and extending his finishes – it may seem rude to you but it will seem enthusiastic to him.

- When talking about an emotional subject try to flatten your pitch more than usual, no swinging highs and lows of nervousness, which he will interpret as hysteria. Leave slightly longer gaps between your own words. If you write out your emotion-provoking speech, then read it aloud to yourself as if you were giving a statistics lecture; you'll pick up the difference intuitively.

- Don't drop hints, be subtle, or think up tactful ways to say things – it's all wasted. Be more direct. It may seem inconsiderate to you but the archetypal logical man will think you are intelligent and know your own mind.

- Don't assume he's not interested or isn't paying attention. If you do you're only interpreting him through your assumptions.

FOR MEN

- If you seem to be talking more, stop and leave a pause for her to come in, encourage her to do it with eye contact, slight nod and smile – she will respond instantly and won't try to keep the subject competitively, like your male friends.

- Real men *can* talk softly – it makes your message all the more intriguing when people need to crane their necks slightly to concentrate on you rather than lean back from the decibel blast – you'll get credit for tactfulness and thoughtfulness.

- Vary your pitch more; getting off the base register at least once in every sentence will lead her to believe you are sincere and involved.

- Try the tangential approach now and then. Conversation is not only about exchanging information. Small talk is to sus out each other's emotional state, it's asking are they still happily involved with you, and it entrains the conversation to the synchrony of rapport. And you thought it was about the reliability of the commuter train to work!

13

The language of independence

Missing the beat is to communication what dropping the baton is to the relay-race on sports day – isolation and rejection! Silences in speech are *not* meaningless, they are integral to the timing and rhythm of speech. Not reciprocating nods, smiles, or small talk with a matching synchrony invites the label 'non-responsive', as does a too-perfect reciprocation (when everything is matched in kind by one the other feels suspicious and manipulated).

This is unfortunate for the non-reciprocator who is simply socially unskilled. But when the mismatch is deliberate, the deviance is taken as dissatisfaction with the relationship. And it's probably true. Reciprocity and similarity mean liking, divergence and mismatch mean protection of personal freedom and unwillingness to be influenced by the other. It can be a statement of dominance and will force the other to reassess the relationship or readjust. When one of the partners is ambivalent about expressing emotion, silence is used as a stylized 'baton-drop' to avoid communicating. Silences between the ending of one speaker's turn and the continuing by the other become the focus of attention. Interruptions, lapses in the flow of conversation, inattentiveness, 'uums' and other such fillers, preceded by 10-second pauses and slower speech rate than the partner all communicate 'Change the subject, I'm bored (or frightened).'

There are two possible responses to a non-responsive partner. One is to speed up and compensate, as if trying to do the con-versational work themselves, (a woman's typical response) and develop almost a compulsion to talk. The other response is to match silence with sullen silence, and wait it out in suspicious withdrawal. The opposite of silence is interruption – which is an attempt to dominate. And men use both silence and interruptions more than any other verbal category. The continually interrupted person (you don't need statistics to work out that this must be a woman most of the time) becomes hesitant, taking interruptions as an expression of impatience, and becomes less and less sure of herself. A few more resilient souls will enter the competition and will talk louder and longer, or step up the tempo to get in what they want to say before they are interrupted again! This can sound like a quarrel. A person who uses both silence and interruption is seen to be dominant, aloof, critical, introspective, and self-sufficient – a pretty good description of a stereotypical male!

An unresponsive partner (to reiterate, it *can* be a woman, one who makes the separate type of relationship) is one who asserts an asynchronous right to control subject topics without repercussions, i.e. denying equal status to the partner's conversational patterns, thus preventing synchronous turn-taking (the most fundamental aspect of communication). A good rule of thumb is that the more a person is attracted to or likes you, the less they pause in responding to you.

Failure to respond with a matching, turn-taking pause makes it seem as if the person is uninterested and the interaction is stressful, carrying undertones of 'You're not worth talking to, you don't exist.' To be responsive requires motivation, energy and attention, an investment the Appollonian type male is unwilling to make.

The Victorian view of sex differences in communication styles was that women chatter and men speak more analytically after greater reflection. A linguist's more objective description is that a man controls the conversation through silence, either by deliberating before replying or by not responding at all, and by consistently refusing to take up some topics. Using a down intonation where a woman would use an up one signals disinterest and will end the conversation.

The silent speech style of the unresponsive male is generalized to body motion, which reflects private and repressed emotional states and thoughts. Lower rates of speech (as there must be if there is more silence) are associated with a decrease in limb movements, particularly upper limbs and head. But they are unaware that mimed acts of the lower body are likely to be the inverse of what is held down on top. Rubbing, scratching, stroking, jiggling, all suggesting a self-touching that is perhaps a reflection of what is missing in the life of the strong, silent male.

The unresponsive male of the previous chapters has several origins which serve to locate him somewhere on the unresponsiveness dimension. At one end is the normal man, brought up according to sex role socialization standards and who has different definition of intimacy than a woman (Chapter 6), a misunderstanding that can eventually be overcome, with awareness and tolerance. At the other end is the Appollonian male, on whom all the Hollywood wild west characters seem to be based. This is a much more difficult nut to crack since the Appollonian male is a mysogynist who exploits and disrespects women, to the point of hatred in some extreme cases. Then in the middle are men with the normal amount of desire but a slightly above normal amount of fear, a combination that doesn't promise easy communication.

Most of us aren't aware of altering our speech and communication style to regulate the independence we need from the other when we're in the withdrawal downswing of the circadian cycle. But it is instantly detected by the other. The threat is not clear, only a vague misgiving starts to pervade the relationship but it is easily dismissed in the optimistic upswing which slips us into the mood for intimacy, involvement and affection.

As time goes on things get worse, because romantic love minimizes misunderstanding. It fills in gaps and when eventually misreading of intentions, flaring tempers over small matters, petty bickering and such arise over incompatible speech styles the couple are apt to think that love has faded. Not realizing that the way they talk to each other IS the problem they read all the Good Communication books and see that all can be resolved, by talking more to each other. The result is a mutually aggravating spiral that just intensifies the conflict. More of the cause makes more of the result – and a conviction by her that he is selfish and by him that she is irrational.

The similarities that attracted them were the ability to synchronize body language and speech and the compelling opposites were the complementary sex-linked traits ('masculine' competence and 'feminine' softness – remember the list in Chapter 8 of stereotypical male and female qualities). But being a man or a woman affects your communication style and speech patterns. Keeping synchronous communication up is a great strain when career, children, time and the bills keep pressing us into the diverger and converger shorthand for communication. Such stress makes men and women turn different ways as illustrated in Chapter 8, and slowly enter a variant of the pursuer-withdrawal cycle or else both become less involved, which is reflected in their language of independence.

Cycles of divergence

Every creative act, from talking spontaneously to conducting symphonies, takes place in body movements, and every human interaction has its appropriate movements and gestures which can be suppressed only at the expense of personal growth. Cultural norms shape them, there are different rhythms for different cultures – but each group shares them. Cultural clashes and colliding rhythms make communication difficult, but when enough people share rhythms powerful speeches are made and pyramids get built and couples get along.

Differences in communication styles break the rhythm and are unperceived causes of incompatibility. The strain we feel trying to maintain a good conversation with someone we feel isn't listening, or appears to be indifferent, uncooperative, cold, irrational or rude is the strain of not being able to establish a conversational rhythm. Like armies that march in step and wood choppers who swing axes to song, everything is easier with the right rhythm.

When a converging speech rhythm vies with a diverging one there is a gradual transition from thinking of oneself as part of a couple back to thinking of oneself as a separate person again. A competitive style will always win over a cooperative one, and the diverger swamps the subtleties of the converger. Cause and effect are two way, clashing styles breed conflicting feelings which shift them both towards a more diverging rhythm which eventually leads to breakdown when the length of the withdrawal cycles exceed the length of the intimacy cycles. That happens when tense arousal overrides the circadian energy rhythm. And fear, uncertainty, ambivalence, insensitivity are all expressed by a diverging style which eventually infects the most enthusiastic converger.

The most commonly accepted reason for breaking up is that the couple can't communicate. It's not that they don't talk – but that their talking leads them to fever pitch frustration or apathetic depression. Mariane said:

> If I'd heard Peter once more, if he started on his 'you don't care about me' routine again – I'd have gone bonkers. Seven years was enough. He

started the same way each time, it went on the same each time and it finished the same each time. I would even start to recite the list with him, the times he did the decorating, the gardening, the tenderness that was gone, what was wrong with the children, why didn't I give up that boring job – what he really meant was time-consuming job. I used to try to remonstrate but he'd just get more upset, so I learnt it would be quicker if I just let the tape run. It made me so depressed I didn't even try to change how the conversation was going – just waited hopelessly.

This couple hadn't resolved the first conflict and the relationship had been deteriorating for five years before Mariane took the first step to leave. Ritualized complaining like Peter's states his dissatisfaction, but it destroys trust and goodwill, precisely the opposite effect to what he wanted. He wanted Mariane to change and as his unhappiness became evident to her she did attempt to try harder, to get closer and find out what was wrong. But that seemed to make things worse, the complaints intensified and she slowly removed her emotional investment in the relationship. As each start restating their point of view instead of listening to the other's reaction, turntaking becomes replaced with a monologue like Peter's. And no response, like Mariane.

The most common complaint is that neither will say what they mean, so arguments and bickering pile up over the toothpaste top, the last biscuit or anyone of a hundred little things when the deep structure was 'I'm unsettled by your non-verbal incongruity.' Language partly shapes our thoughts and actions and Peter's communication style was divergent. He loved Mariane but it had taken time to feel comfortable when they first set up home together and he had disappointed Mariane by his vacillations between declarations of undying love and then doubts which led to some backdowns, like renting a flat when she had wanted to buy one, not telling his parents that they were living together, and avoiding discussions of anything that hinted of permanence. He felt pushed, unready for commitment one day and overwhelmingly sure that his love would last an eternity the next day.

Unrealized by them, he had emphasized the language of divergence, and for three years the question of his commitment had been a low-lying rumble which had become a generalized resentment to Mariane, erupting every few months into an explosive situation, where she went off hysterically one way and Peter withdrew ever more determinedly into a silent hostility. They would make it up through sex, which was inevitably so wonderful that they decided they were meant for each other after all and settled down more or less happily for a few more months.

Peter and Mariane, Jack and Jill, John and Jane . . . the names may change but the structure of breakdown is the same. It starts with the identity of one conflicting with the sense of being a couple, either right at the beginning, or at the approach to a later macro-cycle of commitment, or the first child, or a job move – anything that involves a move toward more involvement faster than the person is prepared for. Consequently, the signals of non-involvement are sent, the hints, disgruntled glances, body tension, omitted kisses, complaints and subtle criticism, time spent alone and the speech style is used as a symbolic stand of difference, autonomy and freedom. The diverger becomes increasingly information-orientated. 'Did you pay the telephone bill?' before 'How do you feel today?'

Criticism is a protection against overwhelming closeness, but the criticized partner rarely realizes this, it is taken as a cruel rejection of the hope and love which had forged their bond such a short time ago. It is responded to on the surface level ('No, I'm not' etc.) which obscures the main issue 'I feel as if I'm losing my identity.' This odd feeling of being out of place in a world of couples comes and goes in stages. The uneasiness is dismissed as natural, something everyone goes through but divergent communication styles never get better. They get worse. The relationship then brings out the partner's deficiencies rather than their strengths. When one can't make oneself understood efficiently (as handicapped and stroke patients know) one tends to be dismissed.

Like Clever Hans of Chapter 11, women comment on feelings by reflecting them in a sensitive matching process – their facial expressions, pauses, signs and body language tend to be more integral to their discussion than are men's. But the language of involvement that most women use is denigrated as emotional by the men that use the language of independence, and, just as happened to Clever Hans, the divergers can dominate the convergers.

Breakdown in communication occurs when the closeness of the relationship encourages secrecy rather than openness – the one more concerned with protecting their autonomy and freedom, will shift to the divergent style. He or she will continue or take up something that makes him feel more like the old, single self. Old friends or interests, a course, a hobby, an affair, or any other palliative that reinforces their old idea of themselves. Anything the partner can't share or doesn't know about. Garden sheds, spare rooms and studies are pressed into service, and as secrecy becomes more necessary to protect the new self, a non-verbal and verbal divergent speech style increases, and synchrony decreases.

It can happen over years, as each becomes involved in their life-plans of career and children, the extra monitoring needed to communicate on a convergent level gets pushed aside in a busy life with its competing demands for attention. The relationship may survive forever at a lower level of satisfaction than they could have achieved, but if no alternative is available, divorce or break-up is not usually thought of. One of the most surprising things in my survey was the low level of satisfaction many couples were living in, yet they had no thought of leaving. They had many regrets, disappointments and complaints, but no plans for changing anything. They often appeared to be in a helpless state not believing they *could* do anything about it. The problem was usually seen to be the partner's fault but on the whole having a relationship was better than not having one. 'The happy times made up for the boredom,' and 'What do you expect after 10 years anyway?' seemed to be the general consensus of those living below the average happiness level.

Their level of communication, although out-of-tune and not as involved as it could be, was not too divergent for a total communication breakdown. It could be described as habituated and designed for a busy life, the few words said conveyed much factual information but given the inability of many people, especially men, to decode non-verbal messages accurately, misunderstandings seem impossible to avoid. People who had been outgoing, friendly and responsive, able to attract others easily became, over the years 'relationship-retarded'. They believed their unhappiness meant they were no good at relationships and in addition to blaming their partner, often took a negative view of their own ability to get on with someone else. (I am not including unhappy couples who were committed for life due to religious, economic or family reasons.)

From passion to poison

The more intense love is, the more it involves possession and control as well as protection and help. And the closer it is to anger. This is why even minor resentments should be sorted out before they escalate into a retaliatory spiral. Emotional involvement turns us into big babies, crying for love, approval and attention. Once either feels vaguely wronged our signal detectors of criticism, disapproval and rejection start whirling, and a progression is established. The sensors of the nervous system are turned up to record the instances of unfairness, selfishness, laziness, irresponsibility, lack of care, never being let alone and so on into the 'How much I am loved' register, and when the balance goes into loss, retaliation is mobilized. Vengeance belongs to couples in love! And it is calculated to cause the most harm – withdrawing physically or emotionally can be as threatening as outright violence. The concern of most family therapists is to redistribute the love gone wrong – from wishing to *be* loved and using manipulation to get it, to wishing *to* love and protect the other.

But once a partner is galvanized to right the wrong, the balance of the euphoria and anxiety molecules is disturbed, and little seeds of disappointment grow into big vines of hostility, sending out tendrils of dissatisfaction that spread over the whole relationship, and poison it. Each unresolved cycle of conflict ups the ante even more, and triggers off the primitive survival mechanisms of fight or flight. And it makes it less likely that a loving compromise can be reached, because the hostility elicits blame. The wrong must be righted and the perpetrator castigated, brought to book and made to suffer, not only in direct proportion to the hurt inflicted, but even more – for punishment.

There are three distinct roads to breakdown according to marital research, and they fit very well into the attachment style and relationship style categories as well as the diverger/converger speech styles. Differing speech styles lead each to make inferences about the other – usually the converger will be labelled temperamental and the diverger selfish. Each loses their positive expectation of the future and recognizes that something is missing. When they try harder, which means more of the same thing that caused the perceived coolness, indifference or hysteria, their negative interpretations are merely reinforced, the cycle is intensified.

Body language is now a powerful message carrier adding emotional meaning to the speech style, underlining the unwelcome message. Their sexual life suffers and the actual breakdown starts with male withdrawal into unresponsiveness and attempts to keep control of the woman's freedom in lots of little ways – disapproving comments about her going out with friends and so on. The language of control and divergence reinforced by the body language of non-involvement and power. The synchrony established in early days decreases. Usually it is the woman who first notices she doesn't get a match back from her partner, telling her that their sensory attunement is not indexed physiologically speaking. She will call this a lack of responsiveness. As she starts to make a joke about something she will notice he is staring out the window morosely, or he may decide it's time for a brisk walk just as she'd settled down in the comfortable chair with the Sunday paper. She will start to feel 'on edge' – and what happens from there determines the rest of the relationship.

Because sex is the physically closest of all activities the couple share, it suffers from emotional distance between them. As Jeanne and Simon drew apart, Jeanne went from enjoying the fullest expression of her love she could make to Simon, to recoiling from his touch on any erogenous zone, as if he was a stranger.

Men tend to feel upset and angry more quickly over emotional issues than their wives and furthermore take a longer time to calm down, so they will hide that emotional turmoil under a frozen mask of indifference. The body language is tense, and talking and listening is done with an 'I'm not really here' stance, which infuriates the woman who is trying to talk about the problem. His unpleasant physiological activation of heart rate, skin conductance, and general body activity is translated into the facial muscles, gestures, voice and eyes which is communicated to her, and her nervous system is then also aroused, unpleasantly. This makes things worse for both of them, his inner turmoil increases as her outer frustration does.

Once the problem is acknowledged (no longer just a passing phase) it may be taken to a marriage counsellor, friend or family. But the couple rarely have much idea of what the problem is. 'He/she doesn't care anymore, we're not close anymore, we bicker, quarrel and misunderstand each other' and so on. This is often diagnosed, accurately, as poor communication. But the solutions offered, although helpful, rarely go far enough. Relationship guidance teaches communication skills to increase intimacy, but it is a lengthy and sometimes unsuccessful process that suggests a simple 'you be nice to me and I'll be nice back to you' sort of exchange. Although of some help, it is really missing the main point. The usual recommendations (spend more time with each other, talk more openly and honestly, make a be-nicer contract, reinforce the behaviour you want) can't work if the problem is incompatible speech style and communication style. Very few marriage counsellors recommend matching sentence length, voice volume, silent pauses, turn-taking or rhythms. To change communication style entails changing the couple's idea of masculine and feminine interaction style, and even what it is to be a man or a woman. Real men *can* talk expressively, emotionally and responsively, and femininity *doesn't* have to mean whispering, simpering high-pitched child-like voices.

Although the breakdown starts the same way and there is always a battle about the degree of control and closeness between them, there are three possible outcomes: female withdrawal, male withdrawal, male fighting.

Female withdrawal

If she uses a diverging style herself and tends towards the separate pattern of relating, then she will eventually cease doing things to attract her man's attention. Feeling helpless about creating the spark of responsiveness and rapport again, she will stop trying to match intimacy signals and turn away to other satisfactions – like Barbara of Chapter 5. She will start to live a parallel life, feeling victimized and blamed. With neither 'servicing' the emotional closeness of the relationship, one day it will just stop. No fireworks, just a shrug of the shoulders. Tammy had got to this stage, she and Rex cooperated, ran their home efficiently, but were both involved in separate careers – often joking about meeting each other only on the doorstep or in bed. They had been married two years and kept up their quite separate friends, hardly any of them knew each other and Tammy and Rex tended even to have separate holidays. Well, she liked travelling, and Rex thought it a bore. They had been closer but things didn't stay like that and Rex was so hard to get through to, she just couldn't be bothered. But life was good, maybe in years to come if she met some Prince Charming, she might leave Rex but at the moment she was happy enough. They didn't quarrel and Rex was good around the house, and there were lots of women who couldn't say that, Tammy reasoned. Until the day that Rex was putting the car away and she went into the kitchen to make tea. When he came in and said, 'Where's my cup?' she realized she had set the table for one! And she further realized that she didn't want to share his life anymore either.

The separate style woman is the first of the three types to withdraw emotionally in response to the perceived withdrawal of the man. If she is extroverted and working she is far more likely to divorce quickly – presumably having more social and financial support, as well as less emotional investment. The *parallel* style of relating meant that withdrawing increased their emotional distance, they talked less, took longer to say even that little, and were more hesitant, indirect, and divergent in their speech style than ever. Her withdrawal meant relationship obliteration.

Male withdrawal

A more likely reaction is the woman's attempt to soothe, talk over what's wrong, dissect the emotional problem . . . become more expressive to his lack of responsiveness. As speech style differences have conveyed their unintended message, destroying good communication, she senses his alienation and tries to re-establish bonds, using an ever more convergent speech style. Usually now it's too late, the secret 'new self' identity is revealed along with the new interests, friends and affairs. But the reason is still seen to be within the personality of the other – if they had been more responsive, interesting, attractive, less selfish, and so on – and the relationship is now judged a mistake. The reaction is only a more general withdrawal of the male. The traditional or manic woman is the more likely to seek counselling before resorting to thoughts of separation or divorce.

> I sat there helplessly, said Fay, while Lance said he'd only married me because I wanted to so much. He said he's known all along it wouldn't last but he went along with my wishes. I wanted to ask why it took him 20 years to find out that it wasn't going to last but I felt so let down I just couldn't hear anymore. He was lying, it was NOTHING like that, but I could see he'd totally convinced himself.

Fay's story was repeated everywhere. She had felt the frustration of the non-matching speech styles first, but she had tried harder to please, so that they eventually stayed together 20 years. But her increasing involvement with the local tourist office, at first in a voluntary capacity and finally as a paid executive, gave her so much self-validation that it was reflected in her speech. At 45, her voice had lowered in pitch, sounded more confident and she accommodated without thought to Lance's divergent style, which was when the relationship broke down. They'd had no problems or arguments, but Lance had decided there was more to life than living with the same person in the same house for 20 years, and when the opportunity arose to take a partnership in another town with a younger female colleague he left. Other women, less patient than Fay and less able to find alternative sources of self-validation, would have made the decision to leave themselves, and much earlier.

Once the amount of frustrating communication exceeds the pleasant communication, the decision to leave is made by the one who feels most restricted in their freedom and autonomy – the diverging, ludic attachment style man, who feels too out of place to match the converger, or the converging woman who has got to the stage of having given up so much of her autonomy, needs to leave the relationship to get back to her old idea of herself. The leaver will look for anything that justifies him or her, from the relationship being forged by accident, false pretences, pressure, mistake, *anything* so long as it was not personal choice. This is a clear statement of non-involvement, and used by the ludic attachment style man in full flight away from intimacy.

The male fighter

The traditional couple move to a *complementary* style of relating, with the husband using the dominant, diverging speech style and the wife the placating convergent. Thus they wind the pursuer-withdrawal cycle one spiral up. The male, with his greater vulnerability to unpleasant physiological arousal, dons his emotional armour, tightens his facial muscles, avoids eye-contact and turns away from the source of this emotional upheaval. 'Be rational', he mumbles which *infuriates* her and elevates her emotional arousal. He 'stonewalls' thus amplifying her emotions and their physiological reactions get out of control, which worsens the resentments they feel. Her persuasive converging style brings out the worst possible reaction in him, in the traditional style male, domineering belligerence and sometimes violence.

She asks what's wrong and what can be done with a battery of verbal and non-verbal means; he closes down totally and uses threats, shouting and loud refusals to be 'coerced', if she persists. But he doesn't want her to leave, he just wants her to shut up. She is left to figure out the mixed signals of non-verbal involvement, with lack of responsiveness to her verbal initiation. His divergent speech style is saying independence and his body language is saying involvement. A conflict that is transferred to the relationship.

They can go on for years in collusion, never discussing their real worries of how involved they are with each other, because they can't get a handle on it. This problem is so nebulous to most couples they can't pinpoint it. As things deteriorate, the monitoring and balancing of involvement and independence needs is condensed into a shorthand routine, that assumes everything is OK if nothing is said. Signs of dissatisfaction are actively dismissed with 'She'll be alright tomorrow', instead of explored, as the couple get on with life and work. A communication system based on the habituated acquiescence of the traditional couple (the divergent man controlling the speech style), can only function as well as the intense monitoring of the early years when nothing else in life changes. But of course it does. Men get promoted, demoted, made redundant, and women are changed by the experience of childbirth, for example, and they turn to each other for emotional support. But the habituated style of communication they have developed is not complex enough to monitor involvement needs, and they go unnoticed. Change is obscured and new information is prevented from disturbing the relationship. Stability is more important than the individuals needs. They know they are not close enough to hear each other's cries for freedom, and they push the alienation of the other back into their court – 'You deal with it, I'm not to blame' is hidden under 'Have a nice day darling' and even more cryptic, time saving conversational devices like 'Cuppa?' and 'What's for dinner?' It's a collaborative effort, each saying 'I'm only prepared to talk about dinner, television, cups of tea, and so on.' The dissatisfied one (the convergent style woman usually) has started to build an emotional defence and the other thinks 'Good, they've got over that silly trouble.' By colluding to keep secrets they preclude the possibility of alleviating the danger. Meanwhile the identity seeker is quietly going through the transition period of detachment.

This stage will go on until there is a reason for change, other friends getting a divorce, the balance of dissatisfaction with the relationship tipping into the negative with illness, money worries, children leaving home and so on. Threats, ridicule and sarcasm usually accompany the woman leaving the pragmatic man, and sometimes they are deterred from leaving by these ploys, but more often the months or years that have been spent building up a new identity now allow the chrysalis to turn into a butterfly and soar away.

The most wounding aspect of the break up for the one being left is the blame and cricitism that the leaver must heap on them in order to justify leaving. Eager though they may be to leave, the biological programme of attachment is brewing away at another level and setting in train the mourning for the relationship that did not succeed. The old partner has to be blamed for this failure and even has to be thoroughly disliked to sever the bonds of attachment. The one being left is in no state to pour oil on troubled waters. As their treacherous partner alternates between hostile recrimination and indecision the *last* reaction they are able to offer is reassurance. But that is what is necessary. But once the freedom fighter has decided (and sometimes this is the other's first intimation if the collusive communication has worked) nothing much is going to change their mind. A simple reassurance of 'I will change' in answer to the complaints of 'You don't care/are a workaholic/sterile/ boring/fat/lazy/watch too much television' is not enough. The freedom fighter will say 'All this time I felt like this and you didn't even know, how can you claim to love me?' They have spent months and years developing alternative lifestyles while the one being left has had only days or a few weeks with the realization that their life is going to change. Very occasionally the freedom fighter will agree to stay, by focusing on the bond and trying to recreate what they were once to each other. The other will go into a frenzy of accommodation, converging, not to say a pandering of the freedom fighter. But it's usually temporary, because it's artificial and makes the converger feel manipulated. The power is with the freedom fighter. '*You* change, or I go', which sets off emotional alienation in the converger this time! Because Barbara and Edward had both changed they were able to negotiate a new beginning – they even formalized it into an unofficial contract. But even they admitted catching themselves from falling back into the same old negative thoughts now and then; memories can be revised but never totally rewritten.

The irony for the innocent partners who are left is that by being such a good team builder, by investing everything in the relationship and giving up outside interests they actually did become less interesting, and by renunciating other sources of self-validation relied too much on their freedom fighter to supply them. As their communication styles become less synchronous with the increasing psychological gap between them, the team builder will try to revive nostalgic memories which are interpreted as meaningless by the freedom fighter. The team builder is left feeling inadequate and to blame. They go through the same process of detachment as the freedom fighter – only later. But it is more serious for them because they haven't had the time to develop a separate sense of self to replace the joint identity the freedom fighter is tearing away. They feel they have no control over the changes in their life and can become isolated and depressed, even suicidal. Being left in the same place exacerbates the loss – the joint possessions left behind symbolize the life created together which is now ruined.

The perceptive partner who is aware of non-verbal communication will have already suggested alternative sources of self-validation, encourage long-held dreams, Himalayan hikes, higher degrees – and offer understanding, or recreate interest by clever ruses. Shirley Eskapa gives examples in her book of women who invited friends with troublesome babies to stay, with the aim of discouraging middle-aged husbands going off with younger women who had or wanted children. Or left their own baby in the back seat of the car so the fleeing husband couldn't board his plane without abandoning it (it worked!).

But neither humour nor kindness comes easily after you've been given a detailed recital of all your worst qualities with several other imaginary ones thrown in for good measure. The turnaround is so staggering it's hard not to fight back in hate and recrimination, or breakdown in clinging dependency and reproach. Most partners are shocked at this betrayal, and fail to realize that this is a psychological imperative. To leave one must emphasize the negatives and accentuate the alternatives – precisely the reverse of the falling in love process. It is mostly temporary, once the separation is officially complete the couple can become friends again or at least cooperate. This is a completion unavailable to those who come home to find a dear John letter on the mantelpiece, but the leaver (usually the ludic type) will be going through a similar trauma of justification and is just not courageous enough to face the counter-accusations.

And the tragedy is, with two normal enough people, even the fighters, fleers and submitters, the alienation needn't happen. Swift intervention, to balance the signals of independence and vary them with non-threatening, involving non-verbal signals is the recipe. But, like Janet of Chapter 2, the usual response is to counter independence forces with extremes of involvement. The more self-validation is denied in the relationship, the more it will be sought elsewhere. The freedom-seekers often described coming home after being with their sources of validation (friends, hobbies and so on) and sitting in the car outside, not wanting to go into a house that no longer felt like home. The security of familiarity had turned into the threat of alienation.

The *symmetrical* pattern of the therapeutic couples meant that their speech style was interchangeable, either could be silent or enthusiastic, sympathetic or distant, but their intuitive communication rule was that whenever one was negative, angry or hostile, the other did not reciprocate in kind, the only time in a relationship when similarity did not pay off. Their higher degree of convergent speech style gave them a better understanding of each other so that the negatives could be handled without resentment. They were not allowed to build up and place a strain on the whole relationship.

The cycles of divergence are as predictable as the other cycles. Change WILL happen, and it must be balanced if it isn't to develop into a spiral of blame, counter-attack, and break up. Monitoring the level of involvement in the relationship through the right kind of communicative interaction allows fine tuning to take place. The impression of emotional overinvolvement of the converger and non-responsiveness of the diverger that each gets from communication style differences becomes a reality for them when the origin was merely in the pause, pitch and timing of speech. Little things mean a lot!

Although the cycles of divergence have the same emotional trauma associated with them, recovery is different according to the different relationship types. The separates and traditional styles have the worst post-divorce record, from being martyrs, overinvesting in the children, giving up a good job for one that involves unthinking routine or becoming depressed and vindictive.

The therapeutics, once separated, were free to see again the good qualities in the other without pain, to see them realistically and to keep contact through family events so that the period of life they shared together was not in vain.

No statistics are available on whether the therapeutic divorce less often than separate or traditional relationships, but if the level of conflict is any guide then the therapeutics have the least of it. Divorce mediation and counselling is much more likely to be a satisfactory process for them than the other two relationship styles. Although the description of the three styles is written as if both individuals are one of a kind, in practice there are mixed types – six possible combinations, which slightly alter the relationship characteristics. But it is possible to call the interaction between the couple predominantly traditional, predominantly therapeutic or predominantly separate relationship types. And each and every one of them will struggle with the balancing of the forces of involvement and independence.

Another study of divorced couples with children found that some couples themselves (apart from the children) maintained a friendly relationship and many of those who couldn't wished they could. It was certainly beneficial to the children when they did so, even when the wife had married again. The new husband was happy too since he did not have to take on the whole burden of the new ready-made family. Although the circumstances in which the marriage ended affected whether or not a friendship is maintained, the circumstances themselves are related to the attachment style of the individuals, fight (competitive), flight (avoidant), submit (give up self) and secure (the interdependent). Common-sense things like the distance from each other, whether and how many children they have or the time elapsed since the divorce has an influence on whether or not they will remain friends.

Depending on how much they saw each other and how friendly it was when they did (excluding any sexual or romantic involvement) one study was able to classify divorce types into:

Angry associates (25 per cent): These were moderately involved still but the involvement was fraught with conflict. Unable to distinguish between the anger due to their relationship and the anger due to each other's idea of bringing up the children, they tended to quarrel on every occasion, even when just dropping the kids off for a weekend.

Fiery foes (24 per cent): Avoided each other, fought each other through the courts, the children, their friends, their family and made life worse for everyone, especially the children.

Perfect pals (12 per cent): who enjoyed each other's company and stayed interested in each other's lives, phoning to share exciting news or depressing events. They put the children's interests before their own anger and frustration and did not remarry or live with anyone else, both living a child-centred life.

Co-operative colleagues (38 per cent): not quite so involved but they minimized potential conflicts and were mutually supportive of each other, whether each had remarried or not.

The degree of anger was the most distinguishing characteristic, and for the first two groups it was still as alive after three years, even though they nearly all wished there were less bitterness. Even after five years the perfect pals became more distant and the natural history of the conflict cycle came full circle – to detachment. Handling conflict constructively and containing anger are two life skills that can prevent the negative emotions of breakdown making things worse; but understanding the micro-rhythms of communication is the best preventive medicine of all.

14

The language of laughter

What's the difference between a buffalo and a bison?
You can't wash your hands in a buffalo!

The future whispers its mysterious promise to us in the form of fantasy, which is probably about the only ability that distinguishes the human species from the rest of the animal kingdom. We are a story-telling species – from campfires and Homeric sagas to the novels that win the literary prizes. Consider the significance of libraries of fiction, repeating the endless variations of the human story.

The stories we tell ourselves alter our perception of ourselves and our relationships. We choose the love stories we are willing to incorporate into our lives – so that we end up with the love style that comes from the organizing myths of our culture incorporating a world picture that explains why people are attracted to each other, how they should live together and in general sanctifies the social order and gives the individual a map of life's path.

Attracting each other was the first stage of this shared story and attachment, (a sometimes lifetime struggle of overcoming their fear of close contact) is the next, resulting in an affection to which, like drugs, money and cream cakes, we become tolerant, needing more of the same to get half the effect. Love is actually very like a drug, with the same neurochemical emotional underpinnings. The fantasies that sustain our imagination turn to practicality and we don't try to regenerate them – feeling perhaps that it's time to 'settle down'. Familiarity and availability can dull the senses, and if you're waiting for a revival of love and passion and tenderness it won't happen on its own. Changes must create and maintain love and attachment.

In nearly all relationships there is a predictable deterioration process. Seeds of unresolved conflict start to sprout, as each stage evolves, but even in well-balanced relationships of securely attached couples there is a tolerance build up, or adaptation. This is the ever-present danger of stagnation.

Even happily married couples with no thought of separation voiced secret desires to go back to the period of love and vitality, when all their emotional energy was concentrated on each other. Just as the biological act of giving birth is automatic and not necessarily related to good parenting which requires voluntary commitment, the biological idealization of a partner comes almost involuntarily but requires commitment to maintain intimacy and rapport.

Chemistry of human transaction

The novelty of passion erodes quickly. In the first chapter the male fade out was described, which left many women feeling betrayed, angry, desperate and fearful that they were no longer loved. Men were somewhat dismayed at their diminishing sexual drive, but less often concluded that lack of love was the cause. The powerful passions that exist at the beginnings of most relationships lead the couple to believe that they will always be able to interest and arouse each other. In this stage they can be said to be addicted to each other, they have a biological imprint underwritten by the same chemical that the opiates (the body's natural morphine) are derived from.

As the couple become 'desensitized' to the drug of love, their feelings of optimism and joy in each other decrease slightly and each becomes slightly more selfish, putting their own needs first, which diverts energy away from the relationship. Preoccupation of each with job, career, interest, children or extended family are daily small rejections to the other, which further emotionally distances them. Much energy goes into taking stock of who is contributing more or less, getting the better deal out of the relationship and so on. Arguments at this stage revolve around who didn't do what – like in Jeanne and Simon's case. When couples are too frightened to communicate for fear of the other's potential wrath, their behaviour becomes the criteria for how much the other cares; so when behaviour isn't up to expectations the conclusion is that the other doesn't care!

While the separates can continue to live in this state of emotional suspension, the traditional in their relationships start to make demands and test each other's commitment. The therapeutically orientated relationships, with their modicum of unresolved conflict and their capacity for intimacy, will be philosophically accepting of the downturn. In all cases though the ploy is to get the other person to care more than oneself and then they are more vulnerable – it's easier to break up if you never 'let go' and that is more likely to be a male game than a female one, the booby prize being progressive detachment.

The breakdown of the insecurely attached, the anxious, avoidant and ambivalent, was described in the chapter on divergence of communication-styles. Resentment, anger and criticism precipitate a vicious cycle of accusation, blame and defensiveness, even to the point of trying to prove each other wrong over trivial matters, and now emerge with ever-increasing frequency.

But the securely attached also have their problems, ironically born out of their very reliability and consistency – which makes them predictable. The duality of the human condition is that we want control and predictability until we get too much of it, then we become blasé, or in the drug addict's language, tolerant. These are however, slow cycles of decline, patience occasionally turning to impatience, sensitivity to roughness and gentleness to sharpness. Barriers are erected against further disappointment and little by little different attachments replace the eroding emotional bonds. The relationship, while satisfying basic sexual, companionship, social and financial needs, fails to meet the changing wants or grow enough to support the couple's increasing complexities and responsibilities. They both feel stifled in between the pleasant routines and lack the energy to overcome boredom and stagnation.

Commitment may still be enough to keep the relationship together – and the traditional family asks for no more than tangible evidence that they are united. Gracie Fields attributed her lengthy marriage to the example of commitment her mother had illustrated to her. Every family member had to turn up for Sunday lunch and Christmas, no matter how far they had to travel – a shared family ritual. Sometimes though, in the traditional family, communication obscures much private disharmony, but the objective standard with its 'one for all and all for one' philosophy can withstand much internal fragmentation.

A strong family for the therapeutic couples is based more on the subjective components of emotional support, the ability to communicate and encourage each other according to their own lights. This is how a therapeutic couple can live together extremely happily for years and yet, with hardly any fireworks, split up. Their expectations of relationships are high, so that any diminution in their happiness means they may shake hands and go on to find others with whom they can recreate that zest. Commitment is less important than the quality of their experience – their own subjective definition of what makes them feel good.

Happiness for them is the euphoric state that resonates through their bioelectrical systems, and it stagnates if we linger too long in the past or the future. This reverberation needs an ongoing response to trigger and maintain euphoric happiness, otherwise things become stale and relationships lose their psychological homoeostasis. People from war-torn or poverty-stricken homes nevertheless often look back on them as the happiest of their lives because of the quality of caring, sharing and loving engendered by the optimism, enthusiasm and hope for the future they had. Their later riches or success never seem to have the same vibrancy.

Couples can start with an emotional distance between them like the separates, or develop it as a result of their communication, breaking down in any one of the macro-cycles, or due to the gender-based differences in communication symbolized in communication styles of divergence. But there is another route: a slow build up of tolerance that dulls the novelty and attachment of an emotionally close couple. This reduction in endorphin functioning is felt as boredom; life with no challenge or risk or variety palls very quickly for the sensation-seeker and eventually for all, except perhaps for a few anxiety-loaded angst addicts.

The way out of the adaptation anchorage is variety, novelty and low level but constant change. If the background is kept constant (old friends, same neighbourhood) the foreground should be a passing parade of new interests, hobbies, challenges, courses and so on. These are all long-term means of keeping up the endorphins of attachment.

The laughing therapy: the biochemical basis of enjoyment

Using creativity to combine old elements into new patterns of perception is one definition of humour; it's the quickest way to change arousal levels and has been shown to be the biggest single influence in keeping a relationship alive and happy. As Clare said:

> From the day I first met Robin he kept coming up with all these schoolboy jokes like: Where are the Andes? At the bottom of your wristies! Where was the Magna Carta signed? At the bottom. Why did the biscuit cry? Because its mother had been awafer so long! I thought they were silly – but laughed in spite of myself and then gradually I used to pick up good teasers I'd heard and try and remember them for Robin. We got almost into a joke competition routine and I remember the first time I thought this is really good fun – I'd hope no one could hear us going on like two 12 year olds, but I noticed it made a sort of lightening in the relationship. My first marriage was deadly serious, everything done by the book – for each of us, the perfect husband and wife but it was boring for me, we got into such a routine that I knew exactly what he would be doing every Thursday at 8 a.m. (putting the rubbish out) and me every Saturday at 10 a.m. (buying vegetables in the market). Almost everything we said was functional. We would discuss things like politics or other issues but in a serious way. Robin makes me feel like a schoolgirl again. He sends me funny postcards now and then from imaginary people like the anonymous tax collector or my fairy godmother or the committee for the protection of trainee husbands which make me laugh and give me a bird's eye view of life. Even though I know there's no good fairy sending me postcards promising me all sorts of fantasies, it does help me start another day at the office in a good mood.

Clare is describing how humour helps her keep the rhythms of their life going, their micro-cycles in harmony and their endorphins flowing. Humour is playing games with categories, mixing and matching on the basis of a set of rules that is a caricature of the real rules. For instance, bison and basin are similar in length, part of speech and sound like a joke – to ask what the difference is between a buffalo and a bear is no joke at all.

Jokes work on the same principle as the micro-cycles of arousal and relaxation, first arousal, the stress of not understanding, an incongruity to be resolved – and are consumed momentarily as we run through all the possible similarities and differences we have categorized in our semantic network. Then the truth dawns, the stressful incongruity is resolved and the relief flips us into relaxation mode.

People who make a serious business out of humour can predict how funny a joke will be rated based on how incongruent the categories posed are. And also how long it will take people to get the point: 1 to 3 seconds is correlated with the rise in arousal, anxiety or embarrassment as we flounder helplessly, juggling concepts that could resolve the incongruity – and then the relief, pleasure and feelings of control as we figure it out, or are told the answer.

The underlying physiological mechanism is the evolution of humour from the stress response. It's no different to manipulating arousal by a cold shower or hot bath, playing games, having a cigarette, a drink, or anything we use to calm us down or perk us up. A well worked out stage performance is manipulating audience arousal levels all the time – a bit of suspense, activity followed by quiet reflection and understanding. The comedian alternates pathos and ludicrousness with precision timing, the singer and music score uses pitch, tone and note to the same effect, and the dancer alternates speed and complexity of movement.

Spoken jokes are a social phenomenon – have you noticed how often arousal levels are enhanced by the presence of another? – but jokes are only part of humour, which has been examined by philosophers, psychologists, sociologists and comedy writers. There are many types of humour, but all have the communality of the biological payoff of releasing us briefly from reality, throwing up alternatives, detecting multiple meanings in the situation and enhancing our feelings of well being, thus increasing endorphin production, immunological efficiency and other physiological benefits. It is a microcosm of the bigger arousal/withdrawal cycles.

There are male jokes – used as a ritual of conviviality which get attention by breaking the 'cognitive set' of the group. Men tend to use these jokes as a substitute for the emotional intimacy which evolves easily in a women's group. Making a joke is the reverse of listening. When men don't laugh at women's jokes and vice versa, they each assume the other sex has very little sense of humour, but since the sexes differ in their perception of the world, what strikes them as funny is also likely to be different. Then the dominant group will have their version of what's funny perceived as normal, and this dominant strand of humour is represented by all the male comics. This group has been joined by one or two brave female comic loners in the last few years, something that would have been impossible

20 years ago, when it was the general opinion that women had no sense of humour.

So it's clear that socialization heavily biases sex-differences in humour. Little girls are taught that loud jokes like the boys guffaw at are rude and unfeminine. Women laugh at male jokes though, in their role as team builders and supporters. But women's witicisms are perceived as catty and therefore not to be laughed at. Analysis of styles of jokes have noted that male jokes tend to be more sarcastic than women's, the purpose being to command attention and control or change the consciousness of the group, while women's jokes are more to do with tension relief, jokes about the social situation they are in and so forth, all to promote a cooperative intimacy.

A humorous response implies you can see beyond the immediate, using a playful creativity, while all about are tearing their hair out. It provides clues for the labelling of experience, and is the best response to the negative spiral described in the chapter on diverging communication. Remember, the possible responses were emotional withdrawal, non-responsiveness or male domination. When people are angry and upset, body changes occur. An increase in the pulse rate and blood pressure, faster blood circulation and breathing, increased muscular tension and digestive changes – all originating in a little area of the brain, the hypothalamus, an emotional coordination centre. Once stimulated it can remain active and take more time to disseminate than it took to be aroused. This is an important fact in trying to understand the mechanism of conflict. Threats, frustration, resentment, confusion can instantly trigger off a negative physiological emotional state which takes longer to die away and interrupts the micro-cycles of intimacy and withdrawal. In the interval, the facial muscles and other non-verbal body language express this physiological state and this does irreparable damage to the relationship, unless the couple find a channel for the release of their feelings, and a method for at least a temporary resolution of the issue.

It is physiologically impossible to arrive at a rational resolution when still emotionally aroused. Most people find that they can agree it was nothing to get so upset over, or there was an explanation, but they don't feel like getting close again until the physiological upheaval settles down. Those few moments of silent withdrawal elicit the negative response in the other – at an unaware physiological level, so, off it starts again – to the puzzlement of each, who then blame each other.

In all cases, a critical, thoughtless, insensitive, rude or otherwise negative remark or behaviour can be met with humour – even humour with a punch line. Although research shows the forgiving, loving response is the defuser in negative escalation, this can get to be a pattern, and inevitably, in the long-term, exploited. Which increases the likelihood of the negative behaviour. To vary undiluted forgiveness with a spice of humour, or cutting punch line increases a partner's interest and enjoyment – and endorphin flow. Humour is also a more assertive and self-esteem enhancing response. Repeatedly turning the other cheek is only good advice when you're wearing a face guard, and anyway it leads to being taken for granted. Humour is a powerful reinforcer and an antidote to the diseases that kill people through stress disorder.

As a coping response, humour allows you to change your appraisal of the situation. Good leaders are those who perceive the multiple levels of meaning in any situation – the funny side in a desperate situation, and then change the group's perception of their misery. Using humour as an emergency stop gap in the negative spiral cancels out the stressful effects of the anger and upset. A good laugh blocks the stress chemicals and speeds up the endorphin flow.

William Frey calls laughing 'internal jogging'; it accelerates breathing and increases oxygen consumption. A robust laugh gives the muscles of the face, shoulders, diaphragm and abdomen a vigorous work out. With convulsive side splitting laughter even the leg and arm muscles get involved. Then, as laughter subsides, relaxation drops the heart rate and respiration rate to below normal levels and anger dissipates as calm pervades. Laughing 100/200 times a day is equal to 10 minutes of rowing, says Frey.

Clowning around is taken seriously by some US hospitals, who employ clowns to get up to all sorts of antics on the children's wards – often satirizing the tragic situation of the children. A clown 'doctor' might give a clown 'patient' an anaesthetic by punching him on the nose and then transplanting a red nose onto him – but trouble, the nose rejects the patient!

Dr Jonathan Miller has obviously given humour a lot of thought. An example he likes to give as an explanation of humour is two explorers up to their necks in a swamp with one of them saying 'Say what you like Carruthers, quicksand or no, I've half a mind to struggle'! Have you noticed how often laughter goes with anxiety? In one experiment medical students were told to take blood from a rat, one half was also told that it might bite. When these obedient students trooped along to take the rat out of the cage they found it was a toy rat and they all enjoyed the joke. But the group who had been told they were ferocious rats (the anxious ones) rolled around the floor laughing compared to the others.

Joking about your own misery was captured perfectly by that wonderful pair of comedians who went from talking about their families being so poor they lived in a cardboard box to living in a hole in the road. Reducing anxiety is behind all the stereotyping jokes. We also laugh at those whose behaviour is strange, deviant or unpredictable, so in many ways humour is a sort of social control mechanism as well.

Much humour depends on linking incongruous but similar elements. For instance, 'another bomb scare at King's Cross' invites tedium, whereas 'another bow and arrow scare at King's Cross' is funny for its ludicrousness but still gets the point across. To answer an enquiry as to whether you'll be Mother (to pour out the tea) is difficult for a female up and coming manager, to refuse is bad grace, to accept is putting herself in the subordinate female position. A humorous answer violating traditional expectations would be something like 'No thanks, I'm on the pill.'

Such reframing the situation to one's advantage by linking similar elements out of context becomes easier with practice, and newspaper headlines are good examples. A disciplinarian headmaster referred to as Ayatollah Smith (when it was the Iranian revolution in the news) or a play on words like 'My mother made me a transvestite' to which the response could be 'If I send her the wool will she make me one?'

Ridiculous displacements, like cartoons depicting road painters blacking in both sides of the road to leave a light middle band can be used in humorous banter effectively. Humour, exploration, play and art all depend on novelty, surprise, incongruity and the unexpected, and relationships can benefit from the same principle. Even sex can be fun – passion doesn't preclude it. Pillow-fights, hide and seek games, 'surprise' parcels of ridiculous gifts, competitions for silly things, and so on, all go to change the chemistry of adaptation.

Humour is rapidly comprehensible and quickly forgotten – but the change of arousal level stays. Humour takes us out of ourselves and our one-track concerns, and momentarily replaces them with a new and novel perception of the same old thing. A shared joke is a synchronous, emotionally positive event from which we tend to generalize many other synchronies.

Joking is just as much a communication system as words, for to make a joke in response to something negative sends the message 'I don't want to fight, I want to change the situation, the context, the emotional climate, tread water until we sort it out.' When Jeanne thought Simon was going out too much with the boys, she didn't seethe in unexpressed resentment at him treating the home like a hotel. Instead she laid the table with the best crockery, got herself up in a frilly white apron, black tights with high heels and met him at the door with a menu-card (with prices) when he came in from work. Simon appreciated the joke, and the skimpy get-up and Jeanne got her point across without accusations, counter defences and blame.

Tranquillity and turbulence

A shared sense of humour, helps keep the rhythm matched between a couple, their physical coordination good, their moods matched, sex drive in synchrony, and intimacy cycles converging.

Anger erupts as spontaneously as laughter – but picking a quarrel is easier than making a joke in an angry state. The ability to make up is very much part of a fruitful quarrel. To be constructive and not damaging, a row should eventually be resolved in discussion, laughter and an ease of tension. As children we have anger discouraged, so when it wells up unexpectedly and in response to the one we're supposed to love, it's often repressed, and comes out in a slow nagging needling, which blights a potentially good relationship. If either of the couple withdraw the anger becomes blocked and congealed. The painful conflict must be resolved as soon after its arousal as possible, to avoid it being repressed and carried over into the next cycle of conflict. But we have been taught from babyhood on (especially girls), to avoid confrontation and challenge, so we hide it from others, even sometimes, ourselves. Until the expression of rightful anger (and I use rightful to distinguish from the exploitative dominating anger of the traditional male), becomes accepted as an inevitable biological reaction to the frustration of drives toward involvement or independence, the constructive, fruitful release of aggression which can clear the air and lead to a better mutual understanding is unlikely. When two people are secure enough in their love to reveal the less attractive sides of their nature they help each other to overcome or accept with better grace their weaknesses.

As long as we continue to categorize emotions into good and bad, acceptable and intolerant, we remain prey to guilt and the consequent repression which channels our anger underground to sour the relationship through little irritations, major resentments, feelings of being obligated or imposed on, as the anger drips away underground. Emotion takes precedence over objectivity and instead of debating issues that are eventually resolved, the emotion escalates into fury, and gets out of control.

Reframing the situation humorously is the best de-escalator. Josephine described her rising irritation every time she drove into their drive in her husband's car. Before she'd even got out, he would be rushing out of the house, not to greet her gladly but to cast an eye over the paintwork for any dents and scrapes:

> He did it *every* time, even when it was dark he'd put the porch light on, not to light my way, but the better to see any damage! It infuriated me because I have never had any sort of accident and he's had three. So one day I saw a picture of an electron microscope in a catalogue at work which gave me an idea. I cut it out, borrowed the boy next door's microscope kit and put it in the car. Then the next time I came in the drive and he popped out like a jack-in-the-box, I leapt out and handed him the microscope kit and asked if that would do until the electron microscope I showed him the picture of arrived, and then he could see any damage I'd done really properly! We make new jokes about it every time now – anyway he's *never* rushed out again so blatantly, so I don't get annoyed like before. He thought the microscope was pretty funny, so did the neighbours and I got a reputation for being a bit of a wit – so I tend to voice all my complaints a bit more humorously now.

A joke a day keeps the divorce court away

The benefits of humour are both long and short term. Fun, laughter and joking are immediate and involving, and therefore militate against stagnation. Changing perspectives of daily situations time and time again gives the mind and reality a holiday as all alternative, ludicrous possibilities are imagined.

Both work and relationships can be tremendously enhanced by seeing them in terms of opportunities for fun, rather than viewing them as a serious business to be worked at – a common advice given to couples and guaranteed to alter their perception more negatively than the advice have fun!

We seem to have an implicit association in our brains that long-term means serious and that fun can't be lasting. Some American companies have taken the humour research to heart and set up Fun and Joy committees at work. Seminars are given in fun-planning, competitions are organized for hula hoop contests, telephone booth stuffing, bubble gum blowing, tacky dress up days, historical figure mime days, and prizes given for creativeness.

The prize for the company is the extra creativity in work (yes, they do get round to it eventually). Because everyone joins in the fun events, there is less hierarchy maintained in the company – well, if you'd seen your managing director and line manager dressed up as a clothes line with their wife's knickers drying on it, you wouldn't look at them in quite the same way again, would you? This may sound another mad Californian craze but it is true that people who have seen humorous films solve problems better later on – the suggestion is that the endorphins released on laughing act as nerve cell connectors and create neural networks that allow us to think better. Jokes defuse tension and creativity and productivity in meetings.

Humour gives us some control over even a bad situation, which gives credence to the idea that much humour is born out of desperation, after all, if you can't change the situation you have to change your attitude as Dr Miller observed in his Carruthers in quicksand joke. The problem for us all is wanting to be in control of our lives which means remaining consistent, secure, predictable, *but*, we also hunger for sudden change, the mysterious unknown, which we fantasize will transform us. The exciting stranger who beckons us on to exotic horizons becomes part of the habitual scenery, sonnets become short sentences, and then finally grunts . . . and suddenly, we're out-of-touch, out-of-synchrony, and out of love.

Table 14.1 How to make a relationship more playful

Make a conscious effort to:

- Set fun goals and balance periods of seriousness against periods of fun.

- Keep a list of fun things to do together when you need a top-up:
  humorous videos
  teddy bear picnics
  going skating, or anything you've never done
  set up family sports days, with prizes for the 8-legged race,
  (both of you and the dog)
  impromptu parties for dubious celebrations, like anniversaries of composers, the cat's birthday, some long forgotten invention, Ghengis Khan's wedding anniversary.

- Have competitions with points awarded and penalties accumulated for feminist transgressions, chauvinistic actions, exciting cooking, soothing remarks, stimulating observations, terrible painting or whatever . . . anything that turns you on.

- All these things develop imagination and stimulate creativity and give you a *laugh*.

- Enlist your partner in the 'fun enterprize' – compare your idea of fun and humour. Do totally useless things together every few days, it's not really wasted time, but providing essential time-out pauses in a life too mechanized and efficient for creative feelings of well-being. Keep things in perspective. Remember: a joke a day keeps the divorce court away.

Epilogue

Everything about relationships is symbolic of the transformation of feelings.

First, attracting a partner is achieved by the subtle indications of interest, then the symbolic body language is introduced to synchronize their feelings.

Commitment brings fear of intimacy, and the ambivalent emotions that cycle between involvement and independence are expressed in every muscle, every sense and every word. Eventually most of us learn to trust each other and integrate our spasmodic conflicting feelings of tension, anger and longing for love. The micro-cycles of intimacy and withdrawal blend smoothly like primary colours shading into new harmonies, with their individual strength and rawness being cajoled into an ebb and flow of affection and tranquillity.

Then the blind spots in the relationship maze become clearer. We detect dead-end alleys, find other routes through the blockages, discover other paths to travel on. The unheard, unfelt and unseen that still touched us comes into focus from the twilight world of half-knowing and shifts the centre of feeling from the self to the relationship.

Through the macro-cycles of crisis and conservation, courtship, commitment, career, children, mid-life and retirement, energy and stability replace the cycles of negativity. Narratives of relationship then direct the functional, repetitive patterns that set the tone of the family, lay down paradigms for behaviour and overcome past hurts and fantasies that don't stand the test of time.

Only connect . . . watch, match, monitor . . . and respond. The symbolic will always hint at the underlying reality.

Don't say, 'We're not compatible, let's divorce,' say, 'We're not speaking the same language, let's change.'

Appendix 1

Glossary

Alpha rhythm
an electrical pattern in the brain when a person is in a relaxed but awake state. It represents the turnover of all the neurochemicals that underlie our changing moods and emotions.

Circadian rhythms
daily rhythmical changes which are normally synchronized to the 24-hour light/dark cycle. Most living things change regularly in predictable harmony to this 24-hour cycle, and it indicates a biological clock within us wound up by the brain.

Ethology
ethologists observe animals in their natural state and extrapolate from that to the evolution of human behaviour. Their work is important when trying to decide whether we are born with some human behaviour – such as aggression, maternal instinct, cooperation – or whether it is learned.

Neurohormones
chemical molecules in the blood and brain which have different effects on growth, movement, sexual behaviour, perception, memory, mood and emotions – anything that makes us human. A biochemist separates the body hormones from the brain ones because they are made by different means within the body.

ENDORPHINS are one of these neuro-hormones, more specifically they belong to the general class of opiates, and they have a similar effect to opium. Even the ancient Greeks referred to the well-being produced from poppy seeds and Thomas de Quincy in his *Confessions of an English Opium Eater* advised all those in pain to buy relief and happiness for one penny. A lot of those who took his advice became addicted, as did later millions, when morphine and heroin, which have a similar chemical formulae, were manufactured in the laboratory.

The discovery that the body makes its own 'natural morphine' in response to stress and injury has led to the active search for sub-types of opiates, of which there are several. Endorphins and enkephalins are the two mentioned throughout this book, and their actions regulate our emotional state.

Oscillator

a mechanism within the body that coordinates the millions of different rhythms, so they are all working with each other. When they get out of phase we feel fatigued, irritable and fall ill.

Appendix 2

The MOT of relationships

The concept of quality has improved productivity, staff-relations, turnover and absenteeism. It is a psychological technique that enhances the motivation of those in organizations to provide a quality product or service, and it promises more output for less input.

This concept has revolutionized business methods, at least in America, the country of iconoclasts. Things don't happen for the best automatically. Like water, they wind down the slope of least resistance. But bridges, wings and wheels mean a short-cut. The dictum is *not* work harder – but work more efficiently. With insight, commitment and creativity everything goes better and the individual actually spends less energy to get higher quality.

Troubled organizations waste time and money on doing things wrong, duplicating them, losing or breaking them. Relationships are the same. A few of the right words at the right time in the intimacy arousal v. intimacy overload cycle will save hours of fruitless and frustrating discussion, petty bickering and puzzling behaviour.

Inefficient organizations produce goods and services that frequently deviate from the ideal specification and then install 'hotlines' so that when a system or staff member fails, a patch-up apology operation swings into action. But this itself becomes an expectation and the lower standard eventually becomes the norm. Just as there are workers who spend their whole working lives apologizing and rectifying mistakes in the organization some couples spend their relationship life patching up hurts that should

310 The Rhythms of Love

never have happened in the first place.

Inward looking organizations have standards based on what they can actually do. Error estimates get established as the norm and when some energetic beaver does excell they are lauded as unique while everyone else settles back to the comfortable old norm. Inward looking relationships are the same. The only 'quality-control' they have is the 'performance standard' set by their parents. A generation ago marriages were based on different rationale and criteria for happiness than today. And many relationships stagger along on the 'could be better/could be worse' principle until those low octane beliefs become so fixed that any other way is too much effort. Both the relationship and organization have no idea how much better things could have been. Old family businesses and humdrum relationships ignore new technologies, concepts, techniques and enrichments that make relationships and organizations fully-functioning and life enhancing.

Finally neither the managers of the organization or the participants of the relationship see the signs or acknowledge the mistakes. They find excuses – 'It'll be alright when the old foreman leaves/once the holidays are over/father goes to live in a sheltered home/the children leave school – or something.' Serious underlying structural problems that should be tackled at the core are put down to one-off situations that will go away at some time in the future. 'We can handle it,' say couples and managers – until the company goes bankrupt or the relationship collapses.

The new concepts in the American business world that turn loss-making companies around are quality vaccines that 'immunize' the company and raise antibodies against organizational decay. The vaccine works in a culture that changes attitude and motivation rather than policies, rules and control. It is prepared from three actions: determination, education and implementation.

Determination evolves when managers decide they have had enough and are not going to take any more. *Education* is the process of creating a common language of quality in the organization so that everyone understands what is necessary. *Implementation* is putting the new insights into action because knowing is not always doing – not long-term anyway. Like maintaining the ideal weight so painfully achieved, the short-term goal was easier than the long-term one of permanent loss – *because* most dieters only look ahead to the day when they get finally into a size 10. Relationships enter a new phase with commitment, the wedding day is only the start of the story but is celebrated as the final goal.

If you can think of your relationship as a product, one that needs research and development, costing, marketing, and quality control, then you can immunize it with your own emotional vaccine. The product you have manufactured is love, and the idealization that came so involuntarily is the packaging that has to be kept fresh and up-to-date. The love styles are the means of production which must be agreed on beforehand.

First steps to *relationship quality control* are to define a quality relationship. Each should, alone, clarify their original expectations, current disappointments and future desires. Write them down. Then discuss together all the alternative 'products'. The passionate manics portrayed by most novelists, or the 'good friend' Darby and Joan models of many television serials (use the questionnaire as a guide). Identify problems, positive and negative trends, communication blocks, how they relate to their relationship goals and beliefs in relationships of others (do *not* give them the benefit of your analysis). This is all to help you construct a definition of what might be, to exchange what is for what could be. Once something is conceptualized clearly, it tends to come into existence. Most people intuitively assess and compare their relationship to others, but not usually in such a structured way. To commit to paper a mission statement, with roles defined, is to establish a 'relationship culture' and it is this that enables each to treat each other as they want to be treated.

The stage of *determination* in relationships is reached when the couple believe that they can choose the relationship they want, that its ups and downs are their responsibility and the idealization needs preserving. *Education* starts with jettisoning conventional wisdom. Even if 45 million other couples do something a certain way, it can still be wrong for you. Once you've worked out your joint preferences (including sex-role characteristics) and established your love-style, trust and commitment follow, and the fear of intimacy is reduced. But whatever you agree, him Tarzan, her Jane or vice-versa, each has to acknowledge equal commitment and importance to each other.

Knowing each other's hopes, fears, ambitions, strengths and weaknesses, and intimacy overload threshold, establishes a communication of body and brain that allows complete understanding and support of each other. Then you create the conditions for a quality relationship. *Implementation* means maintaining it. Once you've selected your quality product, and determined the requirements needed for maintenance, you need quality control. It's just as hard to have a mediocre or bad relationship as a good one – actually harder.

Like Barbara and Edward, find a password, or framed copy of 'our last argument' or something indicating 'the bad old days', before you take the relationship in hand to create more quality. Keep your goals clear. Think of the consequences of your actions. If singing in the bath at 3 a.m. is irritating to your early rising partner then you're not maintaining quality. Every couple knows exactly how to needle an Achilles heel, but quality couples resist the short-term satisfaction of minor revenge and ask instead why the other needed to be so annoying. What had they themselves contributed? For most people positive actions are only a matter of thought beforehand, which then guides the action. Even a psyche crippled by anxiety or hostility has *some* choice.

Choosing to maintain a quality relationship means continual monitoring of the other's mood fluctuations in order to respond to the intimacy enhancement period and get on with something else in the intimacy-overload downswing. Staying in touch physically, sleeping together, getting up at the same time, expanding similar levels of energy every day . . . not necessarily together but making sure that when you are together you are both similarly alert or similarly fatigued or matched somewhere between. This may be impossible sometimes and you will need to find symbolic ways of keeping in touch, but it must be managed for a good proportion of the time in order to stay physiologically in sync. Develop techniques for de-escalating the other when tension does push you out of sync.

John and Ann had developed a tension disspeller which excused John's thoughtless remarks when he came in tired and uptight. It was built on an old joke. He had spent two years in the army after school and his mother had hoped he would make a career in the services. But he bought himself out wanting to start his own business rebuilding vintage cars and his mother had shaken her head sadly and sighed 'Oh John, I don't think the army did you any good at all. You would have looked so nice in an officer's uniform too.' When Ann does a perfect imitation of mother in response to a thoughtless or irritable action by John it reminds them both that he is liable to withdraw or explode under tension and the resulting giggle restores their sense of balance. It has become a signal for Ann to communicate that she understands and doesn't take offence and John is relieved that he is understood and consequently he finds it easier to maintain quality, or, as he would say, snap out of it.

Then the micro-cycles of communication (the speech patterns

and muscle movements) that signal the degree of involvement and independence each is negotiating start to converge and the couple are able to weather the stresses of the macro-cycles and the differences of life paths.

Appendix 3

Questionnaires used

Love-style questionnaire

The scale is:
1. Almost never true
2. Rarely true
3. Usually, or nearly true
4. Almost always true

If your response matches the number after the question ring it, if not, leave it and go on to the next question.

1. You consider your childhood less happy than the average   S=1   M=3

2. You were discontent with life (work etc.) at the time your encounter began   S=1   M=3

3. You were never in love before this relationship   P=2

4. You want to be in love or have love as a security   L=1   M=4   P=3

5. You have a clearly defined ideal image of your desired partner   LSM=1   P=4

6. You felt a strong gut reaction to your partner on the first encounter   LM=2   S=1

7. You are preoccupied with thoughts about him or her   LS=1   M=4

8. You believe your partner's interest is at least as great as yours — M=1 S=2 LP=3

9. You are eager to see your love almost every day (this was true from the beginning) — L=1 SP=2 M=4

10. You soon believed this could become a permanent relationship — LM=1 S=2 P=3

11. You see warning signs of trouble but ignore them — L=1 P=2 M=4

12. You deliberately restrain frequency of contact with partner — SMP=3 L=4

13. You restrict display of your feelings with your loved one — S=2 MP=3 L=4

14. You discuss future plans with him or her — LS=2 P=4

15. You discuss a range of topics, experiences with partner — L=2 P=4

16. You try to control relationship but feel you've lost control — LS=1 M=4

17. You lose the ability to be first to terminate relationships — L=1 P=2 M=4

18. You try to force your love to show more feeling, commitment — L=1 M=4

19. You analyse the relationship, weigh it in your mind — S=1 M=3 P=4

20. You believe in the sincerity of your partner — M=3

21. You blame your partner for difficulties of relationship — L=2 LM=3

22. You are jealous to the point of conflict, scenes, threats etc. — LSP=1 M=4

23. Tactile, sensual contact is very important to you — S=1 P=2

24. You take the quality of sexual rapport as a test of love — L=3 S=1 P=2

25. You are willing to work out sexual problems, improve technique — LM=2 P=3

26. You have a continued high rate of sex, tactile contact throughout the relationship — SMP=2

27. You declare your love first, well ahead of partner — L=1 S=2 M=4

28. You consider love life your most important
    activity, even essential   L=1 SP=2 M=4

29. You are prepared to give all for love,
    once underway   L=1 SP=2 M=4

30. You are willing to suffer abuse, even
    ridicule from partner   LP=1 S=2 M=4

31. Your relationship is marked by frequent
    differences of opinion, anxiety   SP=2 LM=4

32. If the relationship ends it will be with lasting
    bitterness, trauma for you   LSP=2 M=4

Now add up your L,S,P, and M scores into 4 separate columns, of
Ludus, Storge, Pragma and Mania and look up those scores below
to get your final score on each love-style.

To use the table: add up your scores on each of the four measures.
   For each love-style locate your score in the first score column and
then look across to the appropriate column on the right to read off
your normalized score, ie., if you scored 17 on Storge, check down
the First Score column until you reach 17, then move across to the
Storge column and read off the normalized score, in this case 42.5.
   It is this normalized score that you compare the strength of your
love-styles with, either your own trends or to see how close you are
to your partner's love-style. The higher the score, the stronger the
trend.

Your Score	Ludus	Storge	Mania	Pragma
1	2.0	2.5	1.1	1.7
2	4.1	5.0	2.3	3.4
3	6.1	7.5	3.4	5.2
4	8.2	10.0	4.5	6.9
5	10.2	12.5	5.7	8.6
6	12.2	15.0	6.8	10.3
7	14.3	17.5	8.0	12.1
8	16.3	20.0	9.1	13.8
9	18.4	22.5	10.2	15.5
10	20.4	25.0	11.4	17.2

Your Score	Ludus	Storge	Mania	Pragma
11	22.4	27.5	12.5	19.0
12	24.5	30.0	13.6	20.7
13	26.5	32.5	14.8	22.4
14	28.6	35.0	15.9	24.1
15	30.6	37.5	17.0	25.9
16	32.7	40.0	18.2	27.6
17	34.7	42.5	19.3	29.3
18	36.7	45.0	20.5	31.0
19	38.8	47.5	21.6	32.8
20	40.8	50.0	22.7	34.5
21	42.9	52.5	23.9	36.2
22	44.9	55.0	25.0	37.9
23	46.9	57.5	26.1	39.7
24	49.0	60.0	27.3	41.4
25	51.0	62.5	28.4	43.1
26	53.1	65.0	29.5	44.8
27	55.1	67.5	30.7	46.6
28	57.1	70.0	31.8	48.3
29	59.2	72.5	33.0	50.0
30	61.2	75.0	34.1	51.7
31	63.3	77.5	35.2	53.4
32	65.3	80.0	36.4	55.2
33	67.3	82.5	37.5	56.9
34	69.4	85.0	38.6	58.6
35	71.4	87.5	39.8	60.3
36	73.5	90.0	40.9	62.1
37	75.5	92.5	42.0	63.8
38	77.6	95.0	43.2	65.5
39	79.6	97.5	44.3	67.2
40	81.6	100.0	45.5	69.0
41	83.7		46.6	70.7
42	85.7		47.7	72.4
43	87.8		48.9	74.1
44	89.8		50.0	75.9
45	91.8		51.1	77.6
46	93.9		52.3	79.3
47	95.9		53.4	81.0
48	98.0		54.5	82.8
49	100.0		55.7	84.5

Your Score	Ludus	Storge	Mania	Pragma
50			56.8	86.2
51			58.0	87.9
52			59.1	89.7
53			60.2	91.4
54			61.4	93.1
55			62.5	94.8
56			63.6	96.6
57			64.8	98.3
58			65.9	100.0
59			67.0	
60			68.2	
61			69.3	
62			70.5	
63			71.6	
64			72.7	
65			73.9	
66			75.0	
67			76.1	
68			77.3	
69			78.4	
70			79.5	
71			80.7	
72			81.8	
73			83.0	
74			84.1	
75			85.2	
76			86.4	
77			87.5	
78			88.6	
79			89.8	
80			90.9	
81			92.0	
82			93.2	
83			95.3	
84			95.5	
85			96.6	
86			97.7	
87			98.9	
88			100.0	
89			101.1	

* Adapted from John Lees *Love-styles* (Abacus Press 1973)

Relationship questionnaire

The score is your judgement of how often a particular activity or behaviour occurs in your relationship. Do it alone first, then compare your answers with your partner to get your different perceptions on your communication and relationship style.

Part One

Score: 7 for always, 6 for usually, 5 for often, 4 for occasionally, 3 for not often, 2 for usually not, 1 for never.

1. We talk about the future of our relationship.
2. We share responsibility for deciding when, for how long, and at what speed chores around the house should be completed.
3. We go out together to public places in the community such as zoos, sporting events, public parks, museums, libraries, etc.
4. My partner has taken holidays without me (even if only a day or two).
5. We try to resolve our disagreements immediately.
6. We embrace in public places.
7. We tell each other how much we love or care about each other.
8. We go to bed and get up at the same time.
9. My partner encourages me to use my talents, even if it means some inconvenience to him/her.
10. Most of our friends know each other.
11. We talk more about feelings and affection than about tasks and accomplishments.
12. We feel a need to resolve the disagreements or oppositions that arise between us.
13. My partner reassures and comforts me when I am feeling low.
14. My partner expresses his/her feelings and reactions to me.
15. I get the feeling that my partner can read my mind.
16. We eat our meals (the ones at home) at the same time every day.
17. We seek new friends and outside experiences.
18. I have my own private workspace or study, den, garage, spare bedroom.
19. We cook and eat our meals separately, even when we are both at home.

20. I have taken separate vacations from my spouse even if only for a day or two.

21. I feel free to ask my partner to communicate his/her true feelings to me.

22. In our house, we keep a fairly regular daily time schedule.

23. If I can avoid arguing about some problems, they will disappear.

24. My partner has his/her own private space, room, study, shed.

25. We serve the main meal at the same time every day.

26. If I am working or concentrating on something, I ignore the presence of my partner.

27. When I am angry with my partner I'll say nothing rather than something that I will be sorry for later.

28. We openly express our disagreements with each other.

29. Our time schedule varies quite a bit from day to day.

Part two

Give yourself: 7 for strongly agree
6 for agree
5 for moderately agree
4 maybe, undecided
3 moderately disagree
2 disagree
1 strongly disagree

30. Life is filled with so many contradictions that I am not certain how to interpret what it all means.

31. We cooperate well in resolving our conflicts.

32. I think that we joke around and have more fun than most couples.

33. Unfaithfulness in marriage is inexcusable.

34. Relationships should not interfere with each person's pursuit to discover his or her own potential.

35. Often the only way to gain perspective on a situation is to see its absurdity.

36. Our wedding ceremony was (or will be) very important to us.

37. Pictures, mementoes, and other objects that have a special meaning for a couple should be displayed in their home so that others can see them.

38. A good motto for our relationship is 'Care deeply but remain composed'.

39. It is important for a couple or family to attend church, and if possible, together.

40. I think it is important for one to have some private space which is separate from one's partner and is considered their own.

41. Children should be taught the traditions and customs which are their heritage.

42. Once family plans are made, they should not be changed without a very good reason.

43. Family secrets should not be shared with friends, no matter how close they are.

44. Our society, as we see it, needs to regain faith in the law and in our institutions.

45. The meaning of life and our purpose in it is very clear to us.

46. The ideal relationship is one which is marked by novelty, humour and spontaneity.

47. In close relationships there should be no constraints or restrictions on individual freedom.

48. There seem to be many minor crises in our lives.

49. A woman should take her husband's last name when she marries.

50. We can go for long periods of time without spending much time together as a couple.

51. We communicate to one another with a greater range and intensity of feelings than most couples I know.

52. It is better to hide one's true feelings in order to avoid hurting your partner.

53. In a close relationship privacy is more important than togetherness.

54. In a relationship, each individual should be permitted to establish the daily rhythm and time schedule that suits them best.

Now distribute your points into three categories according to the following plan:

TRADITIONAL: 3, 10, 16, 22, 25, 26, 28, 33, 36, 37, 38, 39, 41, 42, 43, 44, 45, 49.

SEPARATE: 4, 18, 19, 20, 23, 24, 27, 30, 34, 35, 40, 46, 47, 48, 50, 52, 53, 54.

THERAPEUTIC: 1, 2, 5, 6, 7, 8, 9, 11, 12, 13, 14, 15, 17, 21, 29, 31, 32, 51.

The lowest possible in any category is 18 and the highest 126. 90 or above on any scale puts you in the higher than average bracket.

(Adapted from: Mary Anne Kirkpatrick: *Between Husbands & Wives* (Sage Series on Interpersonal Communication, 1988).

Appendix 4

Bibliography

Since this is not an academic book, only the major, easily obtainable references are listed in the categories on which the book is based.

The physio-chemistry of love and attraction

Bandura, A. *et. al.* 'Perceived Self-Efficacy in Coping with Cognitive Stressors and Opoid Activation'

Birchall, A. 'A whiff of happiness' in *New Scientist* 25 Aug 1980

Campbell, B. *Successful Women, Angry Men* Arrow Books, 1988

Casale, G. *et. al.* 'Circadian Rhythms of beta-endorphin in the aged' *Gerontologie* 18, 1985

Diamond, J. 'I want a Girl Just Like The Girl . . .' in *Discover*, Nov 1986

Dominion, J. *Marital Therapy*, Penguin, 1976

Doty, R.L. 'Olfactory Communication in Humans' in *Chemical Senses*, Vol 6, 1981

Ficher, I.V. 'Marital compatibility in sensation seeking traits as a factor in marital adjustment' in *J.Sex Marital Therapy*, Vol 7, part 1, 1981

Frankenhaeuser, M. 'Quality of Life; Criteria for Behavioural adjustment' *Internat.J Psychol.* Vol 12, no 2, 1977

Frecska, E. *et al.* 'Social Bonding in the Modulation of the Physiology of Ritual Trance' in *Ethos*, Vol 17, p 70-87, 1989

Gottman, J.M. 'Assessing the role of Emotion in Marriage'; in *Behavioural Assessment 8*, 1986

Haier *et al*. 'Psychiatric Vulnerability' in; *Arch Gen Psychiatry*, Vol 37, 1990

Hofer, M.A. 'Relationships as Regulators; A psychobiologic Perspective on Bereavement' in; *Psychosomatic Medicine*, Vol 46, no 3, 1984

Johansson, F. *et. al*. 'Personality Traits in Chronic Pain Patients related to Endorphin Levels in Cerebrospinal Fluid' in *Psychiatry Research*, Vol 1, 1979

Kulcsar, Z. *et al*. 'Endogenous Opiod Functions and Personality' in *European Journal of Personality*, Vol 1, 1987

Liebowitz, M.R. *The Chemistry of Love*, Berkley Books, 1984

Lynch, G. (Ed.), *Neurobiology of Human Learning and Memory*, Guildford Press, N.Y., 1984

Lynch, T. and Anchor, K. 'Current status of the B-Endorphin and Self-Regulation: Health Enhancement through Applied Neuro-sciences' *Clinical Biofeedback and Health*, 10, no 1, 1987

Money, J. *Love and Love-Sickness. The Science of Sex and Gender Differences in Pair Bonding*, Johns Hopkins Press, 1981

Panksepp *et al*. 'Brain opiods and social emotions' *Brain & Behaviour*, Vol 10, 1985

Roy, A. *et al*. 'Extraversion in Pathological Gamblers' in *Arch Gen Psychiatry*, Vol 46, 1989

Schwartz, J. & Roques, B. 'Opiod peptides as intracellular messengers' in *Biomedicine*, 32, 1980

Thayer, R.E. *The Biopsychology of Mood and Arousal*, Oxford University Press, 1989

Tucker, D. and Williamson, P. *Neural Control*

Young, S. 'Something in the air; picking out relatives by smell', *New Scientist*, 12 May, 1988

Sex differences in language perception and use

Deakins, A. 'Advances in gender and language studies', in *New ideas in Psychol.*, Vol 9, no 1, 1991

Graddol, D. and Swann, J. *Gender Voices*, Basil Blackwell, 1990

Kramarae, C. *Women and Men Speaking*, Newbury House, 1981

Spender, D. *Man Made Language*, Routledge & Kegan Paul, 1980
— *Reflecting Men at Twice their Normal Size*

Tannen, D. *You Just Don't Understand*, Virago Press, 1991

Thorne, B. and Henley, N. *Language and Sex; Difference and Dominance*, Newbury House, 1975

Sex differences in everything else

Colheart, M. 'Sex and Learning Differences', *New Behaviour*, Vol 1, no 2, May 1975

Daly, M. and Wilson, M. 'Sex and strategy', *New Scientist*, 4 Jan 1979

Durden-Smith, J. *et al. Sex and the Brain*, Pan Original, 1983

Hardy, Sarah, *The Woman that Never Evolved,* 1981

Kimura, D. 'Male Brain, Female Brain: The Hidden Difference', in *Psychology Today*, Nov 1985

Lippa, R. 'The naive perception of masculinity-femininity on the basis of expressive cues' in *J. of Research in Personality*, Vol 12, 1978

Lloyd, Barbara, 'Rules of the gender game' in *New Scientist*, 2 Dec, 1989

Miller, Laurence, 'Aphasias and aprosodias' in *Psy. Today* (U.S. edition), February 1988

Rossi, A. *Gender and the Life Course*, Aldine Publishing, N.Y., 1985

The non-verbal communication of emotions

Davis, F. *Inside Intuition, what we know about non-verbal communication*, McGraw-Hill

Davis, Martha (Ed.), *Interactions Rhythms: Periodicity in communicative Behaviour*, Human Science Press, 1982

Gale, A. and Edwards, J. *Physiological Correlates of Human Behaviour*, Vol 2, Academic Press, 1983

Hall, E.T. *The Dance of Life; the other dimension of time*, Doubleday, 1984

Siegman, A.W. and Siegman, S. *Non-verbal Behaviour and Communication*, Lawrence Erlbaum Associates Inc, 1987

Men and the masculine mould

Cohen, David. *Being a Man*, Routledge, London 1990

Goldberg, H. *The New Male*, Signet, New York 1980

Kiley, Dan. *What to do When he Won't Change*, Grafton, 1987

Relationship Dynamics

Askham, Janet. *Identity and Stability in Marriage*, Cambridge University Press, 1984

Beck, A.T. *Love is Never Enough*, Penguin, 1989

Bernard, Jessie. *The Future of Marriage*, The World Publishing Co., 1972

— *The Female World*, The Free Press, 1981

Bowlby, John. *The Making and Breaking of Affectional Bonds*, 1973

Deci, E. and Ryan, R. *Intrinsic Motivation and Self-Determination in Human Behaviour*, Plenum Press, New York, 1985

Dominian, J. *Marital Breakdown*, Penguin, 1968

Eysenck, H. and Wakefield, J., Forward, S. *et al. Men Who Hate Women and the Women who Love them*, Bantam Press, 1988

Gordon, Barbara. *Jennifer Fever*

Green, Maureen. *Marriage*

Hazan, C. and Shaver, P. 'Romantic love conceptualised as an attachment process' in *Interpersonal Relations and Group Processes*, 1986

Hendrick, C. *et al.* 'Do men and women love differently?' in *J. Social and Personal Relationships*, Vol 1, 1984

Hewley, Nancy. *Body Politics,* Prentice Hall, 1977

Hite, Shere. *Good Guys and Bad Guys*

Horley, Sandra. *The Charm Syndrome*, Papermac, London, 1991

Horney, Karen. *Neurosis and Human Growth; The struggle to self-realisation*, Routledge & Kegan Paul, 1965

Jourard, S.M. *The Healthy Personality*, Wiley, New York, 1980

Miller, Stuart. *Men and Friendship*, Gateway Books, London, 1983

Roth, Barbara. *The Uncivil War*

Rueger, R.A. *The Joy of Touch*, Thorsons, London, 1981

Schaefer, E.S. and Burnett, C. 'Stability and predictability of quality of women's marital relationships and demoralisation', *J. Personality and Social Psychol.*, Vol 3, no 6, 1987

Trachtenberg, P. *The Casanova Complex, Compulsive Lovers and their Women*, Angus & Robertson, United Kingdom, 1989

A comprehensive overview of the history of knowledge about the left and right hemisphere is *Medicine, Mind and the Double Brain* by Anne Harrington, Princeton University Press, 1987.

This book grew out of the research I did for a Phd on Personality and Marital Compatibility. Initially, 1,000 couples completed questionnaires (Eysenck Personality Questionnaires measuring Extroversion, Emotionality Toughmindedness, Impulsivity, Venturesomeness and Empathy) and others on attitudes and beliefs and various aspects of relationship satisfaction. These broad categories of personality turned out not to be the most important element in relationship happiness, and I went on afterwards collecting more data from interviews, workshops and groups and adding more questionnaires as different aspects of relationships became clearer. One of the very first findings that Professor Eysenck and J. Wakefield noticed was that couples seemed happiest when the woman was more emotional than the man, while he was higher on the toughminded scale than she. Almost, they said, as if each was looking for an exaggerated version of a man or a woman.

This led me to look at sex differences in personality, emotion, life-course, perception, experience, self-esteem, happiness and language, which are responsible for so much misunderstanding in relationships. Now the data base has grown to 3,000 couples who have contributed their time and understanding and I have fitted their experiences into a wider framework according to their attachment history, love attitude, relationship and communication style, and quoted other research where it extends and complements mine.

Index